DAWN

SHIFT

by

Patrick J. Jackson

Dawn Shift

Copyright 2012

PJJ Publishing

First Printing, 2019

Revised Second Printing, 2020

Printed in the United States of America

ISBN: 9781699028650

Contents

3

4

AUTHOR'S NOTE

DAWN SHIFT was written with the intention of giving you, the reader, a laugh or two, through funny or interesting real-life police stories. A couple of the stories are not funny, they were included because they were a part of police calls that you may find interesting and give you some introspect on life.

The one thing all of us want in life is to be happy. Plain and simple. This book is not going to make you happy in life, but it should give you a laugh or two. Laughter is good for the soul. Several of the readers from the first edition of DAWN SHIFT said that whenever they needed a laugh, they re-read their favorite chapter of the first edition of DAWN SHIFT. You should follow their lead and re-tell these stories when getting together with friends and family so you can all have a laugh.

HOW TO ENJOY DAWN SHIFT

Many of us are very hesitant to read a book. We're too busy with our lives and we are caught up in a whirlwind of doing "stuff". Get away from the stuff for a couple of minutes, break out your copy of DAWN SHIFT and have a laugh!

DAWN SHIFT is gluten free, contains no GMO's or artificial ingredients and clinically proven to make you a happier person.

Coffee is recommended.

SPECIAL THANKS

Special thanks to Mike Rounds of Rounds, Miller and Associates for his assistance in publishing this book.

and,

Leslie Sears of Les is More Printing and Graphics for her cover work illustrations.

and,

MC Stovall for her assistance editing this book.

ABOUT THE BOOK

DAWN SHIFT is a collection of humorous or interesting short stories based on true events regarding police work. Most of these stories have been hidden from the public for decades but now they are yours to enjoy

DAWN SHIFT also contains some general, interesting information about the way police work is conducted. But the reader should be aware that police work routines differ greatly from one department to the next and by geographical areas.

A small amount of embellishment was incorporated into some of the stories, because, as Mark Twain stated:

"Never let the truth get in the way of a good story."

PROFANITY WARNING

If you have a low tolerance for profanity, please do not purchase this book.

The profanity used in this book is an accurate description of the words or thoughts of the subjects involved. The author did not make them up.

The profanity was included in the book in an effort to paint a true and correct picture of the events described.

It should be noted that some police officers do not use profanity.

Generally, law enforcement agencies do not condone the use of profanity and officers can be subject to disciplinary action for using it.

One officer stated profanity is overlooked by law enforcement agencies during emergency situations, like being shot at by fucking crooks.

DEDICATION

To all those who have served and those currently serving.

A NOTE ABOUT POLICE SHIFTS

Most law enforcement agencies have three shifts. Shift 1 is the midnight or graveyard shift.

On many departments, it is referred to as the "dawn shift" because one gets to watch the sun come up at the end of the shift.

Some officers like working the dawn shift but many don't embrace it because of the difficulty in staying awake. Usually cop wives don't like their husbands working this shift.

Shift 2 is called the "day shift" because it is during the day. Usually cop wives like their husbands working this shift because their husband will be home at night (supposedly) and they can have somewhat of a normal life.

Shift 3 is the "evening shift" because, you guessed it, it is during the evening.

Again, cop wives usually don't like their husbands working this shift because their husbands won't be home at dinner time and watching TV with the family like normal people.

Usually, police departments will stagger the times of each of the shifts to ensure there are sufficient officers in the field at shift change.

One does not want all the officers changing shift at the same time because that is a very convenient time for criminals to plan their heists and avoid being apprehended.

So, let's look at "dawn shift": half the patrol officers that work dawn shift will start at 11:30 p.m. and the other half will start an hour later.

Half the day shift crew will start at 7:30 a.m. and the other half will start an hour later.

For evening shift, half the crew will start at 3:30 p.m. and the other half of the crew will start an hour later.

On some of the larger departments, there is a fourth or even maybe even a fifth shift.

Those shifts field extra cars during peak crime times determined by crime statistics for their communities and they overlap the three shifts listed above.

THESE AREN'T MY PANTS!!!

OFFICER DAVE

Officer Dave has a very sarcastic and even sometimes, caustic sense of humor. He is a self-admitted "Smart Ass" and has the uncanny ability to match wits with anyone he encounters. A nice guy to have at a family bar-b-que, just full of jokes and stories. He is very intelligent. One would not desire to tangle with officer Dave. He's big, strong, smart, and knows a bit of martial arts. The perfect cop to have driving around your neighborhood, keeping an eye out for your wellbeing.

As a new officer, Officer Dave wanted the best field training he could receive. More senior officers convinced him the place to receive this training was in the "ghetto". The ghetto immerses a new officer in some heavy police work. It is the place where you catch the drug dealers, burglars, and bank robbers. Officer Dave believed if he was to become a big, giant, crime fighting machine, he had to volunteer for the "ghetto". If you could handle the "ghetto" you could handle anything.

LAMONT

Lamont grew up in Officer Dave's patrol ghetto. As a child, he knew his father. But when he was seven his father left home. Lamont's mother never told him that his father was serving 40 years to life in state prison for shooting a drug dealer to death.

You see, one night, Lamont's dad shot his drug dealer because the dealer sold him some bad cocaine. It really wasn't cocaine that the drug dealer

12

sold, it was baking soda which doesn't quite have the kick that true cocaine has. One thing led to another and when the drug dealer refused to make the deal good, Lamont's father had to make a statement in the neighborhood: "Don't mess with me."

So, Lamont, his brothers, and his sisters grew up without a father in the home. Momma did her best to teach her children right from wrong and to shield them from the four drug dealers that lived within 20 yards of their humble ghetto apartment. Regardless, when it came to Lamont, the peer pressure from the drug addicts, drug dealers, and prostitutes was too much to resist. He wanted to be "cool" so he quit high school in his freshman year. By the time he was twenty, Lamont had been in jail several times for burglary, car theft, and drugs. Lamont was thankful he never got arrested by the police for the two drive by shootings he participated in with his street gang. That could have been some serious prison time.

One day, Lamont went "shopping" in a nearby affluent city. He went to a shopping mall, picked out a car he liked, broke the window, smashed the driver's column and "hot-wired" the car. Lamont was driving home when he saw red and blue police lights in his rear-view mirror. He was about to meet Officer Dave.

So, Officer Smart-Ass Dave is on patrol in the ghetto during day shift. His patrol car is outfitted with a stolen vehicle tracking device. Officer Dave received a signal on this device that a stolen car was in his patrol area. He started to search for the stolen car. As Officer Dave did so, his radio dispatcher advised Officer Dave's fellow patrolmen as to his position so they could assist him in finding the stolen car and make an arrest.

Officer Dave found the stolen car. Accompanied by two assisting officer's, Officer Dave stopped the stolen car driven by Lamont. Officer Dave made a "Felony" stop on Lamont and his stolen car. A felony car stop is a very formal affair where the cops are high on adrenaline and ready to shoot the occupant(s) of the stolen car if they don't listen carefully and follow instructions. Officer Dave's career is young and so far, he has not had to shoot any crooks. So far, all of them have obeyed when officer Dave has had to point his "B.F.G." (Big Fucking Gun) at them.

Officer Dave pulled Lamont over on a major city thoroughfare. Officer Dave positioned his patrol car behind the one stolen by Lamont. Officer Dave and fellow officers now have the city street blocked off. All of the Officers are pretty serious in that they all have B.F.G.'s pointing at their new friend, Lamont.

Officer Dave uses his police car's public address system to order Lamont out of the stolen car and to walk backwards to Officer Dave's police car. Officer Dave then orders Lamont to the ground. This is called "proning out" the suspect. Officer Dave handcuffs Lamont and searches him for weapons, etc.

During the search, Lamont blurts out:

"Wime I being arrested?"

"For driving a stolen car."

"Snot my car!"

14

To which Smart-Ass Officer Dave replies, "Exactly!"

Our Hero, Officer Dave then finds a gun in Lamont's front pants pocket. Officer Dave, in his most smart-assish voice says,

"Well, lookee here, we got a gun!"

"Snot my gun!"

Not missing a beat, Officer Dave replies,

"Well, it's in your pants..."

Lamont yells,

"These aren't my pants!!!"

Officer Dave counters with,

"Well, you're wearing them!"

Weeks later, in court, Lamont made a statement that he had borrowed the pants from "My Friend" the day before and he did not know there was a gun in the pants pocket.

The judge at the hearing ruled that 24 hours was enough time for Lamont to be aware there was a gun in his pants.

Nice try Lamont... Now be a good crook and go to prison...

In our next chapter, we will discuss "My Friend", his partners in crime, and the crimes they have committed.

MY FRIEND, SOME DUDE, SOME GUY, AND A TRUCK LOAD OF MEXICANS

At this time, we need a discussion on the three most notorious criminals in the world.

Your author has interviewed hundreds of law enforcement officers in the United States. A synopsis of those interviews shows that 90% of all crime in the United States is committed by three individuals. The first suspect goes by the name of, *"My Friend"*. This asshole has stolen so much shit, hurt so many people, and has been named by so many associates; he should be shot or hung on sight. Most suspects arrested by law enforcement have been working with or know someone who is working with, *"My Friend"*.

The next individual responsible for most of the crime in the United States is known as *"Some Dude"*. If the police do not believe a suspect's story in that *"My Friend"* committed the crime in question, the suspect will almost always tell the cops that it must have been *"Some Dude" who committed the crime.*

"Some Dude" is usually in the company of *"My Friend"*.

Now, if the cops are questioning a suspect and they convince the suspect that the crime cannot be blamed on *"My Friend"* or *"Some Dude"*, the suspect will blame the crime on *"Some Guy"*.

"Some Guy" is also responsible for much of the crime in the world.

"My Friend", *"Some Dude"*, and *"Some Guy"*

are all masters of disguise and suspects have difficulty describing them.

If you have met or know "*My Friend*", "*Some Dude*", or "*Some Guy*", please call your local law enforcement agency as to their whereabouts. These assholes are busy 24/7 and need to be put away permanently!

Lastly, we need to talk about a group of criminals that were also blamed for many a crime spree: "*A Truckload of Mexicans*".

Many years ago, many Mexican laborers would travel to and from work in the back of pickup trucks. It was not uncommon to see a pickup truck driving around a town with a truck bed full of workers.

Quite often, when a suspect was being questioned by police and he could not convince the police the blame should be laid on "*My Friend*", "*Some Dude*", or "*Some Guy*", "*A Truckload of Mexicans*" were always handy for laying the blame on.

It is believed that "*A Truckload of Mexicans*" is responsible for the other 10% of crime in North America. The "*A Truckload of Mexicans*" was always on the road travelling from one town to another.

They operated in both Mexico and the United States and were experts at crossing the border undetected.

"*A Truckload of Mexicans*" were ready at a minute's notice to drive their dirty, unidentifiable pickup truck to any town in North America where they needed to be blamed for a crime.

Author's Note

Many State legislatures passed laws making it illegal for passengers to ride in the back of pickup truck beds.

Just as the horse and buggy have gone the way of the old west, the truckload of Mexicans has disappeared.

Their participation in the criminal justice system will be missed; they can't be blamed for anymore crimes...

THERE AIN'T NO NEED FOR THAT...

OFFICER PETE

Picture a beautiful, sunny, California summer afternoon. It's 3:30 p.m., hot, and Officer Pete has just started his patrol shift. Officer Pete kinda likes the evening shift: starts out with warm, sunny weather and then cools off later when the crooks like to come out of hiding. With any luck, Officer Pete will arrest a notorious criminal before his shift ends. If not, he will settle for just another wayward soul that stumbled (or drove) across his path.

Officer Pete was a hard charging type of guy. He and his peers had a kind of ongoing "bet" in that the first officer to take someone to jail for any significant crime earned esteem, or, unofficial "fellow cop points" for the shift; it was a sign of doing your job...There were no prizes, just bragging rights, being proud of doing a good job, and maybe a couple of cold beers at the end of shift.

Officer Pete drove out of the station parking lot, down a frontage road and entered the freeway. He had to drive a mile to get to his beat area. As Officer Pete merged onto the freeway, he spotted an older mini pick-up truck with a camper shell in the fast lane. The truck wasn't really that old, but it looked that way. It had some body damage, faded paint, and was covered with dust. There was no reason to stop the truck except that it "jumped" from the fast lane into the slow lane and cut off another car.

"Yeah, it "jumped" from one lane to another. Nobody is going to believe that crap. How in

the hell do I describe that in a police report?"

The pickup truck continued hauling ass down the freeway and cut off several more cars. Remember the car that cut you off and you wished a cop was there to do something about it? Well, in this story, a cop was there, Officer Pete, and he did something about it!

Officer Pete pulled the truck over to the shoulder of the freeway. He walked up to the driver's door with the utmost care, using all his senses to detect anything out of the ordinary. But wait, this was no "ordinary stop". This is the "truck that jumps on the freeway" stop. Better be extra alert. Anyone can pull out a gun or suddenly attack you. Cops always have to be on their guard.

As Officer Pete walked up to the driver's door, he looked through the rear camper shell window and got a small clue as to what was happening. The truck cab had an open pass through window to the truck bed area. Deputy Pete was looking at the bonanza of all retirement accounts in the truck bed area. Based upon Officer Pete's training and experience, the truck bed contained approximately 557 empty beer cans. *(No, Officer Pete didn't count them, that figure was made up for this story. But, it's pretty close…).*

Officer Pete contacted the driver with the usual, "hello". This "hello" greeting is the point where the cop is getting a feel for the situation and is taking in all that their senses can handle. Officer Pete's nostrils received the 'ole "tons of stale beer and cigarette smoke" signal from the inside of the pickup truck; it smelled like a good 'ole country western bar in there.

20

Officer Pete asked the driver to step to the rear of the truck so Officer Pete would not have to stand near the traffic lane and possibly get run over. If that would happen, Officer Pete would not be able to enjoy those cold post shift beers that always tasted good on summer nights.

HOSS

The driver of the pickup truck got out and stumbled to the back of the truck while using the side of the truck like a handrail to keep his balance. The driver could best be described as, "Hoss." No, he wasn't six feet tall and two hundred fifty pounds. He was five foot six and one hundred sixty pounds. But, everything about him said, "Hoss".

Hoss had a real live cowboy hat, fully equipped with a real, brown sweat line around the headband and covered with a smooth layer of corral dust. The hat was bent in the front for easy tipping to ladies. The sides were curled up in correct cattle ranch protocol and in accordance with proper country western dress standards. Hoss is a white male, about 55 years old but looks 75 or more due to being kicked by horses his whole life and drinking too many alcoholic beverages. He spent most of his life out in the sun and his thin, weathered, red-tanned face was testament thereto. Hoss's earth toned, plaid western shirt and dusty blue jeans cried, "I'm a Cowboy!!!!!" But wait, there's more! Hoss was wearing a huge, official, scratched-up, silver and gold rodeo buckle with a 25-year-old sweat stained leather belt. His wardrobe was completed with dirty 'ole, pointed-up at the toes, cowboy boots.

Officer Pete is staring eye to eye with the

21

official, retired, rodeo star poster boy!!! Yeee-Haw!!!! Let's have a cold one!!! But, we can't, because Hoss already drank 'em all...

Hoss' breath smells like fresh beer. His eyes are red, watery and sad looking. He can't keep his balance and keeps leaning against his truck for balance. It's hard to tell if Hoss' speech is slurred because he might just talk that way naturally. Who knows?

At this point, Officer Pete knows what he has to do, but in a way, he doesn't want to do it. Hoss is definitely a public safety threat: he is totally wasted. Officer Pete has to arrest him because if he lets Hoss go and he gets back into his truck and hurts or kills somebody, Officer Pete will be the one paying a big price for not protecting the public.

I get paid to get Hoss off the street even though I wish there was another way. If I don't do it, he'll just drive around drunk until he kills somebody. We can't have that...

Well, Hoss is going to jail for sure. I'll just make the procedure as painless as possible for him. I got a feelin' he's been there before.

Hoss digs his driver's license out of his sweat stained brown leather wallet. Officer Pete explains to Hoss that he must administer a couple of tests to see how much Hoss had to drink; or really, how shit faced Hoss is...

Hoss, in a perfect country western drawl states,

"There ain't no neeeed for that..."

You are absolutely right Hoss. You are drunker than heck. You can hardly stand up, but the District Attorney's Office requires us to give you some tests even though you are seriously smashed...Sorry but you have to take the tests Hoss...

The following dialogue occurred between Officer Pete and Hoss:

All of Hoss's statements are made with an official country- western drawl:

"What have you been drinking?"

"Call-la-rrraaa-da Cool-Aid."

"When did you start drinking (today)?"

"Nine-teeeen-for-teee-six."

"No, I asked what time you started drinking today."

"Nine-teeeen-for-teee-six."

"Okay, now we're having some fun. Hoss was drinking Call-la-rrraaa-da Cool-Aid (Coors brand beer), and he started in 1946. Let's see what other fun we can have..."

"When did you stop drinking?"

"Ahh haaaven't..."

"This guy is some character. You just can't make this shit up! At least he isn't lying about

being smash-o'd"

"Okay. Well, I am required to give you a couple of little tests. Do you know the alphabet?"

"You mean A – B – C – D, and all that shit?"

"Okay, now we're having more fun. That almost sounds like a country western song..."

"Yes, A – B – C – D, all the way through to Z"

"Hell, there ain't no neeeed for that..."

"Work with me. I have to ask you these questions. It's part of my job (a.k.a.: *I can't properly take you to jail to sleep off your drunkenness until after we do the tests*)."

"There ain't no neeeed for that"

"Come on, just try it once."

"Okay, you mean A – B – C – D, and all that shit?"

"Yes, A – B – C – D, and all that."

"A – B – C – D – and all that shit...Hell! There ain't no neeeed for that!"

At this point Hoss turns around (almost falling down) and places his hands behind his back for handcuffing.

I think he has done this before.

Officer Pete promptly placed the metal

bracelets on our drunken ranch hand:

"You're right, there ain't no need for that."

Epilogue

Hoss's blood alcohol level was .22 percent which was twice over the lawful limit. This particular trip to Marshall Dillon's jail was Hoss's fourth driving under the influence charge. That means that Hoss was caught and prosecuted four times. He probably drove around drunk hundreds of times in his lifetime.

Officer Pete's story became one of the favorite stories for his family and friends. Now, you have it.

And remember, sometimes,

"There ain't no need for that!"

FUCK YOU STICKS GET OUTTA MY WAY!!!

"5150"
(Pronounced: "Fifty-one-fifty")

Many calls to your local law enforcement agency involve the mentally ill. Some estimate ten percent of police calls involve mentally ill subjects. In recent times these types of calls have skyrocketed.

Some studies have shown subjects with mental illness are sixteen times more likely to be killed by law enforcement and one in four fatal shootings involve mentally ill suspects.

Seeing a need to assist officers with the mentally ill, many agencies began a training program for street officers in how to deal with them. Some agencies formed Crisis Intervention Teams, or, C.I.T. Some were known by a different name: Psychiatric Emergency Response Teams, or, P.E.R.T. Whatever the name used, these teams would try to diffuse situations between the mentally ill and law enforcement and get the mentally ill treated for their condition.

In California, if one is arrested for being mentally ill, it is known as "5150".

"5150" stands for Section 5150 of the California Welfare and Institutions Code. Section 5150 authorizes a Peace Officer or other trained professionals the authority to take persons into custody as a result of a mental health disorder. The person arrested must either be a "danger to others, or to himself or herself, or gravely disabled."

To be a "danger to others", this usually involves threats of harm to others. Being a "danger to self" can involve unsafe acts and threats of suicide. If a person has a condition in which they cannot provide for their basic personal needs for food, clothing, or shelter, they are considered "gravely disabled".

An arrest for section 5150 is not a criminal arrest. It is a civil hold for psychiatric evaluation. After someone is arrested for being "5150", they are taken to a mental health facility where they can be held for up to 72 hours for psychiatric evaluation; longer if the mental health facility manager deems it necessary.

Almost all mental health facilities in America are overcrowded. Mental health problems in the United States are an epidemic.

It's nice to have specialized teams available to deal with the mentally disturbed. However, quite often these teams are not available or busy. Usually the task falls upon the shoulders of the street cop. The street cop may have specialized training, but they know all calls are different and the mentally ill calls are no exception.

Many cops do not like dealing with the mentally ill. They would rather be out catching bank robbers or burglars or enjoying a nice cup of coffee. Encounters with the mentally ill can turn violent in a heartbeat and cops know this. If they have to arrest a mentally ill person, it probably involves a homeless person that will stink up the inside of their patrol car because they haven't showered in weeks (maybe longer). Who wants to wrestle with someone that hasn't showered in decades? Yuck!

Cops know they have to be on high alert when dealing with a Fifty-one-fifty so at the end of their shift they can go home; not the hospital or the morgue and that's the bottom line.

Some "5150" calls don't involve dirty, stinky homeless people. They involve someone that may appear normal but lost something upstairs. This story is one example of that:

OFFICER JIM

Patrol Officer Jim likes being a cop. He is very conscientious in his duties and does not shirk them or look for the easy way out. When he gets a call, he handles it. Jim gets to help the good people and take the crooks to jail. On occasion, he even gets to help the crooks "see the light of day" and change their misguided ways. Officer Jim is in his early 20's, slim, trim, in shape, and will handle anything thrown at him.

The one thing Officer Jim does not like is working the "Dawn Shift". Every normal person is sleeping cozily in their bed. Not Officer Jim. He does not get regular weekends off and on top of that, he has to work the shitty dawn shift hours. But he still likes being a cop.

Knowing he is up against working shitty hours on the "Dawn Shift", Officer Jim looks forward to 8:00 o'clock in the morning. That is the magical time he gets to head for the station. His shift effectively ends at that time unless he receives an emergency call. After changing out of his uniform, he has to somehow magically drive home without falling asleep at the wheel. His one desire is to enter the safe zone of his bed and escape the dreaded "Dawn Shift" experience. A couple of icy cold pre-snooze beers ensure restful sleep.

One beautiful California summer morning at about 7:30 a.m., one half hour before Officer Jim starts the journey back to the station, he receives a radio call of an elderly 5150 lady on a semi remote road in the hills that border the city.

Hold on a friggin' second. I'm supposed to get off in half an hour! If I have to take a crazy person into custody, it'll take me at least four more hours and I've been up all friggin' night!!! What in the hell are you people putting me through? I should have just signed up to work a double shift. Make those lazy day shifters handle the freakin' call, I'm tired…And, are you sure an elderly female is "crazy". 5150's are supposed to be dirty filthy dudes in their twenties or thirties and they stink like shit. They're not Grandmas!

Oh, Officer Jim, you think you know what 5150's are but you don't. You haven't met Grandma Crazy and her *"Fucking Stick Zone"*…

Officer Jim drives to the location of the call. It's a two-lane road bordered by beautiful oak trees and bright green grass courtesy of a recent rain (Yes, sometimes it rains in California). The rising sun is creeping onto the roadway and it is a fight between

29

sunlight and shade. It is starting to get hot.

God, this is really beautiful scenery. What a beautiful day! Too bad I've been up all night fighting sleep. I'd really like for the Department Command Post Motorhome to respond here and set up some lounge chairs in the shade near the side of the road so I could relax. Oh, and the department just hired a couple of good-looking female officers. They are invited to join me for a couple icy cold beers and some nice music...

You can scratch that from your list of things to do today Jim because it ain't happening. Quit dreaming...

The cards are stacked against Officer Jim on this call.

GRANDMA CRAZY

Officer Jim drove down the road where the 5150 was supposed to be. He saw an elderly female or "Grandma" walking down the middle of it. Grandma's general appearance was well dressed and clean, not the typical dirty 5150. She was wearing an old-fashioned semi round 1940's type hat, dark coat, and a dark, below the knee skirt that she was bulging out of. She looked like a generic Grandmother from the 1940's or 50's. One of the nice sweet ones that always show up for family activities and gives you a big bear hug and sloppy, juicy kisses. Grandma held a suitcase in each hand. She was about 5'4", and 250 pounds. Just a little bit chunky. She was looking down at objects in the middle of the roadway and cursing at them. Officer Jim carefully drove by

30

Grandma and saw her staring at a stick middle of the roadway. She took a wild kick at the stick and told it,

"Fuck you stick, get out of the roadway you fucker!!!"

What's going on here? Grandmas don't swear! But this one's got a really filthy mouth. I didn't know Grandmas were allowed to use the "F" word! I wonder if my Grandmothers ever used the "F" word? I never even heard them say the word "shit". Well, whatever, this Grandma is using the "F" word enough to make up for all the other Grandmas in the world that don't swear.

Grandma walked a bit farther, found a rock in the middle of the road, she kicked it too,

"Fuck you rock!"

Officer Jim is now wide awake. He cannot believe little 'ole fat granny is way out in the middle of nowhere and she has such a foul mouth. And, she appears to be crazier than the three stooges!

How did she get here? This is not the city. There isn't a house for miles. I'll bet those cops from the neighboring county dropped her off here because they also know how long it takes to process a crazy person and get them admitted to mental health. That's right, my lazy (they think they are smart) brothers from the neighboring county got a call on Granny. They picked her up, drove her to our city, told her some lies and then went to a phone booth and called 911 to report a crazy person in the

31

roadway. You dirty fuckers, you dirty, dirty little piece of shit fuckers! I've been up all night and now I'm screwed! And, the next shift is supposed to handle these calls, so I don't have to put in for overtime. Ah, shiiiiit! I really don't need this crap.

Our favorite officer drives past Grandma Crazy hoping nobody drives into her during the process. Officer Jim pulls a U-turn, drives back up to Grandma Crazy's location. He turns on his overhead lights to warn other vehicles, and parks on the shoulder of the road. He walks over to Granny Crazy who is still in the middle of the road searching for more sticks and rocks and asks her to walk over to his patrol car to get her out of the road. Officer Jim is obviously very rude to Grandma Crazy at the time; she was busy telling another stick in the roadway to go fuck itself and he interrupted. Grandma Crazy ignored Officer Jim. Officer Jim again nicely asks Grandma Crazy to walk over to his car. Grandma Crazy now notices that Officer Jim has spoken to her. She now finds time to explain to Officer Jim just what position in life he holds:

"Fuck you! And, fuck these sticks!!!!"

"Where's my son?"

"He's supposed to pick me up in his helicopter! Fuck you Motherfucker!""

Helicopter? What kind of shit is this? There isn't an airfield for at least thirty miles. And, who is really fucked here? Is it Grandma, who is already crazy? Is it the fucking sticks in the roadway, the fucking rocks? Or, is it Officer

Jim? The answer is, "Officer Jim" and, he knows it. He can't go home and enjoy emergency pre-sleep cold beers. No cool summer's day bed to slumber in. Nope, none of that shit; because dispatch refused to send the day shift car out to handle this mess of a bizarre call. It's a "No Win" for Officer Jim. According to Grandma Crazy, it's a "Fuck You-Fuck You, Officer Jim" situation.

Officer Jim is totally screwed by two issues of this radio call: the crazy person is elderly and a female. On top of that, she is a grandma! If Officer Jim has to arrest some dirty filthy guy off the street for being crazy, everyone looking on will accept it for what it is. But if Officer Jim has to arrest a little old Grandma for being crazy, Officer Jim will look like a Nazi cop. Grandmas are nice. They spoil you while you are growing up. They buy you gifts you don't deserve. They talk sweetly to you. They cook you nice meals because they want to.

Nazi cops are not nice. They violate the civil rights of Grandmas all over the globe. Everyone hates Nazi, Grandma arresting cops. They are the scourge of the earth! Yes, Officer Jim, you are totally screwed on this one.

A car or two drove by Grandma while she was in the middle of the road but they slowed down and did not hit her or Officer Jim.

Thank God. If they had hit her, it would be my fault because I didn't pull her out of the fucking stick road in time...

Officer Jim knew he must get Grandma out of

the roadway or they would eventually get hit by a car driven by a drunk cowboy that started drinking in 1946. Officer Jim walks up to Grandma, gently grabs her by the arm and tries to guide her off the road. Grandma yells,

"Fuck You!!!"

And with all her might, Grandma Crazy attempts to kick Officer Jim in the balls.

Officer Jim has also been the recipient of hot spilled coffee in the crotch. That he can handle but he does not want to get kicked in the family jewels.

Didn't we mention Officer Jim was slim, trim, and in shape? Did you learn how Officer Jim was not happy with being sent to this radio call after a long night of work and his amount of frustration attached to this incident? Officer Jim was not going to add personal physical injury to his list of complaints if he didn't have to.

Grandma Crazy gave her kick everything she had because Officer Jim must be related to the fucking sticks and rocks on the road. Officer Jim saw Grandma Crazy's foot headed for his crotch. He always tries to stay aware of a suspect's hands and feet. He was ready for Grandma's kick because others have tried it unsuccessfully before her. Officer Jim does not want to get kicked in the family package area. When Grandma Crazy kicked up towards Officer Jim's crotch, he gauged the kick and merely jumped sideways a couple of inches to escape the kick.

Grandma Crazy missed contact with Officer

Jim. She put so much force into her kick that when she missed Officer Jim's crotch, she sent herself flying up into the air. Her body twisted to one side and she came down hard on the roadway, cracking a front tooth in the process.

> *How a woman that fat can send herself airborne is beyond me. The "fucking sticks" really pissed her off!*

> *But now, Grandma Crazy, who looks like a sweet 'ole lady, assaults me and gets a busted tooth. Now, I have to handcuff her big butt and take her to mental health via the emergency room for medical clearance because she busted her own tooth. Who is going to believe this crap? This shit just keeps getting deeper, add another two hours of overtime because of the emergency room visit. I'm still pissed they sent me to this call!!!*

Officer Jim arrives at the local emergency room to have Grandma Crazy treated and cleared for booking into the local mental health facility. So, here is a young cop in his prime, walking dear, sweet, little, old Granny into a hospital while she is hand cuffed and bleeding from the mouth. Everyone who sees the two of them together is going to think that Officer Jim is the biggest Nazi asshole cop alive for picking on little 'ole Granny...

> *Damnit, they sent me to another no-win, shit call!!!*

NURSE ACLU

Officer Jim walks into the E.R. and is directed

35

to a patient bed. Grandma Crazy is very silent as she accompanies Officer Jim. It is this silence and her appearance that attracts the attention of the E.R. staff. Grandma Crazy has a seat on a patient bed. The assisting E.R. nurse walks up to Officer Jim. She is drop dead gorgeous and Officer Jim thinks her beautiful face belongs on the cover of **HOT NURSES TODAY** magazine. Her makeup is perfect.

Focus Jim, FOCUS!

Anyway, our E.R. nurse appears well rested and she probably just started her shift whereas Officer Jim is dragging butt tired. But he can't show it. A sign of tiredness is a sign of weakness.

The nurse glances at little ole sweet Granny who looks like she is dressed for church and then gives Officer Jim that: *"You dirty little mother-fucking Nazi cop!"* look.

You probably went into Grandma's house, dragged her out of bed, beat her up, planted evidence on her, and made up some ridiculous charges because you were bored. I hate cops and you're the reason why! You should be so ashamed of your behavior, I'm calling the ACLU right after we treat poor little 'ole Granny…. You're going to get fired you dirty Nazi Mother Fucker!!!

Officer Jim knows it looks bad. He just has to go through the motions and try to convince everyone he is not a Nazi cop. He tried to be nice to little Granny, but it didn't work. *Nice* doesn't always work with crazy people. *Nice* can get you hurt or killed.

36

I've been up all night. I'm tired, I got screwed with this call. Granny tries to kick the shit out of me and somehow, Damnit, it's my fault!

Nurse ACLU asks Officer Jim in the most condescending tone,

"Why did you (*You Nazi son of a bitch-I hate you more than before*) arrest her?"

Officer Jim quietly responded,

"Well, she's 5150 and tried to kick me in the balls and she tripped and fell. I have to take her to mental health."

Don't fucking second guess me you bitch. I'm the fucking cop here, been up all night, doing my job the best I can, and you have to second guess me. Fuck you and do your job. You hate me because some cop probably gave you a traffic ticket because you talked him into it because you are an authority hating bitch! You hate anyone in a uniform. That shit is all over your face. Don't ask me anymore stupid fucking nurse questions! And, I've changed my mind, I'm not letting your ugly fucking face on the cover of HOT NURSES TODAY magazine! Take that bitch!

Nurse ACLU starts writing on a clipboard.

Yeah, right, Mister Nazi cop…. Nice cover story for being too heavy handed. I'm still calling the ACLU on your fucking ass. You're going to lose your job; we hate cops like you. You're going to pay big for this you dirty fucking lying pig!!! Kiss your job goodbye!

Officer Jim hates it when he is prejudged: Fuck you Nurse ACLU. You were beautiful until you opened your disgusting, prejudiced, fucking mouth. You hate me and I hate you. I would tell you that out loud except I would get in deep shit for swearing in public (even though it is the truth). I like my job so much I will once again hold my tongue when I want so badly to tell someone they are a fucking bitch!

Our favorite E.R. nurse starts to talk to dear 'ole sweet Grandma Crazy and is trying to take her pulse when Granny, saves the day for Officer Jim: Grandma Crazy gets in the face of Nurse ACLU and screams at her as if she was just released from the gates of hell:

"FUCK YOU!!!!! WHERE'S MY SON!? HE'S SUPPOSED TO PICK ME UP IN THE FUCKING HELICOPTER!!!!! FUCK YOU!!!!"

At this moment, Officer Jim is so happy, he has forgotten all about getting home on time. Grandma Crazy has just vindicated him. He now has a witness; even if the witness does hate cops.

I hope Grandma Crazy spit on Nurse ACLU's face when she yelled at her. That should teach that bitch! Payback for thinking I am a fucking Nazi pig cop…

Nurses hate being cursed at. Nurse ACLU is pissed at Grandma Crazy and stops trying to get her vitals. Nurse ACLU turns towards Officer Jim and reluctantly states,

"You're right... the E.R. physician will be right with you."

Yes! Thank God! One ACLU member gone; one to go...

DOCTOR ACLU

A couple of minutes go by and the E.R. doctor shows up. When he sees cute little 'ole Grandma Crazy handcuffed, he looks at Officer Jim with the same disdainful look Nurse ACLU had:

You dirty asshole cops. I hate you too! This is a perfect example of why people hate cops: you beat up on poor little defenseless women! I'm calling the ACLU too fucker! This shit is going to be on 20/20! Kiss your job goodbye Nazi motherfucker!!!

Officer Jim goes through the same routine with the doctor explaining that Grandma is crazy and has a 5150-hold placed on her; she's a bit violent, and we need to get her cleared for mental health.

The E.R. doctor looks at Officer Jim with a look that says:

"Yeah, right. You expect me to believe that line of bullshit, you freakin' Nazi cop? That makes it twice now that you've lied to me. Oh, 20/20 is gonna love this story. You can kiss your Nazi cop ass goodbye motherfucker!

Doctor ACLU then tries to look at Grandma Crazy's broken tooth when all of a sudden, bless her heart, she blurts out at the top of her lungs:

"FUCK YOU!!!!! WHERE'S MY SON!? HE'S SUPPOSED TO PICK ME UP IN THE FUCKING HELICOPTER!!!!! FUCK YOU!!!!"

This time, Officer Jim saw vaporized blood and saliva spew forth from Grandma Crazy's mouth and onto the face of Doctor ACLU.

Take that motherfucker! Things are getting better. The ACLU members now know I am not a liar and one of them got spit on for thinking so. Now if I can just get Nurse ACLU back over to Granny's bed again, we might try to get some blood and saliva spit on her too. And, thank you Grandma Crazy for once again not being able to contain your psychosis and vindicating me in front of the world. I now have another witness that I am not a Nazi cop, and, both of my witnesses now are convinced that you are the one and only, "Grandma Crazy". I am so happy at your performance that I feel like giving you a big kiss except you have blood all over your mouth and you would probably try to kick me in the nuts again. Anyway, thank you so much Granny Crazy... I love you...

Grandma Crazy was eventually cleared by the ACLU emergency room staff and Officer Jim had a thirty-minute drive to the mental health facility where finally, Grandma Crazy will be the responsibility of trained psychiatric staff.

Those cold post shift beers are getting closer and closer!

Officer Jim drove up to the reception door of the mental health facility to drop off Grandma Crazy. A Psych Tech met Officer Jim and he told her what he had: a Crazy Grandma with a chipped tooth. The Psych Tech did not look at Officer Jim like he was a crazy Nazi Pig Cop. There were plenty of varieties of crazy people at the mental health facility and cops don't get second guessed there.

The mental health director (A.K.A. - Head Honcho: Doctor in Charge) did not want to accept Grandma Crazy because their bed space was full, and they had patients sleeping on the floor

Wait a second, I get a late radio call, could have gotten run over in the middle of the road, almost got kicked in the nuts, received hate vibes from the ACLU Emergency Room staff, had to drive all the way over here, and now you tell me you're not going to take her? Is there some secret medical community conspiracy in place today to fuck with Officer Jim? Is this national FUCK WITH OFFICER JIM DAY?

Officer Jim was made to wait while Doctor in Charge checked his 5150 database and learned that Grandma Crazy was in fact from the next county over and she was being regularly treated by a psychiatrist in her hometown. At this point, Officer Jim just wants to drop off Grandma Crazy, go back to his station, turn in his patrol car, turn in his reports, go home and go to sleep. Forget the icy cold after shift beers that support good sleeping health. I'm too tired. Doctor in charge then attempts to get Officer Jim to drive Grandma Crazy to her doctor's office in the neighboring county.

What the fuck? You are refusing to accept her? Alright, no more Mister nice guy.
.
"What's your name? Who is your superior? Ever heard of interfering with a police officer in performance of his duties? It's called 'One Forty-Eight" (148) of the penal code. Oh, the press is going to like this story. Doctor arrested by police for failing to perform his mandated by law duties. Ever heard of the ACLU and 20/20? You are their next story. Need a lawsuit for not taking Granny? I'll be her family's star witness. The ACLU would love to hear about your incompetence. Have I painted a proper picture for you to make a professional decision and help little 'ole granny?"

I think you idiots better re-read section 5150 of the Welfare and Institutions Code because you are responsible for accepting Grandmas that hate fucking sticks and rocks. You are liable for her now. I am not your personal 5150 babysitter. Take her now because I am leaving...

After a brief review of the law and liability, the Doctor in Charge agreed to take Grandma Crazy:

"We'll make room."

Officer Jim drove back to his patrol station, one of the locations of the conspiracy to deprive him of sleep. He was too tired to chew out the dispatchers for sending him on the late call. He was too tired to call the neighboring county and tell them they were

42

fucking assholes for dropping off Grandma Crazy in his beat area. No, he was just too tired to give a shit anymore...

Officer Jim got to bed in the early afternoon. He was so glad to be rid of Grandma Crazy. He totally forgot about his emergency icy cold pre-sleep beers. He was just too tired...

As documented earlier, Grandma Crazy injured herself during the events of this story.

Numerous fucking sticks and fucking rocks were also injured.

CLASSICAL MUSIC ON ELM STREET

Picture a relatively quiet southern California residential neighborhood. The homes are somewhere around the median price range. Not ghetto but not Beverly Hills either; somewhere in between. A lovely neighborhood with well-manicured lawns.

Officer Jim is working the evening shift. It's about 5:30 p.m. and he gets sent to a domestic dispute call in the beautiful neighborhood. A wife just left her home because her husband is acting crazy by breaking up furniture. The wife escaped to the neighbor's house to call the cops because her husband ripped the phone off the wall when she threatened to call the police. Her seven-year-old boy is still in the house and she wants to get him out.

Officer Jim doesn't have any back up, which is not a good idea on domestic violence calls. Domestic Violence calls can be very dangerous and usually at least two officers are sent to them. But this is an unusually busy evening and Officer Jim is going it alone. He must be extra careful.

Officer Jim contacts the wife at the neighbor's home. She is about thirty-five years old. Her husband is going crazy and has threatened to do harm to both her and her son but he hasn't hurt anyone yet. She wants Officer Jim to go with her back to her house so she can crawl through her son's bedroom window and take him out of the house without her crazy husband knowing what happened.

Officer Jim and the wife do just that. She crawls through her son's bedroom window and comes

44

out with him.

At the neighbor's home, Officer Jim advises the wife that up to this point, her husband has not committed a crime to win him a seat in the jail booking cell. (The laws at that time were a bit more lax than they are today).

Officer Jim attempts to contact the husband but he does not answer the door. At this point Officer Jim advises the wife to stay either at the neighbor's or a relative's house and to contact her attorney in the morning. Also, please call us if things escalate. Officer Jim can't arrest the husband unless he is a danger to himself or others. He tells the wife to definitely stay away from the husband.

Officer Jim gets another emergency call and has to leave the scene.

The night goes on with Officer Jim and other patrol cars monitoring the situation on Elm Street. Nothing happens.

This particular night, Officer Jim has to work a double shift in the same beat. That means Officer Jim has to work the dreaded dawn shift directly after his evening shift. But, it's not so bad because his adjoining beat partner on dawn shift is an old friend, Officer Blake.

OFFICER BLAKE

Officer Jim and Officer Blake have been friends since the first day they met. Officer Blake is also very conscientious about his job. Jim and Blake both have a great sense of humor and like to have fun on the job (if that's possible). They are such good friends; they became fishing buddies. So, if things get boring, they can always have a nice cup of coffee and talk about their next fishing trip.

RETIRED POLICE SERGEANT DONUT SHOP OWNER

As soon as Officer Blake hits the street, he and Officer Jim meet at their favorite local donut shop for coffee. The shop is owned by a likeable Retired Police Sergeant from a neighboring police department who is an excellent enabler of Officer Jim's and Blake's lust for coffee. Retired Police Sergeant Donut Shop Owner is in his mid-fifties and still has that "cop" look about him. Officers Blake and Jim respect him because he is much older and has many more years' experience than they do. They respectfully call him, "Sarge". Retired Police Sergeant Donut Shop Owner has the safest donut shop in town because it's like a satellite station for the police department. All the officers pay their respects to Sarge and accept his free coffee. If Sarge has any problems at his donut shop, the 12-gauge pump action shotgun underneath the front counter will handle them.

It's about 1:00 a.m. and Officer Jim advises Officer Blake about the potential crazy husband on Elm Street.

The night is eerily quiet, and a thick fog has rolled into the city. The fog is about twenty feet off the ground.

At least it's not at ground level and we can still see where we're driving.

46

Then it happens at about 2:30 a.m. A call goes out for the house on Elm Street. The Reporting Party (the person who called in), a neighbor, reports loud music and sounds of furniture breaking.

This is going to be weird and interesting...

Officers Jim and Blake drive slowly onto Elm Street. They have their car lights off and they park several houses down from Mister Crazy Husband's house. Our favorite house has all the front windows broken out and one can hear furniture breaking to the cadence of Tchaikovsky's overture of 1812 which is blaring out the front windows and undoubtedly has all the neighbors awake. But these neighbors aren't stupid; they're staying inside their homes. They don't want to be an accident of Mister Crazy Husband.

With the furniture breaking, the loud classical music, and the fog, we have a setting for a Hollywood horror film. We'll call the movie *"Violence in the Elm Street Fog"*, starring Mister Crazy Husband. Costarring Officers Jim and Blake. Musical scores by Tchaikovsky.

The patrol Sergeant that night was Sergeant Phil; he shows up to help out.

Officer Jim sneaks up to one of the front windows of the house to take a peek inside and see what is going on.

Officer Jim has never seen this before. He has a view of the kitchen and part of the family room. It appears as though Mister Crazy Husband has broken as many household items as possible in each of those rooms and had a big pile of broken items in the center of each room.

On the other side of the house the officers could hear the sound of more household items being smashed on the floor and against a wall. Mister Crazy Husband was walking from room to room smashing anything he could get his hands on. Officer Jim got a glimpse of him: he was about 6', 5", around forty-five years old, slender, wearing dress slacks, dress shirt, white cotton garden gloves and he was using a garden rake to rake up the household items he had broken. Officer Jim noticed that one of Mister Crazy Husband's hands was bleeding through the cotton garden glove.

Bingo Dude: You are officially a danger to yourself and you are going to mental health for three days. I do like your choice of music though even though it is a bit loud.

Now the trick is to get Mister Crazy Husband into handcuffs without anyone getting hurt. That would be entirely up to Mister Crazy Husband and if he would follow commands.

Officer Jim advises Officer Blake and Sergeant Phil what he has seen. It is decided to kick in the front door of the house and to take up a position in the bedroom hallway and arrest Mister Crazy Husband for 5150.

They pay us to drive cars fast and to kick in front doors of homes and businesses. Now that's a fun job! But this won't be fun if one of us gets hurt.

Jim and Blake have a plan: Jim will kick in the

front door. Then Jim and Blake will enter the house with Jim low to the ground and Blake behind him standing up higher. That way, if lethal force has to be used, Blake won't shoot Jim in the back and prevent Jim from drinking more coffee that shift. Sergeant Phil brings up the rear, ready to assist with whatever needs to be done like radio for more backup, radio for an ambulance, etc.

The front door is kicked in but Mister Crazy Husband can't hear it because his music is too loud. The trio of officers move as a unit into the foyer and turn right into the first hallway they encounter. They can definitely hear smashing and banging coming from one of the bedrooms. Tchaikovsky is deafening.

It sounds like Mister Crazy Husband is coming back to the area of the front door. Our Officers wait for him to come out.

Mister Crazy Husband comes out of one of the bedrooms and into the hallway and is now six feet away from the officers. Mister Crazy Husband is holding a garden rake at "port arms" or, diagonally across his chest. This rake is a potentially deadly weapon if Mister Crazy Husband decides he wants to try and kick the officer's asses with it. He has a look of astonishment on his face.

Really idiot? What did you think would happen if you decided to break everything in your house at 2:30 in the morning while playing Tchaikovsky as loud as you possibly could and wake up the whole damn neighborhood? Maybe the Nobel Peace Prize Committee would show up to give some kind of award? I don't think so...Instead Mister Crazy Husband,

49

I hope you have real good eyesight because you now have three officers with B.F.G.'s pointing at your freakin' head. We don't want to shoot you, so you better listen to what we say. We're not in a real good mood fucker; you interrupted our coffee break...

Our coffee drinking heroes take no chances and order Mister Crazy Husband down on the floor. Even though he is crazy, Mister Crazy Husband is smart enough to know the officers are not messing around. He complies and is handcuffed without further incident or, "accident".

The house is quickly searched for other people. None are found. Tchaikovsky is turned off and you could hear cheers from the neighbors.

Jim and Blake take Mister Crazy Husband to the hospital to have his bleeding hand stitched up. The treatment at the hospital was uneventful, a couple of stitches on one of his knuckles. Nurse ACLU was nowhere to be found. Doctor ACLU could not be located. Jim and Blake were not Nazi Cop Fuckers this time. This time they arrested the right person, not sweet little ole Grandma Crazy.

It's 6:00 a.m. now and the sun is coming up. After getting Mister Crazy Husband's hand attended to, Jim and Blake put him in the back of Jim's patrol car to drive him to mental health. Mister Crazy Husband is handcuffed behind his back according to police regulations. They are just about to pull out of the hospital parking lot when Mister Crazy Husband blurts out in a somewhat comical voice:

"I'm hungry. How about Taco Bell? I'm

50

buying!

Jim and Blake crack up. They never had an arrestee offer to buy them lunch. But, then again, he was crazy...

THE SHOOTOUT

A BAD DAWN SHIFT

Officer Jim was working patrol on dawn shift again and things just weren't going right. It was a busy shift and a lot of emergency calls were coming in to the station. His beat partner, Officer Blake was at the station booking a prisoner. Because of the high volume of radio calls, Jim didn't get a chance to grab any coffee at the beginning of his shift and everything seemed like a blur to him.

This dawn shift is definitely off balance...

Jim received an emergency call of a burglary in progress at a two-story single-family residence and no back up was available. The residents were upstairs in their bedroom and supposedly holding tight. The burglar was downstairs. It was unknown for sure just how many suspects may have been involved.

Officer Jim was on his own. He was no stranger to danger and was not afraid to handle calls solo.

If you're afraid to face danger, then don't sign up for the police force dumb ass. Go get another job that makes you feel all warm and fuzzy!

Jim knew this call had the potential for being extremely dangerous. He was as cautious as he could be.

The burglar may be armed and I'm going to have to be ready to take him out in a split second. There may be multiple suspects. If so, I can't let any of them get the drop on me from the side or behind. I'm going to use the darkness and my high intensity flashlight to my advantage without giving up my position too much. Always remember: 'We have to go home at the end of shift, No Cop Funerals!'

What if the homeowners are armed and accidentally shoot me? What if I accidentally shoot the homeowners? This shit is stressful, and I haven't even arrived at the scene. Sure, would be nice to have some backup!

Up to this point in his short career, Officer Jim has not had to shoot any bad guys. They had always given up when Officer Jim pointed his B.F.G. at them. But Officer Jim knows that one day he may have to use his B.F.G. to save his life and he has had pretty good training provided by the police department range masters. He's a fair shot using open sights and was also taught to shoot instinctively (with no sights) at a young age. However, instinct shooting is frowned upon by the department.

Jim parks half a block down from the house that is being burglarized. The street has a couple of old streetlights that do not silhouette him very much as he walks toward the house and he is happy about that. He knows he may run into the burglar exiting the house and he is ready for that contingency; one never knows what will happen. Every call is different.

As Jim approaches the house, he sees that the front door is ajar several inches and he hears faint sounds like someone rummaging around inside, maybe the kitchen? Without turning his flashlight on, Jim carefully walks into the foyer and towards the kitchen area. He can see the beam of a flashlight coming from the kitchen area. He has to walk quietly and won't turn his flashlight on until he absolutely has to. He wants the element of surprise. Surprise is good, it doesn't give suspects time to think ahead. Surprise is one of a cop's best friends. Right now, Jim has his two best friends with him: his B.F.G. and his partner, Officer Surprise.

Officer Jim walks into the house. He is five feet from the entrance to the kitchen and all of a sudden, a male subject rounds the corner from the kitchen and is facing Jim. The suspect has a gun in his hand! Jim goes into Ninja mode with lightning speed, points his B.F.G. at the suspect while yelling,

"Drop the fucking gun!"

There is no time lapse here as Officer Jim sees the suspect raising his pistol towards him. Officer Jim wastes him on the spot; he shot the suspect three times and he was down for the count. Another suspect was rounding the corner and Jim shot again, hitting him in the side but the second suspect pulled off a couple rounds and Jim was hit. Not sure if they hit his vest or not; too much adrenalin involved. Another suspect came down the stairs and ran into the kitchen while shooting wildly at Officer Jim and then the unimaginable happened: Jim's gun jammed!

My fucking gun is jammed! I have to kill these fuckers and my gun is jammed!!!

Jim thought the first guy he shot was dead, but he grabbed Jim's legs and tripped him. The two of them are wrestling on the ground all the while Jim is squeezing his trigger harder and harder and nothing happens. Jim is getting tired, he's sweating, he's trying to get his gun cleared to shoot the assholes in the kitchen area and at the same time fight off the first crook who should already be dead. He thought he took him out.

Shit!

The crooks are yelling and screaming. More shots are going off all around Jim. It's pandemonium. Jim is not yelling any commands at this point. He is quiet. It's quite obvious the only language that needs to be spoken here is Smith and Wesson. Nothing more, nothing less.

Jim gets his gun cleared and told the suspect he was wrestling with,

"FUCK YOU!",

as he placed the barrel of his gun on the suspects head and pulled the trigger.

Good night fuckshit! Should have died the first time I shot you!

There are suspects in the kitchen shooting through the kitchen wall adjacent to the foyer where Jim is still laying down. The walls are just wood

55

framing with a drywall covering. The bullets fly right through the drywall with ease.

Jim is injured but doesn't know how bad. He fired as many rounds as he could through the kitchen wall in the hope of killing the suspects on the other side. He hears one of them moaning so he knows he hit one bad guy but rounds keep coming through the wall, hitting Jim in the legs.

When is this shit going to end? Where's my fucking backup?

He's scared shitless, injured, tired, and frustrated over a gun malfunction that never should have happened. He can't reach his portable radio which is on the side of his Sam Brown duty belt. He's still on the floor, he can't move his body. He feels defeated because he can't move his legs and knows this may be his last day on earth, but he has to survive. As hard as he tries, he just can't move his legs.

Shit, I'm probably paralyzed! Fuck!

Jim reloads his pistol and fires several more rounds through the wall.

I may be fucked up but I'm going to try and take as many of you with me as possible!

Jim yells at the suspects:

"FUCK YOU!"

and fires off a volley of rounds through the wall.

Another suspect entered the house through the rear sliding door and was walking slowly through the dinette area towards the spot where Jim was lying in the foyer. The suspect was shooting and laughing at Jim. Jim's pistol jammed again and no matter how hard he pulled the trigger or worked the action to clear malfunction; the pistol wouldn't fire.

I am so fucked again!

And then, like being shocked by a lightning bolt, Jim wakes up.

Holy shit! That shit was so real! What the fuck? My gun doesn't jam; I always keep it clean...

Jim was breathing super heavy. He spent a few minutes lying on his back and waking up in place, amazed he was alive. He tried to move his legs; they were tied up in his bedsheet.

No wonder I thought I was paralyzed; my fucking legs were caught in the bedsheet during the shootout!

He kicked off the paralyzing bedsheet.

It was 1:00 p.m. He had only slept for four hours but that was enough. He was covered in sweat, his bedsheets were soaked, but his sleep was restful; except for that fucked dream!

Now I have to wash the sheets! Create more work for yourself Jim! If your fucking pistol hadn't jammed, we wouldn't have to wash the sheets again! Just when in the hell are we

57

going to have a good shooting dream where the gun never jams?

I can't tell anyone about these damn dreams except for Blake and a few others. I trust only a few of my friends and supervisors with confidential personal information. The others will say I'm crazy or some other stupid shit and make me go in for counseling and see the department psychologist or some other horseshit; then, they'll talk shit about me behind my back and tell everyone I'm losing it upstairs. Nope, I don't trust those fuckers. I'll deal with it.

At least I didn't really get shot! Better go for a run today and get rid of all the residual adrenalin. After that, maybe a dip in the pool and we'll be on the road to recovery!

Jim got up and wanted coffee but there was something more important to do first. Something he just had to do before anything else in life, something more important than coffee: he had to inspect his duty pistol.

Jim carefully unloaded his B.F.G. and checked the chamber twice to make sure it was completely unloaded. He then sighted in on the miniature F.B.I. approved silhouette target on his bedroom wall and dry fired a couple imaginary rounds all the while maintaining good sight alignment and sight picture. He then blew off any dust on his B.F.G., got a cotton swab, placed a small amount of oil on it and oiled the slide rails of his pistol. He then worked the action several times:

Nice and smooth, functioning perfectly. Try to remember your firearm is in perfect working order next time you have that shitty shooting dream. Better yet, next time you have the dream, tell the dispatcher in the dream you are not responding to the burglary call because it is not a real call and you are tired of your fucking gun jamming and having to wash the sheets!

Jim walked to his kitchen.

My legs are working great, I'm definitely not paralyzed!

He made some fresh coffee and took it out to his patio and sat in the hot California sunlight.

It's nice to have some hot sun during the day like a regular person! Moments like this make dawn shift seem like a land that is very, very, far away. A distant land in some make-believe dark fairy tale. Real people don't live in "Dawn Shift Land", only make-believe people do, or cops...

Later, Jim went for a little five-mile, ninety-five-degree heat, punishment run. He deserved some physical punishment after what he put himself through with that terrible dream. Running clears, the head.

BROTHERLY COUNSELING

Later that night, Blake and Jim started their real dawn shift by fueling up with coffee at Retired

Police Sergeant Donut Shop Owner's substation. Blake and Jim walked into the donut shop like they owned the place. Retired Police Sergeant Donut Shop Owner was busy mixing dough and greeted them,

> "How you boys doing?"

> "Excellent to Outstanding Sarge! We need some rocket fuel", replied Blake.

Sarge replied,

> "Always on the menu! How about you Jim?"

> "Everything is fantastico, except for the fucking shooting dream I had this morning. I need some felony coffee Sarge."

As you will remember, Retired Police Sergeant Donut Shop Owner is much older and more experienced than Jim or Blake and he often gave advice whenever he could. After all, he considered Jim and Blake two of "his boys" on the force. Blake, Jim and Retired Police Sergeant Donut Shop Owner had known each other long enough and told each other so many stories that the three trusted one another as if they worked together on the streets. Retired Police Sergeant Donut Shop Owner and Jim had the following exchange:

> "Is that the dream with the trigger that won't pull, or the bullets that dribble out the end of the barrel?"

> "You've had them too?"

"Yeah, I think all cops have them."

"I had the dream where the trigger wouldn't pull and the gun jammed."

"Did you still get to kill a couple of those fuckers?"

"Yeah but I woke up in pouring sweat and got the sheets all wet."

"At least you got to waste a couple of those fuckers. That's good. If you ever get in a real shooting situation, your gun will never jam again in a shooting dream. Or anyways, that's what happened to me. We'll talk about that some other time. Anyway, prior to that, I came up with an idea many years ago and when dispatch tried to resend me to my shitty shooting call dream, I refused. I got in trouble in my dream for not responding, but then I woke up and no more gun malfunctions or sweaty sheets."

"I was thinking something like that this morning after I woke up."

"It's hard to do at first because you feel like you are letting the public down by not responding to an emergency call but you'll get used to it. And, it works".

Sarge grabbed three large Styrofoam coffee cups and the coffee carafe. He started to pour:

"Let's celebrate with some hot coffee."

61

"Thanks for the briefing Sarge."

"No extra charge Jim."

MERCEDES MAN

The adventures of Officers Jim and Blake don't stop. They are once again working another dawn shift together and they are at their favorite donut shop filling up on free coffee supplied by Retired Police Sergeant Donut Shop Owner.

Officers Jim and Blake talk a little bit with Retired Police Sergeant Donut Shop Owner and then take their free coffee out to their patrol cars. They lean against the sides of their patrol cars facing each other while they talk; this way they can watch each other's back. They are discussing department politics and their next fishing trip. They finish half their coffee and get into their patrol cars to check their beats. Each has only half a cup of coffee with a "non-spill" lid. Shouldn't be any hot coffee on crotches tonight.

Officer Jim heads out to his beat area which just so happens to adjoin Officer Blake's beat area. Very convenient, especially because the two of them will undoubtedly have to meet back up again in about an hour for more free emergency coffee.

Officer Blake is already in his beat area because Retired Police Sergeant's Donut Shop is located in it.

It's 2:00 a.m. and Officer Blake drives down one of his main boulevards and sees a newer Mercedes driving towards him without its lights on. Officer Blake makes a U-turn to stop the Mercedes and the Mercedes makes a right turn onto a side street and accelerates to about 80 miles per hour. It appears the driver of the Mercedes doesn't like the police.

Officer Blake radios that he is in pursuit of a dark colored Mercedes and gives the direction of travel and location.

Officer Jim overhears Officer Blake's radio traffic. Officer Jim is very familiar with the street the Mercedes turned onto. The street in question is about 300 feet long, not very well lit, and is a dead-end street. Officer Jim thinks to himself that if a car is travelling at 80 miles per hour, it will very quickly crash into the block wall that is at the end of the street and hidden in the shadows. And guess what? Officer Blake radios that the Mercedes did just that and the suspect ran away from the scene of the crash. Officer Blake radioed a brief description of the suspect, a male in his late twenties, average build, dark clothing.

Mercedes Man had the audacity to be driving in Officer Blake's beat area without turning on his car's headlights. It wasn't Mercedes Man's fault for not turning on the headlights to his car. He was preoccupied because he had just gotten out of prison for auto theft, stole a brand new Mercedes, scored some cocaine, went to a local bar, scored a cocaine whore, and now he thought he was going to find a quiet spot to snort and screw. So, Mercedes Man had a lot of things on his mind that night. The problem is if you are in Officer Blake's patrol beat on dawn shift and you so much as sneeze the wrong way, Officer Blake is going to be there to correct you. That's what Officer Blake gets paid to do: harass people who break the law. If you happen to be a nice person with just a temporary lapse of judgement, you will probably get off with a warning. If not, there is a very good chance Officer Blake will try to find a reason to take you to jail.

Mercedes Man and his temporary girlfriend were driving around looking for a quiet spot when Officer Blake spotted them.

When Mercedes Man saw Officer Blake make a U-turn, he knew Officer Blake was going to try to stop him. They were the only cars on the road. Mercedes Man just spent two years in prison for auto theft. Poor Mercedes Man, he just can't control himself when it comes to stealing cars. He's good at it. It is what he does. And why buy a car when there are so many free ones out there to choose from? Sometimes the car salesmen at the dealerships will leave the keys in the cars for you!

If he was caught again, it would probably be a four or five-year prison sentence. Too long to go without cocaine and women. Mercedes Man knew he had a fast car and he was a good driver. He stood a better than fifty percent chance of getting away.

Mercedes Man had been arrested numerous times for auto theft. Each and every time he steals a car, he thinks he can outsmart the cops. Sometimes he does outsmart the cops and he gives himself a big pat on the back. But sometimes he fails and its back to prison for a couple of years.

Tonight, Mercedes Man thinks he can outsmart the cops. He's driving a newer Mercedes with plenty of power. It's nighttime and he can outrun the cops and then find a place to hide for a while. As soon as he sees Officer Blake make his U-turn, Mercedes Man makes an immediate right turn down the first street he comes to, he then hits the accelerator hard. He knows he's heading for the freeway. The only problem is, there is a block wall between Mercedes Man and the freeway. Mercedes Man obviously doesn't know the neighborhood. Before he knows it, he slams into the block wall, punching a huge hole in it. Mercedes Man leaves his cocaine girlfriend in the stolen Mercedes and immediately runs through the hole in the wall and high tails it away from Officer Blake.

Mercedes Man is having a bad night. He just got out of prison, stole a hot looking Mercedes, scored some coke, and wants to have a little female companionship. Not too much to ask. Then he forgets to turn on his headlights and gets chased by the cops. Now he crashes into a wall and loses his transportation.

At least I can run away from them…

Officer Blake slams to a stop behind the Mercedes and arrests the female companion. Officer Blake advises dispatch of the license number of the Mercedes. Dispatch advises the Mercedes is stolen. Officer Blake radios that the suspect was last seen running southbound, from the wall he had just crashed into.

As previously stated, Officer Jim knows the area very well. He also knows that on the other side of the wall where Mercedes Man was last seen, one must either make an immediate left or right turn onto a dirt maintenance road. The area has no lighting and if one continues running straight instead of turning left or right, they will launch themselves into a seventeen-foot-deep concrete drainage culvert, which is just what Mercedes Man did. He thought he was smart but not this time.

Officer Jim approached the drainage culvert from the opposite side. He searched the culvert with his high intensity flashlight. He doesn't see anything, but he can hear what sounds like a human moaning. Officer Jim uses his superior powers of deduction and thinks that maybe the moans are coming from a man that just ran away from the cops and landed in the culvert and broke his back and or a leg. Officer Jim locates Mercedes Man lying on his back on the bottom of the concrete culvert. Sure enough, Mercedes Man is injured, and he'll be missing this year's track tryouts at state prison.

Mercedes Man is lying flat on his back in the center of the culvert with his knees bent up as if he were about to do some sit-ups. He's wearing a button up shirt and a pair of blue jeans. The jeans have a hole torn in the crotch, obviously caused from his hard impact with the concrete culvert bottom. His right leg looks rather undamaged. His left leg looks pretty good except for the foot. His left foot is twisted to his left and turned around and pointing towards his face. This appears to be very, very painful. Officer Jim radios Officer Blake and advises him he has the suspect in view and he's not going anywhere.

Officer Blake is ecstatic. For a while it looked like Mercedes Man was going to get away.

This is a good night! First, free coffee down at Retired Police Sergeant's Donut Shop and now we have two in custody for auto theft! I love my job...Little Fucker Mercedes Man thought he could get away from me...

Approximately 100 yards from where Mercedes Man launched himself, Officer Blake finds an access into the culvert where the concrete wall is sloped, and one can easily walk down into the culvert. Blake enters the culvert and informs Mercedes Man he is under arrest for auto theft. Officer Blake searches Mercedes Man but does not handcuff him because that would require twisting Mercedes Man's already mangled left foot. And besides, Mercedes Man isn't armed and isn't going anywhere. In addition to one useless foot, he had to break part of his back with that fall.

Officer Jim left his location and drove around to where the Mercedes crashed. He joined Officer Blake in the culvert.

Now, Mercedes Man is in a lot of pain but not so much that he can't stop talking trash to Officer Blake. He's being very disrespectful and will not even tell Officer Blake his name, or other identifying information. Mercedes Man tells Officer Blake,

"Fuck you man, I ain't saying shit to you, you fucker!"

Obviously, Mercedes man has ingested a lot of cocaine because he appears to be in and out of pain.

Yeah, wait till that cocaine high wears off fucker, you're gonna be in so much pain you're gonna wish you were dead.

Officer Jim scans the area of the culvert. The culvert collects drain water from various parts of the city and there is about a half inch of water in the center of the culvert where Mercedes Man is laying.

Mercedes Man landed half in the water and half out of it. In a couple areas of the water Officer Jim discovers something really good: Fish bait! Crawdads are living in the culvert.

> *What a bonus! We catch a car thief and he leads us directly to the secret breeding ground of the fishing bait we need for our next fishing trip. Outstanding! First, free coffee and now this. Thank you Mercedes Man, you're one of the best suspects we have ran into. Ya know, Dawn Shift isn't such a bad thing on nights like this!*

Mercedes Man keeps moaning about his injuries and refusing to talk to Officer Blake. Officer Jim is getting sick of this. It's time to sing the jail song to Mercedes Man. You see, Officers Blake and Jim have a secret talent: they sing a duet to special idiot arrestees that need making fun of. Officer Jim tells Officer Blake that it is time for them to sing their suspect theme song which is sung with a German "oom pah-pah" beat:

> "You're gooooing to jaaaaail, ah-hah-hah-hah…
>
> It's gonna be fun, Oh-Ho-Ho-Ho!"

Mercedes Man screams,

> "FUCK YOU!"

Officer Jim does not appreciate the level of disrespect and potty mouthedness of Mercedes Man:

Fuck me? No, fuck you, you stupid dumb shit...I'm not the one with the broken fucking leg and back dipshit!

Officer Jim states,

"Hey mister smart guy, you probably can't see it but when you crashed   down here you tore a huge hole in your crotch and your privates are very vulnerable right now. I'll tell you just how vulnerable you are because it's too hard for you to move your body and look around and see your predicament. You see, you need to cooperate with us and quit your trash talking and I'll tell you why. You see, I found a bunch of our friends down here in the culvert. Our little friends are called "crawdads". They are like miniature lobsters with sharp claws used for tearing apart flesh.

They like to live in water and they eat meat. They are not vegans. Now, you   probably don't know much about crawdads, but Officer Blake and I do. The only reason why I tell you this is you landed partially in the water, the home of our little crawdad friends. Like I said, they eat meat; they eat it by tearing it apart with their powerful little lobster claws. They also talk to one another; as soon as one crawdad finds some tasty meat to eat, they start this little clicking sound, kinda like a dinner bell and all their little friends come over for dinner and they all tear the meat apart together. All the little crawdads get fed in one big family reunion meat feeding orgy. It looks like there are about one hundred of our little friends down here in the culvert. They look *real hungry.* We fish with them all the time and you have to be real careful with them when you place them on a fishing hook so they don't latch onto you with one of their strong little nasty claws. It hurts like hell and they can draw blood real easy. So, we'll make you a deal, you cooperate and quit your mouthing off and Officer Blake and I will make sure our little friends don't climb through the hole in your crotch and eat your balls for dinner. Sound good?"

Mercedes Man cried out,

"You guys are crazy!"

"Maybe so but the crawdads are hungry.
Looks like they haven't eaten in days.
Oh my, here comes one now..."

"Stop it – you're crazy!"

"Not my fault, crawdads have rights too."

"You're Crazy!"

"Well get with the program!"

Remember that its early in the morning? It's dawn shift. That means that normal people are sleeping comfortably in their beds. As you know, our officers are wide awake with the activity and excitement of having free coffee at Retired Police Sergeant's Donut Shop, getting to chase Mercedes Man, finally getting to meet Mercedes Man in the drainage culvert, and then finding lots of free bonus bait crawdads for their next fishing trip!

Some other civil servants had their dawn shift ruined: The Fire Department. The Fire Department responded to the scene because of Mercedes Man's traffic collision and subsequent injury. Firemen are experts at waking up at a moment's notice, they're really good at it.

They came over to the area of all the activity and made sure the crashed Mercedes was not leaking gas. They then entered the concrete culvert and set up super bright lights to illuminate Mercedes Man's resting place.

Because Mercedes Man could not walk and had potential back injuries, he was going to have to be removed by professionals to prevent further injury. The fire personnel asked for paramedics to respond. The local ambulance company sent two paramedics that appeared to be half asleep.

MUTT AND JEFF

The two paramedics were kind of a Mutt and Jeff team. In the Mutt and Jeff comic strip, Mutt is tall and skinny; Jeff is short and fat. Our paramedic crew for this story was a five-foot-tall skinny eyeglass wearing paramedic who could barely keep his eyes open with his shirt untucked and sticking out the back of his pants.

The other paramedic was six-foot-tall, heavy set, and following orders from his short partner. It was obvious the tall paramedic was getting trained by the shorter paramedic.

As stated, the paramedics were half asleep and they walked up to within four feet of Mercedes Man. The paramedics are basically face to face with Mercedes man. The mangled leg and torn out crotch are lit up by the fire department's lights:

Paramedic Jeff: "What seems to be the problem?"

Mercedes Man: "My foot's broken."

Paramedic Jeff: "Which one?"

Mercedes Man: "The one that's pointing the wrong   fucking way you idiot!"

Officers Blake and Jim couldn't hold it in, they just had to laugh which pissed off Mercedes Man even more.

Mercedes Man was taken to the local hospital emergency room and then booked into the county jail medical ward.

Our favorite officers got off late, but they didn't mind, they had too much fun. They returned to the culvert the next night and retrieved their free fishing bait. They even got some for Retired Police Sergeant Donut Shop Owner, he likes to fish too!

As previously documented, Mercedes Man fucked up his foot and back...

Mercedes Man's Coke Whore was not injured, she was wearing her seat belt.

No crawdads were injured during the events of this story and no balls were eaten.

CHIEF, YOU'RE NOT GOING TO BELIEVE WHAT HAPPENED TODAY

OFFICER DEAN

Officer Dean is quite a colorful character. He served in Vietnam where he survived a plane crash in the Gulf of Tonkin. The crash left him with a broken nose without any cartilage. He was 6' 1", thin, straight black hair combed to the side, with facial features that were somewhere between Lurch of the Addam's Family and Detective Fish from the Barney Miller show. He looked serious most of the time.

When Officer Dean was released from the service, he had a job waiting for him with a local law enforcement agency. Shortly after arriving stateside he was in the police academy and a very colorful career began.

While Officer Dean was in Vietnam, he was instructed to pack all of his military gear in a crate and have it shipped stateside. While in the academy, he received the crate of military gear at his home. He kinda panicked when he opened it up and saw his M-60 machinegun and concussion grenades still inside the crate. He called another police academy classmate who was also a Vietnam veteran and discussed the situation with him. They both knew that Officer Dean was not supposed to be storing an M-60 machinegun and concussion grenades at his home. He could get in deep shit for that.

The two knew there was a military screw up and the simplest solution to properly disposing of the machinegun and concussion grenades was to return them to Uncle Sam.

Officer Dean removed all of his personal effects from the crate and along with his police academy classmate drove to the nearest military base which just so happened to be an air force base.

They drove up to the front gate guard, stopped their car and took the crate out of the truck. Officer Dean told the gate guard,

"I just got back from Vietnam and the government accidentally sent my M-60 and some concussion grenades back to my house with my personal effects. Here they are, thank you."

And with that, Officer Dean and his classmate drove away. The military did not make an issue of it.

OUT OF THE POLICE ACADEMY

So Officer Dean completes his academy training and is later assigned to patrol activities in a southern California city that is home to a "wild animal" park.

Officer Dean's city is going through a metamorphosis. It is a city but surrounded by ranch lands that will one day be transformed into custom homes, businesses and apartment buildings.

Not only does Officer Dean deal with regular police calls, he has to deal with some irregular police calls that do not deal with humans. Officer Dean and his patrol partners all carry livestock ropes in their police calls. When they are not responding to calls of burglaries and robberies in progress, Officer Dean and his partners are responding to calls of livestock in the roadway, "blocking traffic". The livestock range from cattle, sheep, and horses which they inevitably have to rope and lead off the roads. Some of the officers got good at roping animals.

After a couple years on the force, Officer Dean was considered an "old salt".

It's summertime and Officer Dean is working dayshift on a quiet Sunday morning. He is dispatched to a call down the street from the wild animal park. Another animal got loose, a Hippopotamus.

A fun fact about Hippos is that an adult male can reach 8000 pounds. The average weight for a hippo is somewhere around 3,000 pounds. Just a tad bit more than the horses and cattle Officer Dean is accustomed to handling. But that will not deter Officer Dean. No way. He is the resident animal tamer and catcher; he won't let a little hippo get in the way of his stellar animal catching reputation. Nope, this is just another opportunity for Officer Dean to display his superior animal handling skills.

Officer Dean locates the hippo and thanks God because it's not a full-grown hippo. It's still young, only about two to three thousand pounds. Three additional officers assist Officer Dean with his loose animal call. It sounded pretty serious and all.

We've never had a loose hippo.

The hippo is on a major city thoroughfare, munching on the grass on the side of the road.

Dean thinks this is going to be a very simple call.

Officer Dean pulls his police car up to about ten feet from the hippo. The hippo looks at him for a second then goes back to eating grass.

The other Officers pulled up to assist Officer Dean and each one exited their police car with a livestock rope.

All the Officers walk up to the hippo and place their ropes around the neck of the hippo. Each one then ties their rope off on the bumper of Officer Dean's patrol unit.

Simple, Child's play. We've got this one licked. Call dispatch, have them get the hippo owner out here and we're done. Sayonara. Not difficult at all. Now we can add a wild hippo to our list of successfully captured animals. Everybody's gonna be jealous!

Just one little problem: our little hippo decided to walk away from Officer Dean's patrol car while dragging it behind him. The hippo noticed some more grass about twenty feet away and evidently this other grass was higher in nutrients than the grass it had been munching on.

The hippo took up the slack in the ropes and started dragging Dean's police car behind him like it was a toddler's wagon.

What the fuck is that thing doing? It's dragging my patrol unit like it's a little kid's wagon. What if it goes out into the boulevard? What then?

Nice big car crash? Dead hippo? Send all these animals back to Africa, we don't need this. This call is definitely going to shit!

Officer Dean could only watch as his little hippo not only dragged his police car, the hippo managed to drag the police car over the street curb where a tree stump was located. The tree stump was about eighteen inches in diameter and two feet tall. The hippo walked past the tree stump, dragging the police car which ended up hitting the stump right in the middle of Officer Dean's front bumper.

The hippo didn't stop there, he kept dragging the police car because he was trying to reach delicious green grass located further away.

Officer Dean and partners could only watch as the hippo pulled on the police car which was getting dented by the tree stump. They watched in amazement as the hippo pulled the police car and drove the engine into the front seat of the police car, totally ruining the car.

You can't make this stuff up. This is unbelievable. I'm going to get blamed for this. I hope I don't have to pay for the damage...

Oh shit! Why did I come to work today? I should have called in sick and gone fishing or something, or just stayed at home. Why do I carry that stinkin' rope? More trouble than it's worth. The Chief isn't going to believe this. I am so screwed.

An animal trainer from the wild animal park showed up with a short rope to lead the hippo back to its enclosure. On one end of the rope was a spring-loaded clip or ring. The trainer placed this clip inside the hippo's nostrils and walked him back to the wild animal park like he was a little kitten.

Officer Dean had his police car towed to the station. He hitched a ride back to the station with his beat partner.

Dean was furious. He went to the Chief's office:

"Chief, you're not going to believe what happened today..."

"I already heard about it Dean. Sit down, we have to talk."

"Chief, it's not my fault, I thought our ropes would keep the hippo from going anywhere and they didn't do any good!"

"Calm down Dean, I know you've had a long day and you ruined a police car."

"The hippo did it, I swear!"

"Dean, calm down. You're the first to have a hippo ruin their car. I'm thinking about sending you back to patrol training so that you can learn to handle calls more appropriately."

"Chief, I swear, I did everything possible to subdue the hippo."

"Maybe so but I think you at least need some end of shift therapy."

"What do you mean?"

"I mean, I don't want you going home all upset and frustrated by this."

"What?"

The Chief opened one of his desk drawers and pulled out two shot glasses followed by a bottle of Crown Royal.

Dean looked at the glasses and bottle of Crown and asked,

"Am I in trouble or not?"

"Calm down Dean, have a shot of therapy. It's not your fault the car is ruined. I was just kidding with you. The wild animal park has insurance, the department has insurance, we'll get another car."

The Chief poured two shots:

"Now drink some medicine and be healed, it's not your fault, relax."

"Chief,"

"What?"

"Thanks."

"Your Welcome."

Some smart ass posted a sign outside the entrance to the police station parking lot:

"PLEASE LEAVE ALL PETS IN THE PUBLIC

PARKING AREA. DO NOT BRING THEM INTO THE POLICE PARKING LOT (THIS INCLUDES HIPPOS).

ANY QUESTIONS OR CONCERNS, CONTACT OFFICER DEAN, ANIMAL BEHAVIOR COORDINATOR."

Officer Dean was not amused but had to roll with the joke. After all, it wasn't his fault. But, from that day forward, whenever there was a loose animal call, responding officers would ask if Officer Dean was available to assist. Officer Dean just learned to live with it.

The hippo in this story was not harmed.

BWANA

One night Officer Dean gets a call of a loose baby elephant in one of the city's residential neighborhoods. Officer Dean locates the elephant by the side of a residential street and gets his rope out. Officer Dean is assisted by Officer Preston.

For some reason, Officer Preston doesn't get his rope out. He walks over to where Officer Dean and the elephant are standing. The young elephant takes a step toward Officer Preston and nuzzles his truck against Officer Preston's side. The elephant likes Officer Preston! Officer Preston starts walking back in the direction of the wild animal park and the elephant follows his new Daddy, Officer Preston.

Officer Preston obviously has some special way with animals. His parents incorrectly named him "Preston." They should have named him, "Noah."

Officer Dean is enjoying this event and tells Officer Preston to call the elephant "Bwana", or boss. Officer Preston does. He said,

"Come on Bwana, let's get you home" and Bwana followed Officer Preston. No ropes necessary here."

Officer Dean and Preston discussed the matter and decided that it probably wouldn't be a good idea to try and cross the busy street to get to the wild animal park. They didn't want Bwana to get hit by a car.

So, here are two officers walking a baby elephant down a residential street and Officer Dean spots an open garage door with no car inside. Officer Preston walked Bwana into the garage and Officer Dean closed the garage door. Bwana was helping himself to a large bag of dog food and Officer Preston left the garage via the side door.

Officer Dean thought: *Thank God I didn't have to tie it up to the front bumper of my patrol car. I like elephants a lot more than hippos…*

Officers Dean and Preston then walked to the front door of the house and knocked on it. The house was dark but soon the front porch light came on and an elderly gentleman answered the door.

Man:	"What's the problem Officers?'
Officer Dean:	"There's a baby elephant in your garage. It got loose from the wild animal park and we had to put it in your garage until the animal handlers can come and pick it up."
Man:	"A what?" *Are you crazy?*
Officer Dean:	"A baby elephant sir, we're sorry for the inconvenience."

The Man's wife then walked towards the front door while straightening out her bathrobe:

Wife:	"What is it honey, what do the officers want?"
Man: garage."	"There's an elephant in our

Wife:	"A what?" *Are you crazy?*
Man:	"A baby elephant. It got loose from the animal park."
Wife:	"Oh, just leave it. Come back to bed"

And with that, Officers Dean and Preston thanked the couple and left. The next morning an elephant handler came by and picked up Bwana. The animal handler also had to clean up a couple of gifts Bwana had left on the garage floor. Even though they may be just a "baby", baby elephants leave big gifts to clean up.

A week later Officer Preston took his wife and children to the wild animal park to visit Bwana. Bwana remembered Officer Preston and gave him another shoulder rub with his trunk.

THE NIGHT OF THE SCARY TRAIN

OFFICER DAN

Officer Dan was hired by the police department around the same time as Officer Dean. They are friends and rely upon one another while handling dangerous police calls. Officer Dan is a real good cop. He also has some talents. He is an unpaid comedian (a good one) and a fairly good imitator of human voices. But wait, there's more! Officer Dan can also imitate several species of animals. He can also imitate different mechanical devices. He is truly gifted. Officer Dan doesn't go to work to only do police work, he goes to work to have fun. Evidently, he didn't have enough fun when he was a kid and the police department gave him all kinds of toys to play with when things get slow and one needs to entertain oneself.

Remember in the loose Hippo story we mentioned that Officer Dean's city is going through a metamorphosis and growing? Part of this metamorphosis is the city needs an approximately five-mile connector freeway right through the middle of town. The connector will run north to south and assist motorists to bypass surface streets. This was a major construction project and Officer Dan thought it was a good idea.

The project took months to complete and Officer Dan knew that this construction project had potential for some extreme fun. At first, he wasn't quite sure what kind of fun. And then, one night in the middle of dawn shift, it came to him...

At one point in the construction Officer Dan noticed that bull dozers had made a nice flat dirt road, in preparation for pouring concrete. But this wasn't just any dirt road. No, this dirt road had something rustic about its appearance. It reminded Officer Dan of a stagecoach road from the 'ole days. The 'ole days when people travelled by stage coach and railroad.

That's it! It's not an unpaved freeway, it's not a dirt road, it's a potential length of railroad tracks! Yes, it's a railroad and I'm the conductor!

All of this reminded Officer Dan of one of his special imitations, that of an old steam locomotive. He could imitate the sound of a train so well, he impressed even himself. It was sooo realistic.

Officer Dan was very proud of his locomotive imitation. He had always received high marks from family and friends when he performed it for them. But that was a small audience. Nothing like what Officer Dan had in mind. He has a whole city just waiting to take part in his fun.

They don't know it, but they subconsciously want to be entertained by Officer Dan:

People need me, they need entertainment, it's fun!

Thank God the Police Department gave Officer Dan a very loud public address system in his police car. The public address system in the police car was mostly utilized during traffic stops, for advising motorists to pull off to the side of the road for safety reasons or telling bad guys in cars to do exactly what they were told, or they would get shot. The public address system could be turned up to full volume and could be heard miles away if need be. Heck, you could wake up half the city if you had to, it's that loud!

One quiet dawn shift at about 3:00 in the morning, Officer Dan went down to his new railroad playground. He knew tonight was the night.

I'm bored, I can't help myself, I just have to do something fun or I'll go crazy. I can't wait any longer. Everyone will thank me for putting some excitement into their boring lives. It's time to get the train rolling!

At the Northern most point of the unpaved dirt road, Officer Dan started driving southbound down his make-believe railroad tracks. He turned up the public address system in his police car as high as it would go.

Thank you, police department, for all these fun gifts. I owe you!

The police department also gave Officer Dan a train spotlight. It was the police spotlight mounted on the driver's side of his car.

Thank you, police department, for all these fun gifts. I owe you!

Officer Dan turned off his patrol cars headlights so that no one would think he was a car. He drove southbound at a very slow rate all the while, using his left hand, moving his spotlight up and down and side to side just like a real locomotive. He steered his locomotive with his knees. With his right hand, he got on the P.A. system:

"Chug-achuga-chuga-chuga, Choo, choooooooo, chug-achug-achuga, chug-achuga-chuga-chuga chooo, chooooo!"

I can't believe how much fun I'm having! I was bored but now, I'm on top of the world. I've got my train rolling and we're starting to have fun. Fun, fun, fun! I can't believe I get paid to have so much fun!!!

Officer Dan repeated his train sounds for three miles and yes, half the city did hear it.

The Smiths were sleeping comfortably in their bedroom and had their window cracked open to let some fresh air in. They heard the train off in the distance; it was getting louder, it was getting closer, it was headed straight for the Smith home!

Mrs. Smith: "Honey, you here that?   It's a train!"

Mr. Smith: "We don't have any trains here."

Mrs. Smith: "Well it's getting closer, sounds like it's coming right for the house. I'm scared, do something, call the police before it hits the house!"

Officer Dan did a very fine job of waking everyone up that night. Not only had the Smiths called the police, just about everyone listed in the phone book did. Police dispatch was flooded with calls. The city was in a panic!

The next morning there was an article in the local paper about the mystery train in the city and who approved the train tracks.

Good job Officer Dan, you did it again. Another stellar performance.

Now, I know what some of you are thinking, "What a waste of taxpayer dollars. What a waste of police resources, etc."

Not the case, crime actually went down that night because everyone, including the crooks were scared shitless the scary train was going to run them over.

WAKE UP YOU FUCKING MONKEYS!!!

DESTROYED PLAYGROUND

The city ruined Officer Dan's train playground. They paved over his dirt railroad tracks. Now cars buzzed on it at high speeds: too dangerous for a slow-moving locomotive to operate on. Officer Dan misses the scary nighttime train fun. It was one of his best performances.

Sometimes all we have left to hold onto are fond memories...

But in reality, that is not the case for Officer Dan. He still has his police car with the public address system. At least they didn't take that away from him. It would be mortifying if the department took the public address system away from Officer Dan. Then the fun would really be over. And, yes, the train fun is gone but Officer Dan has a good imagination and he can always find something to entertain himself with.

Officer Dan had a backup plan he could always count on. He had some special furry friends. He could always go down to the wild animal park and visit with his friends there. Late at night, his animal friends would be lonely because the park was closed. Officer Dan was quite convinced in his own mind that his animal friends needed him as much as he needed them. They had a special relationship; they loved each other. They had fun together...

Officer Dan missed his scary train set. But when your train set gets ruined and you can't play with it anymore, it's time to play with your stuffed animals. To entertain himself, Officer Dan had his own unique way of turning the closed wild animal park into his very own *Officer Dan's Personal Wild Animal Amusement Park and Fun Center!*

During Officer Dan's days working as a patrol cop, the wild animal park was in full operation and a regular attraction for southern Californians. Though not as big as say Disneyland or Knott's Berry Farm, this was the place to come and see some "wild" animals. All kinds of large cats, monkeys, horses, hippos, camels, and a couple of elephants.

Officer Dan is still assigned to dawn shift. Normally, we would say he is "working" the dawn shift but we don't have a lot of evidence to prove that...

Late at night on dawn shift, if things were slow, Officer Dan would park his police car in the front lot of the wild animal park facing the cages of his friends who were imprisoned there. Officer Dan's friends would usually be sleeping when he arrived at the park. But, thank God the police department gave Officer Dan that very loud public address system. It was the perfect tool for playing with his animal friends late at night while they were sleeping.

Besides being able to perfectly imitate a train locomotive, Officer Dan was an expert in animal talk! Yes, Officer Dan spoke over a dozen animal languages! He was so good at it that just thinking about visiting his furry animal friends and talking to them in their own language sent goose bumps up and down his arms and spine.

Ohhhh, we're gonna have fun! Soooooo much fun!

On the nights that Officer Dan went to visit his friends at the wild animal park, he would turn up the volume on his public address system and notify his friends that he was there. First, he would wake up the animals by having a discussion with his very good friends, the lions. Officer Dan began his lion communication with a long lion growl,

"Rrrrrraaaaaaaarrrrruuuuuuuhhhhhh".

The lions would wake up and talk back to Officer Dan,

"Rrrrrraaaaaaaarrrrruuuuuuuhhhhhh".

This went on for a minute or two; back and forth between Officer Dan and his lion friends until both of them were content in having communicated with each other. It sounded just like a safari recording of lions in the jungle growling at one another, just like one of those wild animal programs on TV.

I'm sooooo good at this and the lions love it when I come and talk to them. I'm so glad we have each other!

Next, it was time for Officer Dan to talk to his most favorite friends, the chimpanzees. This was Officer Dan's most special wild animal park relationship. Officer Dan spoke fluent monkey talk and just had to say "hello" to them after talking to the lions. When Officer Dan and the lions were talking with one another, the monkeys would wake up and begin chirping among themselves. The monkeys were probably worried the nasty lions would get loose one night and eat them. They were especially scared of the big alpha lion out in the parking lot; he sounded a lot bigger than the other lions because he had a much louder growl.

Officer Dan needed special companionship and entertainment only his chimpanzee friends could provide. Officer Dan would once again employ his patrol cars public address system and let his monkey friends know he was there to visit:

"WAKE UP YOU FUCKING MONKEYS! WAKE THE FUCK UP! WHO-WHO WHO-WHOOOHHHAAAAAAAAAAA!!! WAKE UP YOU LITTLE FUCKERS, GET THE FUCK UP! WHOOOOOOO-WHOOOOOOOO WHO-WHOOOHHHAAAAAAAAAAA!!! REVEILLE YOU MOTHERFUCKERS! WAKE THE FUCK UP BITCHES, WAKE THE FUCK UP!!! WHOOOOOOOOOOO-WHOOOOOOO WHO-WHOOOHHHAAAAAAAAAA!!!"

Officer Dan was so good at imitating monkey's that in no time, his little monkey friends were totally awake, yelling and screaming back at Officer Dan, all the while jumping up in the air, rattling and climbing the bars of their cages in a most riotous fashion.

Sometimes it was hard to tell who could speak "monkey" better than whom. Officer Dan was proud of his abilities. He was truly gifted. He never missed a night visiting his monkey friends unless police work got in the way.

He could start a monkey riot in a few seconds and then after basking in his achievement, just drive away, leaving his monkey friends in pandemonium. Officer Dan was truly gifted.

This should be the end of the story but it's not:

One quiet dawn shift, Officer Dan visited his friends at his wild animal amusement park. First, as was customary, Officer Dan paid his respects to the noble lions:

"RRRRRAAAAAAARRRRUUUUUUUHHHHH HH".

However, for some reason, tonight, the lions were not answering back.

Maybe they moved the lions? Maybe the lions are sick? Maybe they were sold to another zoo? No, they wouldn't get rid of the lions, they're probably being used off site on a movie set or something. That's it, they're off site for a movie or something. Maybe a Tarzan episode. That makes sense, the owners wouldn't get rid of them, they're too popular. I hope they didn't take my lion friends away. It just wouldn't be the same without them! I don't have a lot of friends on dawn shift and I won't be able to have any more fun if they took them away. Oh please God, please bring back my lion friends as soon as possible! This is unbearable…

At least I still have my monkey friends to talk to! They wouldn't get rid of the lions and the monkeys. No, that would be too much. We're still going to have some fun!

Officer Dan got back on his public address system and notified his monkey friends to wake up with the usual:

"WAKE UP YOU FUCKING MONKEYS! WAKE THE FUCK UP! WHO-WHO WHO-WHOOOHHHAAAAAAAAAA!!! WAKE UP YOU LITTLE FUCKERS, GET THE FUCK UP! WHOOOOOOO-WHOOOOOOOO WHO-WHOOOHHHAAAAAAAAAAA!!! REVEILLE YOU MOTHERFUCKERS! WAKE THE FUCK UP BITCHES, WAKE THE FUCK UP!!! WHOOOOOOOOOOO-WHOOOOOOO WHO-WHOOOHHHAAAAAAAAAA!!!"

Officer Dan is really punishing the monkeys this night and giving it to them really hard; he is so proud of himself! He's giving them an extra couple minutes of wake-up call because they are not responding the way they usually do; he has to yell extra hard into the public address system. But, like the lions, there is no answer from the monkeys. Officer Dan is shocked, sad and unfulfilled.

Maybe the animal park owners got rid of them too? Maybe the monkeys are sick? I hope they're not sick. They're my best friends. It's why I enjoy coming to work. No more fun with the fuckin' monkeys? No, no, no! I hope they are alright… But, why aren't my friends, the monkeys awake? This is no good. Something's definitely wrong here tonight; I can't believe it.

They probably have the fucking monkeys off site on the same movie set with the lions! Dumb shit, why didn't you think of that sooner?

Why did I even come to work? If I can't talk to my friends what the hell am I going to do for fun tonight? I can't stand it! My friends need

95

to talk to me and talk to me real soon or I just may lose it!!!! What a shitty shift!!!

Just in case the monkeys aren't off site, Officer Dan concentrates and yells into his public address system microphone one more time:

"WAKE UP YOU FUCKING MONKEYS! WAKE THE FUCK UP! WHO-WHO WHO-WHOOOHHHAAAAAAAAAAA!!! WAKE UP YOU LITTLE FUCKERS, GET THE FUCK UP! WHOOOOOOO-WHOOOOOOOO WHO-WHOOOHHHAAAAAAAAAAA!!! REVEILLE YOU MOTHERFUCKERS! WAKE THE FUCK UP BITCHES, WAKE THE FUCK UP!!! WHOOOOOOOOOOOO-WHOOOOOOO WHO-WHOOOHHHAAAAAAAAAA!!!"

As soon as Officer Dan finished this last attempt, his beat partner Officer Dean drives up. Officer Dean is looking very serious and does not look happy.

What is this? Is everybody having a shitty night? I come to work to have fun, but tonight, I don't get any fun. And to make matters worse, my beat partner shows up in a shitty mood and I don't know if I can handle whatever in the hell is bothering him. I'm under a lot of stress right now. My friends aren't here to make me happy! I wish Dean would just leave and handle his own problem. I've got enough of my own.

Officer Dean gets out of his patrol car and walks over to Officer Dan's driver's door which has the window rolled down (the window has to be down

96

so Officer Dan can hear and enjoy the riotous yells and screeches from his monkey friends). Officer Dean's unhappy facial expression does not change as he leans on Officer Dan's driver's door window frame with his forearms. Officer Dean then quietly informs Officer Dan that police dispatch and the watch commander request that Officer Dan please stop transmitting over the police radio band.

Officer Dean explains,

"The whole department is listening to you trying to wake up the fucking monkeys and nobody else can use the radio..."

Officer Dan is mortified; he just stares at Officer Dean with a look of total panic. His exasperation turns to horror. He leans forward in his seat and puts his head in his hands. For once in his life, Officer Dan is speechless.

Oh shit! I've been using the wrong fucking microphone!!!

You see, there are two microphones in a police car. One is the public address system microphone. That is the microphone used for traffic stops, yelling at suspects during felony pullovers, and waking up *fucking monkeys.* The other microphone is the police radio microphone. It is used to talk to police dispatch and to other police cars. It's usually dark out on dawn shift and sometimes because of the darkness and anticipation of waking up fucking monkeys, one could accidentally pick up the wrong microphone. Officer Dan did just that.

There are very strict rules for using the police

97

radio. Police recruits go through a special class in the academy on the proper use and etiquette to be observed when using the police radio. Officer Dan took this special class. The police radio microphone is never to be used for waking up fucking monkeys. Officer Dan screwed up big time. What this all boils down to is that approximately forty patrol cars, several patrol Sergeants, police headquarters, the watch commander, and neighboring departments were wakened the fuck up by Officer Dan's roaring lion monologue and fucking monkey communications:

"WAKE UP YOU FUCKING MONKEYS! WAKE THE FUCK UP! WHO-WHO WHO-WHOOOHHHAAAAAAAAAAA!!! WAKE UP YOU LITTLE FUCKERS, GET THE FUCK UP! WHOOOOOOO-WHOOOOOOOO WHO-WHOOOHHHAAAAAAAAAAA!!! REVEILLE YOU MOTHERFUCKERS! WAKE THE FUCK UP BITCHES, WAKE THE FUCK UP!!! WHOOOOOOOOOOOO-WHOOOOOOO WHO-WHOOOHHHAAAAAAAAAA!!!"

Officer Dan can't believe what he has done.

No wonder my little lion and monkey friends weren't responding. I was using the wrong fucking microphone! I'm in big fucking trouble, they may even fire me. I am sooo fucked! What do I say to my wife? "Honey I'm fired 'cause I roared at the fucking lions and told the monkeys to wake the fuck up!" All my family and friends are gonna laugh at me. What a total fucking embarrassment...Damn it!!! Why didn't I call in sick or something? Why is this happening to me? I knew something was wrong!

Is it my fault I am gifted and can talk to all the animals in their own language? The other officers are probably happy I'm in trouble because those fuckers can't speak animal talk like I can. Shit, shit, shit!

Officer Dan was in deep shit for his little charade and he knew he was in big trouble for monkeying around on the police radio. He also knew that police radios are governed by the Federal Communications Commission and the FCC sometimes monitor police radio use.

I'm going to get my ass reamed by the Watch Commander, then the Chief, then the FCC will take their turn. I am sooooo very, very, fucked!

Nobody knows how hard it is to be me! I have a talent and I have friends in the wild animal park that need me. I can't help myself! I just have to have fun! It's a curse and now, the Chief is gonna kick my ass because of it! I'm losing my job and I'll have to take a job at the wild animal park shoveling elephant shit or some other stupid job! I'm going to lose my job and my wife is going to divorce me…

As it turned out, everyone working that night, including the watch commander, had a sense of humor and they all laughed their asses off listening to Officer Dan yelling over the police radio:

"WAKE UP YOU FUCKING MONKEYS! WAKE THE FUCK UP! WHO-WHO WHO-WHOOOHHHAAAAAAAAAAAA!!! WAKE UP YOU LITTLE FUCKERS, GET THE FUCK UP!

WHOOOOOOO-WHOOOOOOOO WHO-WHOOOHHHAAAAAAAAAA!!! REVEILLE YOU MOTHERFUCKERS! WAKE THE FUCK UP BITCHES, WAKE THE FUCK UP!!! WHOOOOOOOOOOOO-WHOOOOOOO WHO-WHOOOHHHAAAAAAAAAA!!!"

Nobody told the Chief.

The FCC wasn't listening that night.

But, Officer Dan's fellow patrol officers played jokes on him for months to come. They left notes taped to his mailbox that "Cheetah" had called and wants a return phone call. "Cheetah" stopped by and wants to go out for banana splits, etc., etc.

"Cheetah" is the name of the chimpanzee in the original Tarzan films from the 1930's and was one of the animal actors in those episodes.

It took a while, but eventually Officer Dan recovered from the traumatic experience of being found out about his secret passion in life and his love of animals.

No lions or fucking monkeys were injured by Officer Dan during the events in this story. But if monkeys could talk, they probably would tell Officer Dan to leave them the fuck alone.

WILD PONIES

OFFICER JOHN

Officer John had been on the job for a couple of years. He was new to policing but hard charging. He had heard about the heroic exploits of Officers Dean and Dan, the hippopotamus, Bwana, the noble lions, and the fucking monkeys. But that was ancient history, Officers Dean and Dan left patrol and received new assignments. The wild animal park was closed.

The last radio call Officer John wanted at 2:00 a.m. in the morning on dawn shift was a call of numerous horses running down the main boulevard creating a traffic hazard. The horses were running into traffic and sooner or later somebody or some horse was going to get hurt...

Unknown to Officer John, there was a carnival owner that had about a dozen Shetland ponies in his backyard. The ponies were used for kids rides at carnivals and for birthday parties.

Officer John did not have a rope to handle this call. He only had his imagination...

Officer John responded to the area of the loose horses on the boulevard and immediately regretted he did not have a rope. But, what good would one rope do against a dozen loose horses? Nothing. This crap could take all night long trying to get these horses into their corral.

They never taught this crap in the police academy. Shit! Wake some real cowboys up you dumbasses! "My Friend", "Some Dude", and "Some Guy" are out there somewhere in the night getting ready to commit a burglary and I have to corral horses in the middle of the city, "Shit, why me?"

AMERICAN HORSE OWNERS

Horses are communal in nature. They interact well with humans that care for them. They are herd animals and are always looking for food and "greener pastures". Almost everybody likes horses. There is in America, a "cult" of horse fanatics. Most of the cult members cannot get enough of their drug of choice. Given the choice between financial riches and horses, these cult members will almost always choose horses. They will take their financial riches and buy more horses than they can afford to feed. They also have to buy lots of saddles and other equipment to outfit their horses; not to mention tons of hay, oats, horsey treats and veterinarian bills. Don't forget boarding fees, the cost of a new barn, and horse trailer if you could afford it. It's all part of the horse cult package. In short, horses are "legal cocaine" to some.

A small percentage of the American population belongs to the horse cult. The exact number of horses in the U.S. is debatable but it is estimated that two million people own approximately 9.2 million horses. Two-thirds of the cult own more than one horse and fifteen percent own more than five horses each. Texans will be glad to know that once again, they are the biggest and best: there are more horses in Texas than any other state at 1,000,000, followed by California with 698,000 and Florida with 500,000.

The Surgeon General turns a blind eye to this ever growing epidemic. With the advent of the computer age, cult members utilize the internet to help them practice their cult rituals of obtaining more horses and equipment. These addicts need an American Horse Cult Addiction Hotline, but one does not exist.

Some horse cult members chose law enforcement as their vocation. Many American law enforcement agencies encourage the horse cult tradition.

Since 1871, the New York Police Department has maintained a mounted patrol unit consisting of approximately fifty horses. The number fluctuates depending on city finances. The Los Angeles Police Department has about forty horses. The Los Angeles Sheriff's Department has over 180 mounted Officers, many of which are volunteer Reserve Deputies. At the top of the list is the U.S. Border Patrol which rescues wild mustangs for its approximately 200 mounted units.

There are many mounted units around the world and some of the most notable are: The Metropolitan Police Mounted Branch of Greater London, founded in 1860 (about 100 mounts), New South Wales, Australia Mounted Police (approximately 38 mounts), Royal Canadian Mounted

Police (mostly ceremonial), and the Royal Oman Police which includes horses and camels!

SERGEANT FEM

Officer John's field supervisor that night was a newly promoted female sergeant and she was responding to the area of the equine emergency. That would not be a problem except this female sergeant had to let every male officer assigned to *her* shift know that *she* (supposedly) wore the chaps in the family. Officer John didn't have a problem with female senior officers as long as they treated him fairly and knew what they were doing. Not the case with Sergeant Fem. She had a chip on her shoulder for male officers and always had to appear more superior to them.

Officer John had all these loose horses on the boulevard and he really had no idea what he was supposed to do with them. Additionally, his beat partners weren't there to offer advice and help out; they were handling other police calls. If something good didn't happen soon, Officer John was going to be filling out traffic accident reports involving cute little dead ponies.

Wish I could just fire a couple shots in the air like they do in the movies. That should get the little buggers headed back home. The bars are starting to close and soon we'll have a bunch of drunks dodging cute little ponies.

The ponies are on both sides of the road, munching on fresh green grass. Every ten seconds or so, they have to shoot across the roadway to get to the grass on the other side of the road because it might be of higher quality. Cars have to slow down to miss hitting the ponies.

The ponies are just soooo happy to be out of their confining little corral, running around with the freedom enjoyed by their ancestors. Just like hungry little beasts recently released from confinement from Noah's Ark.

What in the heck do I do?

So, somebody left the gate to a horse corral unsecured and all twelve of them got out. Now, they are all over the place...Unfortunately, it is now solely Officer John's problem...

Hope you Shetland Pony owners are sleeping nice and comfy in your beds while I round up your little ponies and spill coffee all over my crotch!

Officer John is not a horse cult member. He does like horseback riding, but it is not a priority in his life. He did spend many a summer afternoon as a young kid getting routinely thrown off a horse his parents were boarding for some neighbors. So, Officer John knows a bit about horses. He's no expert but he does know that you should never let a horse step on you, they weigh more than you do, and it can hurt. Thank God these are Shetland Ponies. Officer John has been stepped on numerous times by his childhood neighbor's Shetland pony and it never hurt.

Thankfully, as a child, Officer John watched many a John Wayne movie and other western flicks. When one needs to get cattle or horses moving, there are just a few things to do: yell at the animals like you know what you're doing, whistle like they do on a cattle drive, and hit your rope against the side of your saddle, or, in this instance, your patrol car.

Knowing that Sergeant Fem would be arriving on the scene within minutes, Officer John had to handle the call before she arrived. If he did not, he would be derided for not handling the simplest of radio calls.

Yeah, Rrrright...

Shetland Ponies were running across the boulevard and drunk drivers were swerving to miss them. Officer John had to take immediate action to prevent one big pony massacre.

JOHN WAYNE

What would John Wayne do in this circumstance? Big John would take complete control and handle the situation and then let the results speak for themselves. *"Let's saddle up and move 'em out, we're burnin' dawn shift."*

Officer John did not have a horse or a rope. So, his patrol car is his horse. Officer John drove his horse past the pony furthest from the horse corral. He turned on his overhead red and blue police unit lights, turned on his siren, slapped the side of his car door with his hand, and yelled over his cruiser's public address system,

"HyaaaDAAAA!"

all the while driving in a snakelike pattern back and forth across the boulevard. This snakelike driving pattern worked and all of the cute little adorable Shetland ponies joined in on one miniature stampede all the way back to their home.

Hey, Big John, We got 'em movin'...It works!

All of the wayward diners landed in their corral.

Unbeknownst to Officer John, Sergeant Fem snuck up and witnessed his unorthodox handling of the call from the shadows.

Officer John was securing the gate to the pony corral when Sergeant Fem contacted him on the radio and told him to meet with her down the street.

They met and Sergeant Fem told Officer John she witnessed his unprofessional handling of the radio call and he was way out of proper police protocol. Sergeant Fem advised him that he should have obtained the assistance of the animal owners and animal control to corral the horses. Officer John got the impression that Sergeant Fem was upset because he handled the radio call without her guidance and superior leadership abilities.

What a poor judge of True Cowboy Talent! Anyone with any common sense would probably praise him. The horse owners would probably invite him over for coffee and trail rides. But noooooo, Sergeant Fem wants to ridicule and find fault because she thinks it is her job to do so. Sergeant Fem is getting on my nerves...

Our candidate for cowboy officer of the year tells Sergeant Fem that the horse owners were nowhere to be found and animal control could not respond till the morning; at which time we would have had several injury car accidents possibly involving injured, if not killed, horses.

Hey Sergeant Fem, do you want me to wait for animal control while these cute little ponies get hit by cars? If we did, you'd have PETA so far up your ass you wouldn't be able to sit for a month! By the way, there is no department protocol for handling loose animals when the owners and animal control cannot respond!

Oh, and guess what Sergeant Fem? I had fun playing John Wayne! Yes, a lot of fun and you didn't get any of it. Now shut the fuck up, go back to the station, and, no Christmas card for you bitch!!!

No Shetland Ponies were injured or harmed during the events of this police call. Officer John scared the shit out of them, but none were injured.

The only injury occurred when Officer John spilled his scalding hot coffee on his crotch at the onset of this radio call, but once the fun began, he forgot about it. He spills coffee on his crotch all the time. Thank God for dark trousers, they camouflage the coffee stains...

LASER BLUE LIGHT

Remember Officer Jim from the "FUCK YOU STICKS GET OUTA MY WAY" chapter? Many years after Grandma Crazy tried to kick Officer Jim in the balls, Officer Jim was reassigned to the Detective Bureau. He liked the Detective Bureau so much that he worked there for many years.

THE DETECTIVE BUREAU

The Detective Bureau consists of several "teams" that specialize in investigating different types of crimes. The "general assignment" Detectives usually are tasked with investigating felony property crimes (thefts), i.e. burglaries, grand thefts, car thefts, etc. Other Detective teams a law enforcement agency might have include: sex crimes, forgery/fraud, narcotics, vice (nasty things and gambling), and major crimes (murders, serious assaults, missing persons, kidnappings), etc.

Large law enforcement organizations normally have all the separate teams listed above and sometimes more like a computer crimes task force. Smaller agencies may combine several of them and the smallest of agencies may only have one or two detectives working all of them.

As a Detective, one can have a big impact on society and criminal activity. A good Detective gets the opportunity to help victims, witnesses, and even suspects on occasion.

DETECTIVE JIM

It took Detective Jim several years to get good

at being a Detective but after a while, one improves and can really get hooked on the assignment. His first four years of being a Detective, he was placed on a general assignment team. Most of his time was spent on residential and commercial burglary cases, grand thefts, and auto thefts.

One aspect of a Detective's job is to interview suspects who have been arrested for felony crimes. A good Detective learns how to read a suspect. This "reading" is based on experience and a kinda sixth sense as to how a suspect thinks. Also, of utmost importance, Detective Jim knows that just because someone is wearing a matching pair of custom-made bracelets (handcuffs), does not mean they are guilty. When Detective Jim is assigned a case, he always tries to prove and disprove the case against the suspect. That way the police and courts don't waste excess time and money on the wrong suspect (besides the moral and ethical implications which are foremost).

Just because someone reports a crime to police, does not necessarily mean it actually happened. Some "Victims" are not. They make false reports for various reasons and motives. Some reports are filed as an act of revenge, some are filed for insurance fraud.

Detective Jim usually works from 8:00 a.m. to 5:00 p.m. with a one-hour lunch somewhere in between. He has so many cases assigned to him that he usually enjoys a working desk lunch and rarely gets off on time. Detective Jim is also subject to being "on-call" for emergencies and after-hours suspect interviews. He's not crazy about the set up, but he loves working in Detectives.

Detective Jim worked with a team of five other general assignment Detectives, which meant the area of their city was divided up into six areas with each detective investigating the crimes committed in their assigned area. One measure of a Detective's effectiveness was in the number of cases he or she closes each month. A high case closure rate is one indicator of good work but not necessarily the final word on job performance. Detective Jim knows this.

When Detective Jim develops a suspect in a case, he prefers to personally arrest the suspect if he can. Oftentimes, this is not possible due to time constraints. There are too many suspects out there in the world and although Detective Jim prefers to arrest his own suspects, he knows it is a better tactical move to have other officers, like the patrol officers or the special enforcement team make the arrest for him. That way, the arrestee thinks the arresting officers are the bad guys because they slapped the cuffs on them. After the arrest, Detective Jim will play the nice guy. Detective Jim is always willing to hear the suspects version of events before he gets them to admit their misdeeds. You see, Detective Jim learned early on in his detective career, he can't, for some reason, play the "bad cop" when interviewing a suspect. The "bad cop – good cop" stuff works on TV, but most suspects are just chomping at the bit to get into an argument with detectives that interview them.

Detective Jim does have a Detective partner that always plays the "bad cop" in interviews. We will cover that in a later story.

When interviewing suspects, Detective Jim learned that a serious but caring approach delivers more confessions. You catch more bees with honey than you do with vinegar. It's a game, but a very serious one. Obtaining a confession from a suspect that will hold up in court is the goal.

TYPES OF CRIMES

Many people are confused about the classifications of crimes, just what an infraction, a misdemeanor, and a felony is. So, for those of you who live in California (and maybe some other states), here they are:

Infraction:

An "Infraction" is a public offense but technically not a "crime". If one commits an infraction, one can be fined but not put in jail or prison. Common infractions include running a stop sign or speeding (as long as the speeding is not excessive and dangerous).

A judge may fine you for running a stop sign, but he /she may not put you in jail for the offense. However, if you fail to appear in court or fail to pay your fine for running the stop sign, either of those violations are misdemeanors and now qualify you for jail time should the judge decide it is warranted.

Misdemeanor:

A "Misdemeanor" is a crime which carries a punishment in the county jail of one year or less and a possible maximum fine of $1,000. Some examples are drunk in public, petty theft (if the theft is a shoplifting offense and the offender has no prior criminal record, or if the value of the stolen property is $950 or less), or disturbing the peace, like yelling at fucking monkeys late at night.

Felony:

A "Felony" is a crime punishable by imprisonment in the State prison (for more than one year). Fines for felonies are usually more than $1,000. Some felonies are punishable by life imprisonment and murder can carry the death penalty. Obviously, felonies are your more serious crimes. Some felonies are called "wobblers", which means they are technically felonies but the District Attorney's Office or a judge may reduce the crime to a misdemeanor if they choose to do so.

THE DIFFERENCE BETWEEN BURGLARY AND ROBBERY

There is much confusion as to what a "burglary" is and what a "robbery" is.

Many lay persons think that every time something is stolen, it is considered a "robbery". Not so:

Burglary:

A "Burglary" is the entering of a building with the "intent" to commit a theft or another felony. So, if little Johnny goes over to the local quick mart *with the intent* to steal a pack of gum, as soon as he sets foot inside the door, he has technically committed a burglary (even without committing the actual theft!). But, how can you prove that without being able to read his mind or him admitting it? You can't unless you have some type of corroborating evidence. Oftentimes the "intent" is ignored, and little Johnny will just get arrested for petty theft of a pack of gum.

Let's say Cindy has a drug problem and she supports it by cashing forged checks at her local bank. Every time Cindy enters the bank to cash her forged checks, she technically commits a burglary because she enters the bank (a building) with the intent to commit another felony (forgery). Technically, Cindy has committed two felonies, burglary and forgery. The District Attorney's Office rarely files both the burglary charge and the forgery charge, but sometimes they do if Cindy has pissed them off too many times.

P.S. – Cindy also supports her drug habit by prostituting herself out! (Prostitution is a misdemeanor)

If someone breaks into your house and steals your big screen T.V., that is a burglary, not a "Robbery".

Robbery:

A "Robbery" is the felonious taking of personal property in the possession of another, from his person or immediate presence, and against his will, accomplished **by means of force or fear."**

Freddy and his buddies belong to a gang. They find somebody walking down the street and beat this person up and steal the victim's cellphone. That's a robbery. You can also do the same thing by pointing a gun at the victim. As long as "force" or fear" are used, you have a robbery. If a detective can prove these little fuckers *planned* to rob someone, that is another felony: *conspiracy.*

Johnny is older now, has a nagging drug habit and needs to get some money to support his drug habit. He acquires a gun, walks into a bank, waits in line, when it's his turn, he shows the gun to the teller, the teller gives Johnny some money, Johnny leaves the bank. Johnny committed a robbery because the bank teller was scared shitless when they saw Johnny's gun.

If Johnny had committed the robbery by passing a note to the teller that read, "I have a gun, give me some money", Johnny still committed a robbery because he instilled **fear** in the bank teller.

Technically what other crime did our little Johnny commit when he walked into the bank? That's right, burglary; because he had *the intent* to enter the bank and commit another felony, robbery. So, Johnny has technically committed two felonies, burglary and robbery. Usually Johnny will only be prosecuted for the robbery.

Let's take a look at burglaries again. Let's say Johnny breaks into your house and steals your TV. That is a burglary. But, if Johnny breaks into your house and you confront him and he pulls a gun on you (or uses some other weapon or "fear"), Johnny also committed a robbery.

Just remember, banks and people are robbed, houses are burglarized.

CHURCH BURGLARIES

Six Church burglaries had occurred in Detective Jim's city. The burglaries were committed on dawn shift while everyone slept. The suspect(s) always entered through the church office door, located the petty cash box, stole the money and left the scene of the crime. There were no leads in the crimes.

Someone is going to hell for breaking into all those churches. We may not catch you but you better pray to Jesus because God sees everything and is not happy you're stealing from Him!

One dawn shift around 2:30a.m., Detective Jim's home phone rang. It was the watch commander asking Detective Jim to come into work to interview a burglar that broke into a church.

Detective Jim asked the watch commander to please have the arresting officer place the burglary suspect in Detective Jim's favorite interview room: Interview Room Number Four. It's his favorite interview room because of its close proximity to the station break room coffee pot.

Detective Jim doesn't know who the church burglar is but he has a gut feeling that this is the guy that has broken into all the other churches.

"So glad I went to bed early. Mister Church Burglar is going down for at least one burglary. Somehow, I have to get him to admit to the others. But first, I have to wake up and get my mind right. I have to be alert. Get some coffee

117

started, take a quick shower, shave, get my suit and tie on and head into work. Screw shaving, it'll take too long. I can shave at the station after the interview is done. If I get this crook to admit to all the church burglaries, nobody is gonna give a shit if I'm shaven or not.

It's going to be ShowTime ladies and gentlemen. Curtain goes up as soon as I arrive at the station. No screen writers, no producers, no directors, no camera crew, just real life actors. Somehow, I have to get this guy to admit to all the church burglaries because I just know he did them. I've got that gut feeling...

Detective Jim arrived at the station and headed straight for the lunchroom coffee pot.

Got to fill up and get wide awake for the performance (interview).

Jim made a fresh pot because some inconsiderate, atrocity committing son of a bitch took the last cup of coffee and didn't make a new pot.

Incompetent asshole! You can't do decent police work without coffee! What the hell are these people thinking anyway? Make a personal note: next call out for an interview, ask the arresting officer to have some coffee ready!

Detective Jim had one cup of coffee at home and drank another on the drive to work but that's never enough. A good cop lives on copious amounts of strong coffee. It also takes Detective Jim longer to

118

wake up the older he gets.

After getting another cup of coffee, Detective Jim met with the arresting officer and basically interviewed the officer before talking to the suspect.

Detective Jim learned that this interview of the arresting officer is extremely important. This is standard operating procedure. Detective Jim can't start the suspect interview until he has all the arrest information available. He not only has to act and look like he knows what's he's doing, he has to KNOW what is going on.

Detective Jim lets the arresting officer explain the events of the arrest. He doesn't write any notes during this first interview of the officer, he just listens. If the arresting officer is new, he or she is likely all hyped up and excited because they caught a burglar. They might not tell the story in the exact sequence of events. So, Detective Jim will patiently interview the officer to get the facts in chronological order. Sometimes these interviews are short, sweet, and simple. Other times they may take a while depending on the circumstances and the number of officers and suspects to interview.

Detective Jim reviewed the arresting officer's version of events a second time and he took notes:

Silent burglary alarm goes off at church, cops are called by the alarm company, cops respond, cops find burglar in church office, cops point B.F.G.'s at suspect, suspect almost shits his pants, cops arrest suspect. No other suspects, cops notice church office doorknob was forced open. Cops attempt to place suspect in police car, suspect barely fits, suspect is driven to station and placed in interview room. Cops call Detective Jim for interview. Pretty simple. Easy story for all to remember.

The goal of a suspect interview is to get to the truth and nothing but the truth. If the suspect committed the crime, Detective Jim needs to get the suspect to admit it. That's the goal. It is not Detective Jim's job to demean the suspect, physically abuse them or anything else. Just the facts and a confession.

But, please don't bullshit me too much; this isn't my first rodeo...

In one way or another, most crimes are connected to either drug or alcohol abuse. Detective Jim knows this. They are the real cause of the problem. Well, not always but Detective Jim says that a lot to his customers (suspects). It's easier for someone to admit to a crime because they have a drug or alcohol problem than to admit to a crime and take full responsibility because they had poor judgement. Hopefully, by the time the interview is concluded, Detective Jim's suspect will be agreeing with him that the crime was not totally the suspect's fault. We first lay blame on drugs or alcohol. Once that foundation is laid, we can revisit how the drugs or alcohol influenced our suspect into committing crimes which otherwise may not have been committed. Detective Jim calls this "getting on the road to recovery". It may sound like bullshit to some but it's true.

One other thing Detective Jim will do prior to the suspect interview is he will run a complete background check to see how much past trouble the suspect has been in and how sophisticated (or not) the suspect is.

The arresting officer told Detective Jim one more item of possible importance: the suspect is a *"really, really, big guy."*

Detective Jim is now going to follow his suspect interview protocol. It's his routine and he follows it nearly every time he conducts an interview:

1. Open interview room door halfway.
2. Lean halfway into interview room. Don't go inside.
3. Look suspect directly in the eyes and introduce yourself in a business-like fashion.
4. Tell suspect you would like to talk to them if they want to.
5. Ask suspect if they have any medical problems.
6. Ask suspect if they are thirsty or hungry.
7. Tell suspect you'll be right back.
8. Leave interview room.

It is very important for Detective Jim to follow his procedure for getting to know his suspect.

Detective Jim doesn't go all the way inside the interview room the first time he meets the suspect. He does this for several reasons. Detective Jim does not want to appear to be in a hurry. He wants to appear kinda laid back to his approach to the suspect, put the suspect at ease if possible. Also, too many mistakes can be made if one is in a hurry.

This interview room and police station is a little

like a hospital. "Doctor, (Detective) Jim" is not in a hurry to treat you, he has a lot of patients waiting for him. You're just one of many. You need "Doctor Jim" more than he needs you. You are the one in need of medical attention. We treat you in the order received. Have a seat, we'll be with you as soon as we can...

Detective Jim has to know if his suspect has a medical problem, etc. Withholding medical care could wipe out a suspect's statement in court. And, he doesn't want anyone having a diabetic coma or a heart attack in the interview room. That could really ruin things...

Detective Jim always asks his suspects if they are thirsty or hungry even though he knows this could be construed by a defense attorney as "buttering up" the suspect to get them to admit to the charges.

Detective Jim makes the same offer to everyone, even those suspects that tell him to "fuck off." He'll always provides water, coffee, or a soda. If the suspect is hungry, there is a snack machine down the hall. Detective Jim doesn't mind spending a couple of bucks on his customers. If the suspect hasn't eaten for quite a while, Detective Jim will even go so far as to order some food from the station jail (even though it's not five-star cuisine, it's better than nothing). He's just a nice guy who cares about his clientele. Who can argue with that?

PAUL BUNYAN

Detective Jim opens the door to the interview

room but does not go inside. There is a big guy sitting on the chair normally occupied by the suspect and he is handcuffed behind his back. He's about thirty years old and big but not fat. Detective Jim introduces himself. The suspect is polite and states he does not have any medical problems. He wants a cup of coffee; with cream please.

Well, he's big, polite, and wants a cup of Detective Jim's truth serum. We are off to a good start ladies and gentlemen. Hopefully this interview goes smoothly, and I'll be done in about an hour or so. But we can't rush it. Sometimes getting a confession can take a while…

The arresting officer approaches Detective Jim:

Well, what do you think?

"My God, that guy is huge, he's a freakin' giant! He should be playing in the NFL but then they'd probably have too many members of the opposing teams on the disabled list."

Detective Jim goes back to the station break room and gets a cup of coffee for his suspect. Detective Jim explains to the arresting officer that even though the suspect is very large, it would be nice to talk to him without the handcuffs on. It would be nice to have the arresting officer within earshot just in case the suspect goes berserk on Detective Jim. One never knows.

Detective Jim enters the interview room and places the suspect's coffee on the interview room table. The suspect is still seated, and Detective Jim asks him if he will remain calm during the interview because, as Detective Jim explained to him,

"I don't want you to go off on me because then I'll have to go Ninja on you and I'm not in the mood for that. Sound good? I know those handcuffs aren't the most comfortable things to be wearing and we can take them off for the interview."

Paul Bunyan said he understood Detective Jim and will not do anything stupid. He knows he's already in enough deep shit.

Still making progress…

Detective Jim asks the suspect to stand up while he takes the handcuffs off. The suspect stands up and Detective Jim immediately wonders to himself if it's such a good idea to take the handcuffs off.

The suspect can only be described as a "Paul Bunyan" type of guy. He's over seven feet tall with broad shoulders, all muscle, no fat. He's even wearing a plaid button up shirt, blue jeans and brown work boots. He looks like a lumberjack! His hands are at least twice the size of Detective Jim's.

Shit Batman, if I have to go Ninja on this guy, I'm going to get my ass kicked more than just a little. First indication he is going off, I'm going for his fucking throat. Can't breathe, can't fight. Simple enough…Hope he stays calm. It'll ruin my fucking morning if he goes off on me…

The handcuffs come off, Paul Bunyan gets his coffee and he is happy. Detective Jim goes through some preliminary background questions and learns Paul Bunyan is homeless: kicked out of his Mother's home for drinking too much (*Reason #1 why we are stealing...*). Paul doesn't have a job (*Reason #2 why we are stealing...*) and has been camping out near one of the city parks. Paul Bunyan asks Detective Jim,

"Please don't tell my Mother about this."

"Aha! We have an area of weakness that might have to be exploited later in the interview. But the way he said it, it might be the wrong button to push. We'll just keep that little morsel of information on standby in case it is needed down the road. Sounds like Mommy is gonna kick his ass when she finds out what her little lumberjack did! Wonder how big Mommy is?"

Detective Jim reads Paul Bunyan his *Miranda rights*, just like on T.V. Paul states he wants to talk.

Bingo! This is going Fantastico! We are one step closer to achieving this morning's goal: complete confession. You may not know it Paul Bunyan but Detective Jim is going to get you back on the road to recovery! That's what we do here! Detective Jim is going to walk you through your life of crime. He is going to get you to admit to one church burglary and then he's going to move onto those other church burglaries that we all know you committed. Yes sir Paul, you're going to be a new person by the time we're done with you!

I'm having fun and, I'm getting paid overtime too! And, I get to drink all the free coffee I

125

want! It's a Win-Win for Detective Jim!

Paul Bunyan explains that he went into the church "for a place to sleep". Detective Jim explains to Paul that he has already mentioned he has a nice spot to sleep near the park. After explaining to Paul that the truth always comes out and it is better not to be hiding (lying about) anything, Paul admits he was going to try to find some money in the church *and then take a nap.*

Paul also admits to something incredible: he didn't use any tools to force his way into the church office. He just grabbed the doorknob with his massive muscular Paul Bunyan hands and turned it until it broke! The doorknobs of the churches are large, strong, commercial doorknobs. They are hard to break with tools let alone human force. Detective Jim cannot believe someone is physically strong enough to force open the church doors when they are locked.

Thank you, God, for having this interview go as smoothly as it has. Please keep Paul Bunyan calm and cool so I don't have to go Ninja on him. Our goal is for a smooth interview. I don't need to mess up my suit and tie. I don't get paid enough to buy new clothes every time I have to get physical with someone. Please keep Paul confessing to crimes he committed.

The interview continues with several breaks and some more truth serum (coffee) for Paul Bunyan. Detective Jim has several case files on the table in the interview room. The pile is about six inches thick. Detective Jim explains to Paul Bunyan that they need to talk about other previous church burglaries. Paul Bunyan denies them all. Probably because he doesn't want his Mother kicking his ass for breaking into more than one church.

But I know he committed the other church burglaries. He knows he committed them. All have the same M.O. (modus operandi or method of operation) as this case. I've got to come up with something or this guy isn't going to crack. I just have to prove to him that I can prove he committed the other church burglaries. Sometimes I feel like a frigging dentist pulling teeth.

BIG FAT DETECTIVE LIAR

If one wants to be a good detective, one needs to learn how to interview suspects and read their body language. Detective Jim deals with flesh and blood persons and has to follow his instincts and get inside their heads. He tells himself it's for their own good. And sometimes, Detective Jim has to do the unthinkable: he has to lie to his customers. Yes, when necessary, Detective Jim will lie to his clients for their own good. And, when in use, the Detective Jim lying machine is a well-oiled and tuned machine.

Deep down inside, suspects want to tell the truth, they need to get shit off their chests, but sometimes they need a little push in the right direction. That's where Detective Jim comes in. That's why they pay him the big bucks. Detective Jim knows how hard it is for some suspects to tell the truth and that is why he does everything he can, within the law, to help his suspects tell the truth and get "back on the road to recovery." So, sometimes lying is necessary for the advancement of the civilized world.

Heck, you suspects always tell me that My Friend, Some Dude, and Some Guy were responsible for the crime. You lie during your interview. Well, here it goes pal, I'm lying to you too. It's for your own good. I'm actually helping you. A lot of cops don't care if you get back on the road to recovery. I do! You should be thanking me for all I do for you! Through my lies, you are getting your life back!!

Remember, the lying is for their own good. It helps them get on the straight and narrow. Detective Jim provides a public service through his lies. And, he's good at it. So good, he should get paid extra for his lies. Detective Jim believes that his lies are superior to most other law enforcement lies. He's not afraid to go outside the box. Some of his lies are just beautiful, fantastic masterpieces! Detective Jim loves helping society through his superior lies.

After about ten minutes of trying to get Paul Bunyan to admit to the other church burglaries, Detective Jim gives up and leaves the interview room. He doesn't display any frustration in front of Paul Bunyan. It wouldn't be proper. To do so would be a sign of weakness. One can only display emotion at certain times and now is not one of those times.

This guy has to think I'm holding a royal flush. If he knows I have a weak case on the other burglaries, he's never going to crack. Who wants to go to state prison? I don't want Paul Bunyan to go to state prison either, but I have to think about the goal: admit to all the burglaries. Is that so much to ask? I don't have any evidence on the other church burglaries. If only I had some solid evidence to throw in his face. Damning evidence. Evidence like they have on C.S.I. Las Vegas!

I have an ace in the hole to get Paul to admit to those other church burglaries. It's called the C.S.I. or Crime Scene Investigation unit. I haven't told Paul Bunyan about all the wonderful evidence the Crime Scene Investigation unit has collected on all the other cases. Oh, this is going to be some inventive work, but fun!

C.S.I. LAS VEGAS

Ever watch C.S.I. on television? Detective Jim does. It's one of his favorite shows. Even though Detective Jim is drinking beer and trying to forget about work, when he is watching C.S.I. Las Vegas, he pays attention. Of course, a lot of the facets of the show aren't true. No one can collect, analyze and compare DNA samples in five minutes. Just doesn't happen. But hey, it's Hollywood and they don't have weeks to mess around. They have a show to get out! However, most of the techniques on the show are current science.

Detective Jim loves to watch the C.S.I. episodes involving the Alternate Light Source, or A.L.S. The A.L.S. is a blue light that allows one to see evidence samples not visible to the naked eye. Detective Jim calls this the "laser blue light". It's really neat science stuff. Detective Jim is not a laboratory scientist, but he needs to know what C.S.I. can and cannot do. He has to stay up to date on the latest technology. Detective Jim also knows that crooks

129

watch TV and are also up to date on the methods used to catch their asses. Detective Jim is a cop, a detective. Part of his job is interviewing and convincing his customers he has all the information about their crimes.

Detective Jim thinks about his favorite show, C.S.I., and how it may help him get Paul Bunyan on the road to recovery. And that's when it hits him:

I should have thought of this before, but I've never had to use it... C.S.I. gets things done in five minutes and we're going to do it too!

C.S.I. has already collected my evidence against Paul Bunyan. I have so much evidence against Paul Bunyan that I completely forgot about it! All I have to do is convince Paul Bunyan how much evidence C.S.I. has collected against him and he should admit to the other burglaries. Let's give it a whirl...

Detective Jim goes to the nearest copier machine and pulls out two fresh pieces of white copy paper. He goes to his desk and removes a blood sample test tube. He also grabs a couple of cotton swabs from his gun cleaning kit.

Play this right, don't act too excited about what you're going to do. Remember you are on stage and the audience needs a believable performance, not one of those fake C.S.I. episodes where they prove every little stinkin' case they get their hands on. Besides, none of this may work. Don't get your hopes up. Take your time and play it right. Act professional.

Coffee break is over, once again, IT'S SHOWTIME!

Detective Jim goes back into the interview room. Paul Bunyan appears to be relaxed. Probably because he thinks the hard part of the interview is over. It's difficult for someone to admit they broke into a building and committed a burglary, especially a church, let alone multiple churches. But confession can be a big relief to someone with a conscience and it appears to Detective Jim that Paul Bunyan has a conscience. He just needs the truth pried out of his big lumberjack head...

> *We have a pretty good relationship right now, we're almost friends. But he still won't admit to the other church burglaries. I know he did them. He kinda trusts me. I'm not attacking him at all. I'm working with him. He needs to trust me more. He needs convincing...I'm gonna have to lie to my friend Paul Bunyan and make it one of my best lies ever. I'm pretty sure I can do it and make it believable. In the end, I'll be helping my new friend...*

Detective Jim takes the sheets of copier paper and places them in front of Paul's big feet. Detective Jim asks Paul Bunyan to stand on top of each piece of paper and then step off of them. Paul does so and then sits when Detective Jim asks him to. Detective Jim asks Paul Bunyan for a voluntary cheek swab for DNA comparison. Paul says,

"Sure".

Detective Jim takes a cotton swab and swabs the inside of one of Paul's cheeks. He then places the swab in the glass blood test tube. Paul Bunyan thinks it's a real DNA swab. Detective Jim collects the sheets of paper and tells Paul he'll be right back.

Through the interview room door, Paul Bunyan can hear Detective Jim telling the crime lab personnel they have to process the pieces of paper and DNA swab immediately.

Okay, hopefully that was a good performance for Paul and he clearly heard me tell my imaginary C.S.I. friends to process the mouth swab and sheets of paper. Let's allow Paul Bunyan to digest that for just a short while. Let's take a little coffee break of our own and then we'll go back and talk to Paul again about those churches he burglarized but doesn't want to admit to. I can't believe that Paul Bunyan doesn't have more trust in his newest best friend, Detective Jim! Trust is everything Paul! It will help you tell the truth about all the nasty things you have done in your life! It will be a positive life altering event. Come on Paul, you want to tell the truth. You want to tell the truth to your new best friend, Detective Jim!

You know you broke into all those other churches. You have to believe that admitting to that is the right thing to do. By telling the truth you will be set free and have a giant weight lifted off your back.

Lastly Paul, you will remove your guilt of having lied to your new best friend, Detective Jim. Each time you told him you did not commit those other burglaries, you lied to Detective Jim. You shouldn't lie to your friends

132

Paul!

You will feel so much better you got all that shit off your chest!

This is taking over an hour. We have to get this show back on the road...

Detective Jim reenters the interview room and explains to Paul Bunyan the importance of telling the truth. There are many reasons for this but first: We need to get the truth out now because if we miss something (like all those other burglaries), it will be quite embarrassing later on Paul. We'd have to file additional charges; people would think you were a liar or something like that.

You don't want anyone thinking you're a liar, do you Paul? If we clear everything up now, people may think you do want to get on the road to recovery and change your life around. And don't forget Paul, you said you had a drinking problem, that's a big factor and I won't forget to include that information in my notes.

We've played this game before. This particular game is a bit unique, but you have to hang in there and do everything just right. One wrong move and Paul Bunyan is going to think you are the biggest bull shitter in the world; which is kinda true. But the game requires you to be one. Paul Bunyan is not playing the game you want but he can change. He's not admitting to those other burglaries because he thinks he got away with them and you don't have any evidence. It's time to pull some tools out of your interviewer's tool kit bag. Lay them on the

133

table. Make Paul know his best course of action is to admit to his mistakes. That's right, we're going to call them "mistakes", not "crimes". The word, "crime" is just such a dirty, filthy little word and conjures up visions of prison cells and terrible food for a couple of years. But the word, "mistakes" is a lot cleaner, softer on the palate, it's doable. It's almost like you "accidentally" broke into those churches. You couldn't help yourself.

He knows he committed those burglaries and we need a complete confession to all crimes...

There's a knock on the interview room door. Detective Jim gets up from his seat and is told by the other actor, or, arresting officer, that there is an important phone call for him from the crime laboratory. Detective Jim asks Paul Bunyan if he needs anything else to drink and Paul declines. Detective Jim excuses himself and says he'll be right back.

It was all choreographed. **OPERATION C.S.I. BULLSHIT** is in full swing. The arresting officer was playing his role perfectly. He even timed the knock on the interview room door just perfectly. And now, Paul Bunyan is wondering what in the heck is going on.

Detective Jim returned to the interview room and took up his seat.

"Paul, you watch T.V. right?"

"Yeah."

"Ever watch C.S.I.?"

"Oh yeah."

"I love that show. You know all the stuff they do on that show is real live stuff? I especially like it when they use that laser blue light to look at fingerprints, blood, and shoeprints in the dark. Have you ever seen them use that?"

"Yeah."

"Remember I got a mouth swab from you earlier and had you stand on the pieces of paper?"

"Yeah."

"Well, the mouth swab is for DNA comparison for DNA samples we collected from all the other church burglaries. The samples were collected   from all the doorknobs and cash boxes. But I just found out they can't be analyzed in five minutes like they do on T.V. But, on those other church burglaries we also have laser blue light footprints.

You see when you and I walked into this interview room, we left footprints all over the place. You can't see them with the naked eye but you can see them if you have a laser blue light like the one C.S.I. uses. In all those other church break-ins, our C.S.I. unit went out there and used their laser blue light just like C.S.I. Las Vegas and found a lot of footprints. They find the footprints with the laser blue light and then they put a ruler next to them and take a picture with a special camera that can take pictures in the dark, just like C.S.I. on T.V. It's amazing. We have hundreds of footprints. One thing about footprints is that they are unique in that you and I may wear the same kind of boots or shoes but your shoes leave a print distinct from mine. Each shoe print is unique because of a person's weight and the way they walk in their shoes. You follow me?"

"Yeah."

"Anyway, like I said, that DNA stuff takes a while to process and I can't get the results right away. But the laser footprints only take about ten minutes. The crime lab took your footprints from the sheets of paper I had you stand on and compared them to the laser blue light footprints from the other churches. They have a computerized database to make the comparisons in only minutes. Remember I told you how important it is to tell the truth and that today is the day we can straighten out any mistakes you have made?"

"Yeah. "

"Well Paul we need to be truthful and clean everything up. I know it's hard to admit to certain things we do in life but today is the day for soul cleansing. We need to get you on the road to recovery. I don't think you actually wanted to break into those other churches Paul. Maybe you were drunk. Maybe you just weren't thinking right."

Boy, that's an understatement…

"You see Paul, I know you did those other

burglaries, but I won't make you tell me the truth. That's not my style. I want you to tell me the truth because you want to tell me the truth.

This interview is taking a little longer than expected but I'm trying to work with you. So, with that said, I know you have a conscience and it is tearing you up a bit. When I left the room here a short while ago it was because I had a call from the crime lab. One of your boot prints is a positive match to one of the other church break ins. The crime lab is checking the other prints found at the other churches and will call me on those too in just a little bit.

Talk to me Paul..."

At this point, Paul's face turned red. He leaned forward in his chair and put his elbows on his knees and his forehead in his massive hands. He stared at the floor and calmly stated,

"If you have those laser foot prints, I did them. Please don't tell my Mother."

Oh yes! Thank you, God, thank you Paul, thank you C.S.I. Las Vegas and thank you laser blue light! I love you all. Hello closed cases. This is a great day...Let's celebrate with more coffee!

During the rest of the interview, Detective Jim and Paul Bunyan went over the other church burglaries in as much detail as Paul Bunyan could remember. Paul Bunyan did not remember each one with clarity. He was living on the street and had a

137

drinking problem. He only remembered committing four of the six church burglaries; very understandable.

He's an alcoholic and just can't remember everything he did. He admitted to four out of six church burglaries, close enough for government work. I can prove the other two by M.O. (Mode or Method of Operation).

Paul told Detective Jim he broke into each church the same way. He manhandled the church office door knobs and broke them with brute force. Detective Jim also spent some time with Paul Bunyan going over Paul's life and some steps he could take to turn it around.

Don't consider this an "interview" room Paul. Consider it Detective Jim's "Rehabilitation Station". You're on the road to recovery. You just have to stop drinking and breaking into churches.

After the interview with Paul Bunyan, Detective Jim walked over to his desk to begin writing his report of the interview. On his desk, laying side by side, were the two pieces of paper he had Paul Bunyan leave his footprints on. Detective Jim threw them in the trash with the fake DNA swab kit.

Hopefully Paul Bunyan turned his life around and now goes to church through the front door.

Detective Jim never told Paul Bunyan's Mother what terrible crimes her son had committed...If she did find out, she probably kicked his ass.

THE CASE OF THE STOLEN BULLDOZER

OFFICER NEILSON

Officer Neilson has been on the job for about ten years. He stands about six foot two, slender, muscular, sports a mustache and has a nose that resembles Cyrano de Bergerac. He is a very experienced officer and possesses an above normal IQ. Because of his high IQ, he is oftentimes alienated from his fellow officers because he is a "KNOW IT ALL". Unfortunately for the human race, he is mostly correct; he just doesn't always possess the tact to communicate effectively with his brethren. Because of this flaw, his peers sometimes find pleasure in pointing out a chink in Officer Neilson's armor. Despite this, Officer Neilson is a go-getter and a problem solver.

On a very hot summer California day, Officer Neilson receives a call of a stolen bulldozer from a rancher on the outskirts of the city. The rancher owned approximately 500 acres of land adjacent to a riverbed that flows all the way to the Pacific Ocean. The rancher has several pieces of heavy equipment for road repair and tilling the earth. One of them just went missing.

On the day this theft was reported, there were no calls for emergency service at Officer Neilson's station. At headquarters, the mood was quiet and subdued to the point that Officer Neilson's Watch

Commander, Lieutenant Cunningham was engrossed in drinking coffee and reading the local newspaper at his desk. Nothing of importance was happening in their community. Just the routine theft report and traffic accident calls.

From his desk, Lieutenant Cunningham subconsciously heard the call of a stolen bulldozer over the station radio, but he thought it was just a report call, a crime reported after the fact, and not a call in progress; no big deal.

Hell, no one thought it was a call in progress until Officer Neilson showed up at the scene.

Neilson drove his patrol car off the main highway and half a mile down a dirt road. He got out of his car and met up with the rancher who was pointing up the riverbed at a cloud of dust about a half of a mile away:

"I think that's my stolen bulldozer!"

"What kind is it?"

"A Cat D-9"

"Wait here."

And with that, Officer Neilson got in his police car and drove up the riverbed after the D-9 bulldozer.

CAT D-9

A "Cat D-9" is short for a Caterpillar company, model D-9 Bulldozer. A true workhorse if there ever was one. The D-9 produces from four to five hundred horsepower and has tracks like a military tank. The D-9 can go a lot of places a regular car or truck can't go, like riverbeds. If the D-9 runs into an obstacle, many times it can just move the object aside with the huge earth moving blade it has mounted on the front of it.

After driving in the sand for about 100 yards, Officer Neilson's patrol car got stuck. He had sand up to the axles of his patrol car and it wasn't going anywhere.

Shit, now what in the hell am I going to do? If I can't catch up to the bulldozer, I can't make a fresh felony arrest and here I am up to my axles in sand! Shit, shit, shit!

At this point, it doesn't matter that the D-9's top speed is about seven miles per hour. The D-9 is about half a mile away and steadily moving farther and farther from Officer Neilson. Officer Neilson isn't going to run after the D-9, it's too hot out. Heat exhaustion and heat stroke are definitely on the menu today if one wants to be stupid enough to go for a jog in the blistering heat. Officer Neilson just watched the cloud of stolen tractor dust get smaller and smaller in the distance. It seemed there was nothing he could do.

And then, something beautiful happened! A huge four-wheel drive truck came lumbering around a bend in the riverbed behind Officer Neilson. The driver pulled up to Officer Neilson,

"Need some help?"

141

JOHN AND LIZ

John and Liz are in their mid-twenties. They met at the local gym by accident one night. Liz stole John's racquetball court. John couldn't get mad at her, she was too beautiful to get upset with and there was a chemical attraction. They ended up playing racquetball on John's court and John almost let Liz beat him at racquetball. Afterwards, the two exchanged phone numbers.

On their second "date", Liz, a horse cult member, invited John on a horseback ride. They had a beautiful summer days ride and agreed to go on another date.

For the third date, John invited Liz to go for a "drive". He didn't tell her where or what kind of drive. John picked up Liz in his, "Four By" to go "four wheeling" in the local riverbed.

It may not sound too romantic, but John drove a pristine 1951 Willy's Pickup Truck with hopped up suspension and Gumbo Monster Mudder Tires. These tires are almost four feet tall and make John's truck look like a monster. Off road, it's almost like riding a horse! Add a gun rack in the rear window and this truck is ready for action.

John's Willy's Truck advertised to the world that he possessed the best-off road vehicle and Liz could hardly wait to go for a ride. She had never gone four wheeling' and it sounded like fun. John's truck had custom bucket seats separated by a custom off road ice cooler that was watertight even if you rolled your truck! But John never rolled his truck.

John and Liz were in the riverbed doing some slow four wheeling, having a fun time taking in the beautiful summer day. The skies were blue, and some of the bushes were still blooming. Liz was totally enjoying her first four wheeling excursion. John was taking the driving easy because he didn't want to scare Liz off. John showed her the custom four wheeling beer cooler stocked with beer and wine coolers. The ride got even more enjoyable. The riverbed was about a hundred yards wide and only had a small stream running through it at that time of year. The driving was easy. No one spilled their drinks.

FOUR WHEELING CULT

John had a deep, dark secret he did not want to share with Liz right away. A secret that could turn her off if she was told at the wrong time. No, now was not the time to let Liz in on the secret four wheeling cult's activities: they are almost as bad as the horse cult.

John and his four wheeling brethren would get off work on Friday evening and meet up at the local liquor store. They would then load up their four wheelers full of beer. From the liquor store, it's a three-mile drive to the riverbed for some extreme four wheeling with their off-road lights and stereos blasting. Sometimes they would get separated from each other in the riverbed and lose contact. Not a problem, that's why God made guns! Just fire a couple of shots in the air and wait for your partners to return fire. It's easy to find one another if you have a loud gun!

No, I have to wait. I can tell Liz about that fun

later. She may be offended by guns. If we keep dating, she may understand my cult activities, I don't know. Doesn't matter right now. I have a beautiful woman in my jeep and we're having a beautiful southern California day in the sandy riverbed. Heehaw! We'll just keep cruising along, have a couple of cold drinks and go home without rolling the truck.

John didn't give a shit about four wheeling or his beer. He couldn't keep his eyes off the beautiful blond sitting next to him. She wore a hint of perfume. It smelled intoxicating to John. Off they went, cruising slowly up the riverbed while drinking icy cold refreshing beverages. Then they drove up on Officer Neilson and his stuck patrol car. As they approached Officer Neilson and his stuck police car, they placed their open alcoholic beverages inside the special 4X4 drink cooler, just to be on the safe side.

When John asked Officer Neilson if he wanted some help, he wasn't kidding. John's 4X4 was famous for pulling some of the largest stuck trucks out of the river bottom.

Officer Neilson thought about John's offer for a second and realized that getting towed out of the river bottom will only solve one problem: getting his patrol unit unstuck. It didn't solve the problem of pursuing after the Cat D-9 and catching the bulldozer thief. And then it came to Officer Neilson:

POSSE COMITATUS

Posse Comitatus is Latin for: *Power of the County.* It is a law that authorizes law enforcement officers to deputize citizens when necessary. It is only used in special circumstances. Circumstances like "My patrol unit isn't cut out for four wheeling!"

Officer Neilson needs a four-wheel drive vehicle faster than the Cat D-9. Officer Neilson believes God just sent him one. Lieutenant Cunningham may get mad at Officer Neilson for commandeering a four-wheeler but ya know what?

Tough Shit. I'm going to do everything I can to catch that bulldozer thief and return an expensive piece of equipment to the owner. That's what they pay me for!

Officer Neilson tells John and Liz there is a stolen bulldozer travelling up the riverbed. He needs John to drive him there safely. Officer Neilson tells John and Liz they are hereby deputized and to follow his orders:

"Don't do anything you're not told to, especially anything stupid."

"Officer, my brother is a cop and I've been on ride alongs with him a couple of times. I have a three-fifty-seven (or, ".357", a popular large caliber pistol) I'm going to give to my lady friend only in case of emergency. I'll be backing you up with my 12-gauge double barrel shotgun only if I have to. I'll be careful."

I can't believe it! I needed a 4X4 and God sent me one. He not only sent me a four-wheeler, He sent one with backup! Things are starting to turn around. I don't need no stinking patrol car! Ya know, it just doesn't get much better than this!

145

Officer Neilson climbed in the bed of the Willy's truck and grabbed a hold of the roll bar. John told him there was a strap attached to the roll bar that Officer Neilson could wrap around his waist so he wouldn't fall when they hit a bump. Officer Neilson strapped himself in,

"John, head for that cloud of dust way the hell up the riverbed."

"You got it!" And John headed after the Cat D-9 like a cat stalking a mouse.

COP TALK

When talking on the radio, cops use what is a called a phonetic alphabet. Each letter has a specific word assigned to it: the letter "A" is "Adam", "B" is "Boy", "C" is "Charles", and so on and so forth...

Cops also use a code for speaking on the radio: numbers to represent what is taking place. Many police agencies use what is called a "Ten Code". Most of us have heard cops say "Ten-Four", or "10-4" in movies. "10-4" means, "message received" or "I heard what you said." Using this code, police dispatch can say a whole lot without actually using words. For example:

"Two-Boy-One ("2B1": a call sign that a patrol car assigned to a certain geographical area), ten-forty-nine ("10-49": injury accident), First and Spring streets, respond code three (Code 3: turn on your pretty red and blue emergency lights and siren and scare the shit out of all the other drivers on the road and make them get out of your way), Fire and Ambulance are ten ninety-seven ("10-97": already on scene)."

Officer Neilson got on his portable radio,

"Station one, two-boy-one (Officer Neilson's call sign), I've commandeered a four by four pickup truck and we're in pursuit of a stolen Caterpillar D-9 heading northbound in the Rio Robles riverbed from the location of call."

Police Dispatcher:

"Two-boy-one, ten-nine? ("10-9" means, "REPEAT") or in this case:

"CONFIRM WHAT THE HELL ARE YOU DOING?"

"Station one, two-boy-one, I've commandeered a four by four pickup truck in the Rio Robles river bottom and we're in pursuit of a stolen Caterpillar D-9 bulldozer heading northbound upriver from the location of call, request a ten-thirty-three ("10-33").

A "10-33" means all the other patrol officers are not to use the radio unless they have a bona fide emergency. Officer Neilson is in pursuit of a felon which could get nasty and he doesn't need any of his fellow officers talking on the radio unnecessarily.

"Station one to all units, ten-thirty-three. Two-boy-one is in pursuit of a stolen Caterpillar D-9 bulldozer, northbound in the Rio Robles river bottom, just north of 17000 Waters Road. Two-boy-one, advise type of vehicle you commandeered?

"Station 1, I'm in a Tan 1950's Willy's truck with large off-road tires."

"Two-boy-one, ten-four. All units, two-boy-one is in a commandeered tan, 1950's Willy's truck with large off-road tires. Any units in the area to assist two-boy-one, advise".

What the dispatcher really wanted to say was:

"Any units in the area of the Rio Robles river bottom, assist two-boy-one on his wild assed wild goose chase of a stolen Caterpillar D-9, just like some of the shit you see on TV. I can't believe this shit is happening! This is really gonna piss off Lieutenant Cunningham!"

But the dispatcher couldn't say that. She has to remain calm and professional. She has to be on her toes and thinking ahead. She also knows that if the shit hits the fan, It's going to be hard to get backup officers out to Officer Neilson; he might still be within city limits but for all practical purposes, he might as well be in the middle of the Sahara desert with back up a hundred miles away. He's in the boondocks and almost inaccessible.

Lieutenant Cunningham had just taken a break from reading the local paper and decided to balance his check book when dispatcher Karen walked into his office:

"Lieutenant, I don't know if you heard but two-boy-one is in the Rio Robles river bottom, in pursuit of a Caterpillar D-9. He commandeered a four by four truck. He may need air support."

148

Everyone in the dispatch area knew Lieutenant Cunningham was going to blow his lid when he heard the news about Officer Neilson and the stolen bulldozer pursuit:

"Damnit! There goes Neilson again, stirring up the pot! Karen see if the copter is available.

Karen came back a minute later: They're unavailable, on a medical flight. Two-boy-one is on his own."

I can kiss my newspaper and quiet afternoon goodbye. Thanks Neilson!

John was an experienced off roader. Without too many bumps, he was closing the distance with the stolen Cat D-9. Officer Neilson told John to drive up alongside of the Cat,

"not too close so we don't get rammed" and be ready to back off in case the suspect has a gun...

John asked Liz,

"You know how to shoot a gun?"

"Been raised with them..." she replied matter of factly.

Been raised with them? You gotta be kidding me! I'm sitting next to a beautiful gal who likes horses, four wheeling, wine coolers, and knows how to use a gun! This is turning out to be a great day...

John reached under his seat, pulled out a .357

magnum revolver and handed it to Liz. She opened the cylinder and checked the rounds: fully loaded with semi jacketed hollow points.

"Where are the speedy loaders?" Liz wanted to know.

"They're in the glove box"

Liz placed the revolver under her left thigh. She opened the glove box and found two speedy loaders which she placed in the shirt pocket of her plaid country western shirt.

"Don't look at my chest, it's not polite!"

John looked away.

Was I that obvious or is she just messing with me?

John slowly closed the distance to the D-9. It was being driven by a male in his thirties, heavyset, long dirty blond hair, dirty blue jeans, dirty white t-shirt covered with dirt and beer stains on the front. It's hard to drink beer without spilling it when you're in the river bottom driving a stolen bulldozer!

A forest green Ford four by four truck appeared to the right of John's Willy's Truck. Officer Neilson's portable radio blared,

"Station one, two-boy-two, ten ninety-seven with two-boy-one. I've commandeered a green Ford four by four and we're trying to stop the bulldozer."

I can't believe it; Officer Steve is here. He

learned how to commandeer a four by four too! He's a man after my own heart. Way to go Steve! Free beers for you down at the cop bar tonight my man!!!

The cavalry has arrived...Well, maybe not the whole cavalry troop but at least one more trooper showed up for the rodeo...

Karen repeated,

"Two-boy-two, ten-ninety-seven."

"Lieutenant, two-boy-two is with two-boy-one. He also commandeered a four by four."

"I heard, I heard damnit! What is this, **NATIONAL COMMANDEER A FOUR BY FOUR IN THE DAMN RIVER BOTTOM DAY?!**"

Karen smartly replied,

"I've been asking the city to get rid of that damn river bottom for years, but they just don't listen."

Officer Neilson was holding onto the roll bar of the Willy's with his left hand and in his right hand he had his .357 magnum service revolver. He was getting ready for the big moment. The Big "BFG Moment". That moment when he got to point his BFG in the face of the suspect and tell him to stop what he is doing, or he is going to blow his fucking shit away. Yes, Officer Neilson loved the BFG moment!

The bulldozer thief lumbered up the riverbed wearing a shit eatin' grin. He was having a great time. He had no idea that in less than a minute, Officer Neilson was going to hold a big fat BFG party just for him!

BILLY BOB

Our bulldozer thief, "Billy Bob" was thirty-one years old. He had just moved out west to escape his past in the Midwest. He had only been in California two weeks when he stumbled upon the rancher's Caterpillar D-9. The rancher left the keys under the seat and the bulldozer just screamed, **"STEAL ME!"** to Billy Bob. So, he did. This wasn't the first time Billy Bob had stolen a D-9. He's stolen so many pieces of heavy equipment, he's lost count. In reality, he can't remember because he was drunk when he stole most of them and his drinking memory isn't that good.

Billy Bob was having a fun time driving the bulldozer up the riverbed. He still had four beers left in his six pack and it was a beautiful day to go joy riding. He didn't really steal the bulldozer. No, it was given to him. It wasn't his fault the rancher left the keys in such an accessible spot!

John pulled up on the left side of the D-9 but kept a safe distance between the two vehicles. He knew if Mister D-9 thief tried to ram his Willy's, the D-9 would win; it was just too big and rugged. John was careful...

The shit eatin' grin disappeared from the face of Billy Bob when he looked left and saw the Willy's truck pull up alongside. It wasn't the appearance of the Willy's so much but the crazy cop in the truck bed yelling at him about blowing his fucking shit away, or

152

something like that. The cop was also waving around a huge gun with a barrel that looked like a cannon. Officer Neilson was having his BFG moment and enjoying it!

How did this happen? This shit only happens in movies. The fucking cops here must know everything. I thought for sure I would get away with this and now there's a cop with a Big Fucking Cannon pointed at me and that fucking thing might go off if they hit a bump!

Billy Bob is not quite sure what to do. He was never a fast thinker. Situations like this always took a toll on his ability to think clearly. He wasn't quite sure what to do. Then Billy Bob saw the other four-wheel drive truck with officer Steve on his right side. Billy Bob's heart was racing, and he could feel his blood pressure rise:

SHIT!!!! Another crazy cop waiving his gun! This just keeps getting worse! Should I keep on going? I might get away. Probably not though…Why do I always get caught? Shit!

Billy Bob stopped the bulldozer and took it out of gear. He just sat there with the engine idling and thought about his options.

Should I give up or try to make a slow run for it? I might get away if I can find a spot in the river bottom their trucks can't go. They might not shoot me. But then, they might. If I get away, they might send a helicopter after me. Shit, it's hard to think. The cops are yelling at me too much. I can't hear myself think…

Billy Bob was a special kind of stupid. Sometimes he would make a good decision and then change his mind at the last second and do something stupid. This was one of those times. He could go either way. Secretly he was hoping he could give himself up without getting shot. He had been shot at before back home and it scared the living shit out of him. He had burglarized a home and the owner came down from an upstairs bedroom and fired off a shot just as Billy Bob was running out the front door. Billy wasn't hit by the bullet, but it barely missed him. He didn't want that happening again. He might get hit this time and he heard it really hurts if you get shot. Billy Bob did something smart. He put his hands in the air.

Officer Neilson got out of the Willy's truck bed and walked towards Billy Bob and yelled at him:

"Don't mess around. I'll blow your shit away if you don't listen!"

Billy Bob put the bulldozer back in gear. John opened his driver's door, stood up on the rocker panel and placed his double-barreled shotgun over the roof of his truck and aimed it at Billy Bob:

"Dude, you better listen to the officer here because if you don't, you are getting both barrels of this shotgun!"

Officer Steve was now yelling more loudly than before for Billy Bob to get off the fucking bulldozer. There was more yelling about blowing Billy Bob's shit away...

Liz had her revolver in her right hand and pointed it out her window at Billy Bob and screamed,

"Get off the fucking bulldozer fucker!"

She noticed her hand was shaking a bit, so she steadied her pistol with her other hand. She had a right to be a bit nervous. This was her first B.F.G. felony stop!

Billy Bob was freaking out. He saw the BFG's, he saw John's shotgun. He saw Liz's BFG and that her hand was shaking a bit. He still couldn't believe he got caught and that there were four guns pointed at him. The cops continued yelling at him that they were going to blow his shit away. They won't shut up!

"Alright, alright! Don't fucking shoot! Put the fucking guns away!!! Don't shoot me. Please don't shoot me!"

Officer Neilson yelled back,

"Get off the bulldozer and lay down on the ground, I'm ready to fucking shoot your ass and call it an 'accident'. Now get the fuck down! Keep your hands where I can see them!"

Billy Bob turned off the bulldozer and jumped down. He kept his hands open and to the side of his body. He didn't want to be an "accident."

"I don't have any guns, don't shoot."

Officer Neilson kept his pistol pointed at Billy Bob's chest and told him to get the fuck on the ground and lay face down. Billy Bob was all too happy to oblige. Officer Neilson handcuffed Billy Bob and searched him. The stolen bulldozer pursuit was officially over. Officer Neilson told John and Liz,

"You can put the guns away now"

Officer Neilson got on his portable radio,

"Station one, two-boy-one, code four, ten-fifteen one suspect, lift the ten-thirty-three." Which means,

"No further assistance needed, one suspect is in custody, and you may now let all the other patrol units use the police radio band for their boring report calls."

Dispatcher Karen repeated for all the other patrol units to hear,

"Two-boy-one, code four, ten-fifteen one, ten-thirty-three lifted." Over Officer Neilson's portable radio, a dozen police microphones clicked on and off; an unofficial signal to Officer Neilson from his brethren that weren't involved in the pursuit that they were happy Officer Neilson and Officer Steve were successful in their pursuit and came out of it safely.

In his watch commander's office, Lieutenant Cunningham heard the radio clicking too,

"Damnit, I hate it when they do that! They're just encouraging him. Karen, let me know when Neilson gets to the station, I want to talk to him! All this pot stirring crap. He's always getting into shit like this!"

Karen complied,

"Two-boy-one, eleven ninety-eight the watch commander when ten-eighty-one." Or, in other words,

"Officer Neilson, you pissed off the watch commander again. Big surprise there! Please meet with him in his office to get your ass chewed when you arrive at the station of love."

Neilson just swore to himself and radioed back,

"Station-one, two-boy-one, ten four."

Neilson didn't give a damn. He just arrested a felon and recovered thousands of dollars' worth of stolen property. He was still high from the BFG adrenalin rush.

Nope, nobody is gonna fuck up my beautiful BFG day!

Officer Steve walked up to Officer Neilson and said,

"Lieutenant Cunningham hates it when we do things like this. You probably gave him a brain aneurysm."

"Yeah, well that's too bad. I was sent here to do a job and the job got done."

Officer Neilson got a big grin on his face,

"And besides, I had a lot of fun, didn't you?"

"Hell yes!"

"It's days like this that makes beer taste so good! Let's get back to the ranch."

Officers Neilson and Steve placed Billy Bob in the back of the Ford four by four and hopped in beside him. John and Liz followed in the Willy's, and the rancher followed in his Cat. It was one big happy felony river bottom caravan!

On the drive back to the ranch, Officer Neilson asked Billy Bob,

"So, what are you on parole for?"

"Who said I'm on parole?"

"You're either on parole or probation, which is it?"

"Probation.'

"What's the charge?"

"Theft."

"Oh, I see we're playing a word game. What kind of theft? Petty theft, like taking candy from a drugstore? Or maybe, something a little bit bigger like say, grand theft? Like maybe grand theft auto? Or grand theft of farm equipment? Help me out here."

Billy Bob shook his head,

"Grand Theft Auto. Shit!."

Officer Neilson looked at Officer Steve and just grinned.

Once back at the ranch, the rancher thanked Officers Neilson and Steve and told them he was going to write a letter to the city council and the police chief as to what a fantastic job they did in recovering his stolen bulldozer.

Oh yeah Lieutenant Cunningham. I'm fifteen minutes away from you chewing my ass for doing my job but I'm about two days away from getting a commendation for it. Until then, Officer Steve and I are going to keep it our personal little secret. You'll find out about it well after you chew our asses. I'm going to post a copy of our commendation on all the station bulletin boards. Everyone is going to know about it. You can rip them down, but I'll just put up another one!

Officer Neilson went to the trunk of his police car and got out a camera,

"We're taking pictures! I've got a work photo album and I have to have photos of this. I'll make copies and send them to everyone!"

They all took turns taking photos with each other. They even had Billy Bob in some of the photos!

John and Liz hooked up a tow strap to Officer Neilson's patrol car and easily pulled it out of the sand. Officer Neilson was extremely thankful for that kind gesture because if he had to call a tow truck, the police department would have to pay for the price of the tow and that would give Lieutenant Cunningham another thing to be angry about.

Technically, up to this point, Lieutenant Cunningham didn't really have a valid reason to be upset with Officer Neilson. Officer Neilson went outside the box to solve a problem, but he didn't break any department rules or regulations. However, Lieutenant Cunningham could give Officer Neilson some heat for stupidly trying to drive in the sandy river bottom in a police cruiser. Thanks to John and his big assed Gumbo Monster Mudder tires, that isn't a problem. Officer Neilson's patrol car is unstuck and he's not even going to mention it to anyone. It never happened. If Lieutenant Cunningham does find out about it, he'll play it down,

Oh yeah, I went off road for a little while and the front tires got stuck but it wasn't a problem. They came right out. That's when the four by four came by and helped catch the crook. It's not an issue.

Officer Neilson again thanked John and Liz for all their help, especially being there as back up in case Officer Steve had not arrived. Officer Neilson offered to give them some money for gas even though there really wasn't that much driving involved.

John told Officer Neilson,

"Hell, we should be paying you. We had a blast helping out!"

Billy Bob was placed in the backseat of Officer Steve's police car (the police car that did not get stuck in the sandy river bottom). Officer Steve drove Billy Bob to the police station for an interview by detectives and booking.

Officer Neilson drove to the station to face Lieutenant Cunningham and his expected *stirring the pot ass chew tirade.* Neilson wasn't going to let his watch commander's attitude ruin a perfectly beautiful felony day!

Mister Rancher thanked John and Liz for all their help and they all drank a beer together.

On the way to the police station, Officer Steve asked Billy Bob,

"Dude, do you have gas or what?"

"No."

"Well, what the hell am I smellin'?"

"I think I shit my pants."

"You think you shit your pants or you DID shit your pants?"

"I shit my pants. I couldn't help it! All of you were waiving guns around and that woman was shaking her gun and I thought she was going to shoot me too."

"All right, we'll get you cleaned up at the station and if you don't say anything about it, I won't either."

"Thanks man."

Officer Neilson reported into the watch commander's office as ordered. Lieutenant Cunningham was seated at his desk. He wasn't happy. Cunningham told Neilson to have a seat.

Cunningham got up from his chair and closed the office door to have a little heart to heart with Neilson.

"I don't like the way you handled that call Neilson. You're always stirring the pot."

"I did what I had to do, as I see it, there was no way around it. I don't drive a magical fairy tale police car that turns itself into a four-wheel drive vehicle to chase people down in the river bottom."

Now's my chance to be a smart ass and get away with it...

"I think Officer Steve and I did a good job, a great job. Maybe you should write us a commendation for our superior police work?"

A commendation? How about a reprimand?

"With all due respect Lieutenant, you run the shift, but you aren't able to supervise in the field. You're stuck to your watch commander's desk (And your newspaper and your checkbook that needs balancing). The city relies on its officers to make command decisions and that's what we did today. We recovered property worth tens of thousands of dollars and made a prominent citizen very, very happy. That's what we're supposed to do.

"I'm not taking a reprimand off the table."

"Well, I can't stop you from doing that. If you write me up, you'll be hearing from the police

162

union attorney. The whole ordeal is going to give me mental anguish I didn't ask for. I'm already having the onset of emotional distress. I think I'm getting a case of diarrhea as we speak.

After I am exonerated, and I will be, I will probably have to sue for emotional distress and harassment. Oh, I almost forgot, the suspect has out of state warrants for burglary and sexual assault. We not only arrested a thief for grand theft, we took a pervert of the streets.

I wonder if the rancher contributes to any of the city councilmembers when they are up for reelection? He probably does.

The rancher was such a nice guy. It felt good doing something positive for such an upstanding member of the community and nobody got hurt."

"You can leave Neilson. Just stay out of the river bottom from now on."

Yeah, rrright. I'll stay out of the river bottom as long as I don't get any more calls there. You're just pissed you never got to handle any calls like this one and have so much damn fun in the process...After I book Billy Bob, my shift is over and Officer Steve and I are going to have icy cold felony beers down at the cop bar and you're not invited fucker!

John and Liz left the rancher and continued their four wheeling up the riverbed. They were full of adrenalin and thought how they made a good team backing up Officer Neilson.

They had one frosty cold adult beverage after another and eventually relaxed from all the excitement. They stopped to stretch their legs. They had their first kiss.

They got home late that night.

They later married . . ..

YOUR HONOR, I'M AN ALCOHOLIC AND I NEED HELP!

GUSTAVO

Gustavo was a simple man. He was a nice person when he wasn't drunk. If he wouldn't drink, he could lead a normal life like anyone else. The problem is that Gustavo liked to drink, and he was almost always drunk.

Gustavo had a habit of drinking in public and going to jail for public intoxication. He and the cops had a special relationship. Gustavo got drunk, the cops showed up, Gustavo went to jail. Gustavo would dry out for thirty to sixty days in jail, get released and start the cycle over.

ALCOHOLICS AND JAILS

Many people are not aware of it, but many poor alcoholics that cannot take care of themselves are still alive today because of the jail system and the medical staffs that work there. Jail medical staffs are experts in treating alcoholics and keeping them alive. Gustavo was kept alive during many a bout with extreme alcohol withdrawals because of jail medical staffs. And, Gustavo knew this.

Jails have inmate workers. To be a worker, the cops must have some level of trust in them; at least some level of trust more than other inmates. After Gustavo got arrested and sobered up, he was always made an inmate worker.

Every time Gustavo went to jail, he got his old job back: Inmate Car Wash Supervisor. He was in charge of washing all the police cars. Gustavo obtained this esteemed position because he was older than most inmates, didn't get into trouble while he was in jail and knew how to run a car wash crew. Normally most inmates don't like to be told what to do by another inmate, but Gustavo was like a beloved Uncle to the other inmates. He was *Tio Gustavo* (Spanish for: Uncle Gustavo). Tio Gustavo assisted younger inmates with their adjustment to jail life (if they hadn't been in jail before) and was their unofficial jail counselor. The cops liked Gustavo because he was older and helped keep things running calm in jail.

So Gustavo's program went something like this: He'd get drunk, get arrested, go to jail. He'd stay in jail for a couple of days to sober up and then get released on his promise to show up in court in about ten days or so.

Most people that get arrested for being drunk in public don't have to return to court or if they do, rarely have to serve additional jail time. Public Intoxication is considered a low-grade misdemeanor. However, there is an exception to this rule. If someone is a professional drunk, they get jail time and probation. Gustavo is a professional drunk and he always gets additional jail time. The cops don't mind it because they get to have the best Inmate Car Wash Supervisor on the planet in charge of keeping their cars clean. It's a symbiotic relationship of sorts.

After one of his arrests for being drunk in public, Gustavo was routinely ordered to return to court for sentencing. Gustavo was still drinking, and he felt like he needed to once again stay in jail for an extended time and dry out. So, on his appointed day in court, Gustavo went to the courthouse to see the judge. He expected to get a thirty- or sixty-day sentence. He deserves it and he needs it to stay alive.

On Gustavo's court date, the courtroom was full of a wide variety of misdemeanor cases to be heard, defendants to be sentenced, etc. When Gustavo's case was called, he walked up to the defendant's table. He knows where it is because he's a professional and has been there many a time.

The regular judge in Gustavo's courtroom is on vacation and a visiting judge is in on the bench. The regular judge knows Gustavo and his drinking problem and always sentences Gustavo to jail time because he is well aware Gustavo needs it to sober up.

The visiting judge is new to the bench and Gustavo's courtroom. He is not at all familiar with Gustavo or his drinking problem. The judge advised Gustavo of the charge of Public Intoxication filed against him and asked Gustavo how he plead to the charge.

"Guilty your Honor. I need at least a sixty-day jail sentence."

The judge was taken aback as most defendants don't want to go to jail, let alone a sixty-day sentence.

The judge imposed a year's probation with a 30-day suspended sentence on Gustavo. The judge didn't think Gustavo needed to go to jail. If Gustavo violates his probation, like getting drunk again, which will happen, then Gustavo will have to come back into court and get sentenced all over and then go to jail. Gustavo knows he cannot control his drinking and needs to immediately go to jail to dry out.

Normally, if a judge sees a particular defendant in his courtroom on a regular basis, that defendant gets lots of jail time and probation. This judge is not familiar with Gustavo's past. Also, Gustavo is being very humble and respectful. Gustavo isn't blaming the judge for his drinking problem; he blames himself which is unusual. So, Gustavo is respectful; he just wants to check himself into the jail rehabilitation center for professional drunks. Gustavo can't afford a real rehab center and he knows the county jail works just fine for his rehab needs.

Gustavo, not happy with his sentence, asks the judge:

"Your Honor, may I say something?"

"Yes, go ahead."

"Your Honor, I'm an alcoholic and I deserve to go to jail for sixty days. I need to dry out."

"No Mister Gustavo, I see you here today and I think you can manage on your own, you'll just be taking up valuable jail bed space"

"Really? "Valuable bed space"? Do you know who I am you rookie judge? I'm the Inmate Car Wash Supervisor. Get your facts straight! I've got a fucking drinking problem and may die from it if I don't dry out in jail. Now give me some jail time!"

"Your Honor, I know when I need to dry out and I know I'm just going to get arrested again tonight because I can't stop drinking and I'm afraid I'm going to kill myself. So please sir, sentence me to at least sixty days in jail"

"No Mister Gustavo, I don't think you're listening to me. I'm the judge here, not you, you don't tell me what to do. You may leave the court room, you're dismissed."

"But your Honor..."

The judge is losing patience:

"What Mister Gustavo?"

Gustavo blurted out:

"FUCK YOU!"

With the slam of his gavel the judge blurted out:

"THIRTY DAYS!"

Gustavo again blurted out again:

"FUCK YOU!"

Another slam of the gavel:

"SIXTY DAYS!"

'Thank you, your honor."

Everyone in the courtroom except for Gustavo and the judge was laughing their heads off. It's amazing how two simple words can sometimes help you achieve your goals in life.

BRO, I'M GONNA KILL MYSELF

NETWORKING

To be good at his job, Detective Jim had to interact with many different groups of people. First and foremost, he had to work with his peers and supervisors. Also, networking with law enforcement agencies near and far was sometimes necessary and required to solve cases, etc. There were also victims, witnesses and suspects to deal with on a daily basis. Detectives also work with the District Attorney's Office and sometimes the Public Defender's Office and/or private attorneys. Don't forget the crime lab and C.S.I. - Detective Jim often waited on results from the crime lab before he could proceed on a case. There was another group he dealt with:

INFORMANTS

There is a subcategory of witnesses that police have to deal with. They are called "informants". Informants provide information to law enforcement. Anonymous informants are just that, they wish to be "anonymous". They usually call the police department and leave a tip for the cops. Some of these anonymous informants are criminals wishing to turn in their competitors and increase their own customer base, like in drug sales. Some anonymous informants just want to turn someone in for revenge. Some anonymous informants are called "citizen informants". They provide information to stop criminal activity for the good of society.

"Paid informants" get money for the information they provide. These informants give information as a first or second job. Some police departments have special budgets to fund these paid informants in an effort to keep crime down in their community. Most paid informants associate with the criminal elements in society on a daily basis and they know what's going on. They gain the confidence of criminals; learn what crimes they are committing and then pass the information on to the police in exchange for a paycheck. Beats working for a living.

Many informants are recruited by the police after they have been arrested. This occurs quite frequently in drug cases: the cops arrest a low-level drug dealer, "little guy". They then get this "little guy" to "roll over" on his "connection", the next drug dealer up the food chain. So, this "connection" gets busted and the cops try to recruit him to set up the next person in the food chain and on and on it goes. Almost everybody cooperates with the cops to get a lighter sentence or a dismissed case.

There are also informants that don't really consider themselves informants. They like cops and police work and give information for their own pleasure. They believe they are a type of "citizen cop". It makes them happy because they can play cop. Detective Jim calls this type of informant a "groupie informant", for lack of a better term.

DAREN

Detective Jim had a groupie informant named Daren. Daren had a problem: he was an alcoholic; but, a functional alcoholic. He lived on the streets but would find casual labor or revert to begging to fund his lust for alcohol.

172

Each day Daren would work or beg just enough to pay for a cheap hotel room, some fast food, and a pint of whiskey. He casually associated with the criminal element because he had no real home and people in similar situations as Daren's are attracted to each other like magnets.

Daren usually called his friends at the police department when he was drinking and bored. From his cheap motel room, he would call his friends at the Detective Bureau and report any suspicious activity he noticed. Daren called all his Detective friends "Bro".

One day at 10:30 a.m., Detective Jim received a phone call at his desk. It was the Detective secretary advising she was transferring a phone call from Daren.

Daren was calling using a prepaid cellphone; he was extremely inebriated. His speech was slurred to the max and he told Detective Jim,

"Bro, I'm gonna kill myself".

Detective Jim was busy and the last thing he needed was to handle a suicidal groupie informant, but Detective Jim felt he owed something to Daren. They had a long history and every once in a while, Daren "cracked" a case for Detective Jim.

Detective Jim told Daren to relax and not to think suicidal thoughts and maybe he should go check himself into the local hospital or something.

Daren slurred,

"No Bro, I don't want to kill myself but I've been

drinking for five days straight, I'm drunk, I can't stop, I'm seeing things, I can't take it, I'm going to keep drinking 'till I kill myself."

Detective Jim believed Daren was going to die if he didn't get the help he needed. And where could Daren get that help? Daren didn't have medical insurance. How about the county jail and the professional medical staff that are experts at keeping alcoholics alive? Yup, that's the answer.

"Daren, we have to get you arrested so you can go to jail and get dried   out"

"How do we do that?"

"I'll take care of it, you just stay on the line, okay?"

"Okay"

"Don't leave me now, I have to go to another phone for a second. What's your room number?'"

"207"

"Okay, hang on, don't leave the phone"

"Okay"

Detective Jim went to another phone and called police dispatch. He asked the dispatcher to send an officer out to room 207 of Daren's motel. There was a really drunk subject outside that room, and he was falling down and could not care for his own safety. The dispatcher stated a car was on the way.

"Daren, you there?"

"Yeah"

"Okay, listen to me real carefully, there is a police officer on his way to your room. Keep your phone on so I can hear what's going on. I want you to stand outside your door and when the policeman gets there, I want you to act real drunk and fall down on the ground, you got it?"

"Yeah"

"Okay, do as I say because the officer cannot arrest you for being drunk in public if you are inside your motel room, you have to be outside the room   and appear really drunk. When the officer gets there, tell him you are drunk and fall down, okay?"

"Okay"

A uniformed officer shows up in the walkway leading to Daren's room.

"Okay I can see him; he's walking toward me"

"How far away is he?"

"About fifty feet."

"Okay, when he's about ten feet away tell him your drunk and fall down" "Okay"

Ten seconds later:

"Officer, I'm really drunk…"

Detective Jim hears the sound of Daren falling to the ground. He hears Daren tell the officer again that he is really drunk. Detective Jim can also hear the officer tell Daren to just go back inside his room and sleep it off. Daren comes back on the line:

"He won't arrest me. He says I can just go back inside the room and sleep it off"

"Hold the phone close to your ear so he can't hear me."

"Okay"

"Daren, I want you to stand up slowly like you're really drunk. Lean on the walkway handrail like you can't keep your balance. Look the officer in the eye and tell him, 'Fuck You!' But, don't touch the officer. Got it?

"Got it."

Detective Jim had to use the last tool in his arsenal to get Daren arrested and receive the treatment he needed. That tool, the words" Fuck You!" are like catnip to a cop. Cops come unglued at being cursed at and disrespected. Most of the time anyway.

A couple of seconds go by as Daren follows his instructions and gets to his feet while using the handrail to balance himself.

Hey Officer, "FUUUUCK YOU!"

Detective Jim can hear the sounds of a scuffle and then the ratcheting of handcuffs being placed on Daren. Daren dropped his cellphone when he was arrested by the Officer. The Officer picked up Daren's cellphone and seeing that there was a call on the line asked:

"Who's this?"

"This is Detective Jim. Did you arrest that asshole?"

"Yeah I did. Dispatch said he was really drunk and they were right."

"Good. That prick called me up and had been telling me to go fuck myself and threatening me all morning. Good thing you showed up and arrested him. No telling what kinda shit he would have gotten into. Good job."

"Thanks, I have to go book this asshole."

"Bye."

"Bye."

And that is yet another example of how law enforcement saves lives with just two simple words.

I NOW PRONOUNCE YOU DIVORCED

OFFICER SCOTTY

Ever since his childhood, Officer Scotty knew what he wanted to be when he grew up: a policeman. He is a three-year veteran of the police department. Officer Scotty was in his mid-twenties, short in stature, average build, and a permanent look on his face as if he is constantly sizing up the world around him. Even though he is not considered an "Old Salt", he has handled enough police calls to know what is going on in the world. Scotty has an extremely high IQ. Scotty was a bona fide member of Mensa which means he scored in the 98th percentile for the IQ test they administer. Even though he could have been a rocket scientist, he chose law enforcement. It was his calling.

JOSEPH WAMBAUGH

During several calls that Officer Scotty handled, he almost got in trouble for his sense of humor. Like several of his police comrades, he sometimes just can't control his humor. It's not really Officer Scotty's fault, you see, when Officer Scotty was a kid, he fell in love with two books written by the world famous police author Joseph Wambaugh, a former Los Angeles Police Department Detective Sergeant. Wambaugh is known as the 'Grand Master' of Police Novels. The two books Scotty held so dear to his heart were The New Centurions and The Choirboys. These two books were produced into movies. Some of the characters were not exactly the role models one would want in police work, but Scotty could relate to some of their humorous pranks.

MR. AND MRS. TRASH

Mr. and Mrs. Trash lived in the center of town in a middle-income neighborhood. The neighborhood wasn't trashy except for the home rented by Mr. and Mrs. Trash. They were in their early fifties, on welfare, and decided that after twenty-five years of marriage they were not happy being married to one another.

It all began around noon one hot summer day. Mr. and Mrs. Trash were continually arguing, and the surrounding neighbors just couldn't take the yelling and screaming anymore. The day shift police officers were sent out to the Trash home twice in an attempt to quell the disturbances. The officers advised the Trashes to go to court and get a divorce. After the officers left, the trashes continued to argue.

Officer Scotty was working the evening shift that day and he was assigned the beat area where the Trashes lived. Three hours into his shift, Officer Scotty was sent to the Trash home for yet another disturbance call. Police dispatch advised this is the third time officers had been sent to the home that day. Officer Scotty was sent to the home without a back-up officer which if you will recall is not usual protocol. He has to be extra careful because he too knows domestic violence calls can turn to shit really quick.

On his way to the Trash residence, Officer Scotty received a call on his mobile phone from police dispatch. It was dispatcher Cindy:

"Hey Scotty, just to give you a heads up, the neighbors are also really pissed at the Trashes. We received an anonymous call from

179

one neighbor. He said the Trashes have been arguing for days and he can't take it anymore. He also said if the police can't take care of it, he's got a gun and he will. Be extra careful."

"I will and thanks for the heads-up Cindy."

Great, now I'm going to a domestic dispute call without backup and a neighbor wants to play vigilante and blow up the neighborhood.

Officer Scotty parked two doors down from the Trash residence and can hear yelling coming from the Trash house. He walks slowly up to the house all the while listening to what the argument is about. The front door and front windows of the house are wide open; probably to get a breeze through the house because of the hot weather. Officer Scotty cautiously approaches the area of the open front door. Without standing directly in front of it, he calls inside and states his presence. Mr. and Mrs. Trash walked outside to meet Officer Scotty

Mr. and Mrs. Trash are dressed like they live on a farm. They are not dirty, but they appear very unkempt. Both are missing several teeth. Officer Scotty scans the area for a banjo player. He finds none.

Officer Scotty: "What seems to be the problem?"

Mr. Trash: "I can't be married to her any longer. We don't get along and she won't shut up!"

Mrs. Trash: "Me too, we can't agree on anything"

Officer Scotty:	"You two been drinking today"
Mr. Trash:	"Just a couple of beers but we're not drunk."
Mrs. Trash:	"I wish he were drunk, he's easier to get along with when he's drunk. Your officers were out here twice today, and they didn't help a bit."
Officer Scotty:	"Well, what did they tell you?"
Mr. Trash:	"They told us to go get a divorce."
Officer Scotty:	"Well, why don't you two do that?"
Mrs. Trash:	"Our car is broken, and we can't drive to the courthouse and we don't have any money for that. We need a divorce!"
Officer Scotty:	"Why don't one of you leave the house so you will stop arguing?"
Mr. Trash:	"We have nowhere to go and no money."
Officer Scotty:	"Would you stop arguing if you got a divorce?"
Mrs. Trash:	"Oh yeah."
Mr. Trash:	"Of course, why not? We'd be divorced and happy."

Boy, this conversation really makes sense.

Officer Scotty is thinking he is not dealing with the smartest people in the world. None of this makes sense to him except that the Trashes are very simple minded.

It's time to have some fun with the Trashes. I think I can settle this matter in proper trashy style, and they'll buy it. I don't have a back-up officer, therefore, no witnesses except for Mr. and Mrs. Trash. It's time to break out some Wambaugh.

In Joseph Wambaugh's book *THE NEW CENTURIONS*, one of the characters is named Whitey Duncan, a crusty old police officer who had a flair for handling problems. At one point, Whitey and his partner are dispatched to a domestic dispute and the couple involved wanted a divorce to live peacefully together *(if that makes any sense at all but then again, we aren't dealing with the smartest of people here)*. Officer Whitey Duncan performs the divorce by having the married couple place one of their hands on his badge while Whitey recites some appropriate language to sound official. Whitey pronounces the couple divorced and everyone is happy. Only problem is, it's not legal. Whitey doesn't care as he knows he's dealing with some candidates that will never make it through rocket science school. Whitey solves the problem and effectively keeps the peace through an illegal divorce.

Officer Scotty: "Do you two have any firearms in the house?'

Mr. Trash: "No sir."

Mrs. Trash:	"Good thing..."
Officer Scotty:	"Okay, let's walk inside into the living room. I think I can help you."
Mrs. Trash:	"Finally, those other officers didn't help a bit."

All three walk inside the house and into the living room. It's unkempt but not necessarily dirty. Officer Scotty expected it to be a bit dirtier but he's glad it isn't. He hates dirty homes.

I can't believe this, I read Wambaugh when I was a young kid and here I am using that knowledge to provide a public service, keep the peace, but above all, have some fun! And, I don't think I'll get caught!

Officer Scotty:	"Okay, you folks want a divorce, but you can't afford one?"
Mrs. Trash:	"That's right."
Mr. Trash:	"Yes sir."
Officer Scotty:	"And if you get a divorce, you'll be happy and will quit arguing?"
Mr. Trash:	"Of course."
Mrs. Trash:	"Yeah."

Officer Scotty: "It's a good thing they sent me to this call. I have the answer for you. What you need is a confidential, common law divorce. We can take care of this right now. I have special training for this. The other officers that came out here earlier would have done it but they did not take the special State of California Common Law Divorce Training Class."

Mrs. Trash: "Oh, that explains why they didn't help us"

Mr. Trash: "That's great"

Officer Scotty: "I need each of you to place your right hands over your hearts and place your left hand on my badge."

The Trashes do as Officer Scotty instructed.

Officer Scotty: "By the power vested in me in the State of California I now pronounce you both divorced in accordance with the common law. You are now divorced."

Mrs. Trash cried out,

"Oh thank you" while lunging at Officer Scotty and applying a huge bear hug.

Next, Mr. Trash grabbed Officer Scotty's hand

184

for a shake and stated:

"Thank you sir, this is a big help, now we don't have to argue. You're the first Officer to help us."

Officer Scotty left the Trash house. He was proud of his use of Wambaugh Wisdom. He was laughing hysterically inside. He couldn't believe what he had just done. He also knew he couldn't tell anyone about the incident for many years to come. Maybe not until after he retired. For once, the Trash neighborhood was quiet. There was a sense of calm.

When Officer Scotty returned to the police station at the end of his shift, he was summoned over the station P.A. system that dispatch wanted to see him. The dispatch center was crammed with desks, phones, microphones, and paper everywhere.

He walked into the dispatch center where several female dispatchers were at their consoles of phones and radio microphones. As he entered, he asked,

"Someone wanted to see me?"

Dispatcher Cindy jumped to her feet and walked up into Officer Scotty's personal zone. The other dispatchers were on the phone. In a quiet voice, Dispatcher Cindy stated,

"We received a phone call from the Trashes. They just wanted to thank you again for divorcing them. They said how lucky they were to have you show up to divorce them because you had the special divorce training through

185

the State of California; or something like that."

Cindy smiled and winked at Officer Scotty. She continued,

"And we here at dispatch want to thank you too because now, we aren't sending cars over to the Trash house and wasting valuable police resources. The watch commander doesn't need to know, it's our little secret..."

Wink, wink.

Officer Scotty smiled and said,

"Don't thank me, thank the teachers that taught Joseph Wambaugh how to write and the ones that taught me how to read.

Cindy, please forgive me but I've had a really trashy day and I need to go home and drink some beers."

"Have one for me."

PLEASE KICK MY ASS

CYCLE OF ASS KICKING

We all have met or know someone who is generally unhappy with their life. These people are angry most of the time and social misfits. They hate themselves and other people and are almost always looking for a fight. They want and need their asses kicked on a regular basis.

Once the angry person gets their ass kicked, they usually don't need it kicked for some time. The time varies. But, they eventually forget about their last ass kicking, the anger returns, and they need their ass kicked again. This cycle is referred to as the 'CYCLE OF ASS KICKING.'

BIKER BARRY
SCOOTER TRASH

Biker Barry was in his early thirties. Tall, big, long bushy black hair, wears black oil stained motorcycle leathers, rides an oil leaking chopper motorcycle and belongs to an "outlaw" motorcycle gang. He is one of the most feared members of his motorcycle club. He is uncontrollable when under the influence of alcohol and drugs. Usually when he is "high", it is from both drugs and alcohol because Biker Barry has to escape reality and the anger inside him. But, when Biker Barry is high, the anger comes out in a flood. He had spent his fair share of time in jail for his explosive behavior and lust for alcohol and drugs.

From time to time, police organizations hold seminars dealing with outlaw motorcycle gangs. In those seminars, Biker Barry would be described as "Scooter Trash"; he's just a dirty piece of garbage.

OFFICER ROCCO

Officer Rocco joined the force after serving six years in the military. He wasn't that tall but he was stocky and strong. He grew up in a New York neighborhood where he learned to not put up with anybody's crap. He was a patient officer but ready at a moment's notice to take care of business.

LET'S ALL GET DRUNK!

One hot summer night, a popular downtown bar was full of patrons. Everybody was drinking and dancing and just having a great time. Half the clientele were drunk. Biker Barry and his motorcycle club buddies wanted to get out and have some fun too. A group of eight thirsty bikers headed for the popular watering hole. As they pulled into the parking lot, the rumble of their bikes could be heard inside the bar and everyone had a feeling that something bad was going to happen. And it did.

Barry and his biker bros entered the bar and everybody noticed them immediately. They nudged their way up to the bar and ordered drinks, two rounds because the first beer went down almost as fast as it was poured.

Yup, we're going to drink and kick some ass tonight!

Barry was eyeing all the women folk with a lustful eye. For a while, everybody kept to themselves. Barry went into the bathroom, took a piss and snorted a line of crank (methamphetamine).

Like throwing a match on gasoline!

When Barry returned from the bathroom, everybody knew something was different about him. He seemed angrier and meaner then when he first arrived at the bar.

Barry was starting to get loud and was talking trash. He was staring at one of the girls in the bar and she felt uncomfortable. Her boyfriend told her to ignore the piece of shit (Barry). The boyfriend said this to his girlfriend but said it loud enough for Barry to hear. The boyfriend had consumed five beers and was feelin' pretty badass himself; he wasn't going to let Biker Barry ruin his evening by eyefucking his gal.

Barry didn't like being called a piece of shit and the next thing you know, he was on his feet and challenging the boyfriend to a fight. No one remembers who threw the first punch but the fight was on. Some of Barry's bros joined in and so did the friends of the boyfriend. The bartender was pushing all the fighters outside as best he could with all the punching, kicking, and swearing.

Nobody hit the bartender. Hitting the bartender was equivalent to attacking a minister or rabbi. No, you don't touch the bartender. He won't let you back inside his bar if you do!

The fight was now in the parking lot and the sirens could be heard off in the distance. Everybody was bleeding. The cops showed up just as everyone had achieved getting their asses kicked to an almost acceptable level. That is, everyone except for Biker Barry.

A Sergeant and five officers, including Officer Rocco arrived at the scene. They quickly separated all the fighters. More police sirens could be heard in the distance. All the fighters were quiet, that is, except for Biker Barry.

I'm drunk and high on crank. I haven't had my ass kicked sufficiently...

Would somebody please kick my ass just a little bit more? Is that too much to ask?

Biker Barry wouldn't quit trash talking the boyfriend. Officer Rocco told him to shut up and don't say anything.

Most "outlaw" motorcycle members realize that once the cops show up to a scene with guns, nightsticks, pepper spray and handcuffs, the fun is over. They try their best to not go to jail.

Who wants to spend the night in jail? Not worth it. We had some fun, now, it's over...

But sometimes, Biker Barry just doesn't have a "STOP" button:

"You're just a fucking cop! FUCK YOU!"

Officer Rocco is now a little bit pissed...

Biker Barry took a step towards the boyfriend,

"And fuck you too dude, you're dead!"

Officer Rocco:

"Stop right there and put your hands behind your back, you're under arrest."

Biker Barry swung and hit a glancing blow off of Officer Rocco's jaw. That was it:

Good job Barry, you just accomplished pissing off Officer Rocco; he's now very, very pissed!

Ass kicking school is open boys and girls! Biker Barry wants his ass kicked and he's going to get his wish. Some people just demand it!

Because he was so much taller than Officer Rocco, Biker Barry was going to be the recipient of the unapproved police hair pull take down maneuver:

Officer Rocco side stepped Biker Barry, grabbed him by his long hair and pulled him down to the ground. As this happened, Biker Barry was trying to land more punches and some kicks on Officer Rocco but none landed solid.

In pulling Biker Barry to the ground, Officer Rocco *accidentally* landed on top of his head, smashing it into the pavement.

Shit Barry! That must have hurt! I'm so fucking sorry you piece of scooter shit!

Officer Rocco administered a couple of 'civil rights' and a couple of 'civil lefts' to Biker Barry. He then applied a choke hold and choked his ass out:

I really don't know what it is about the choke hold but nighty-night Barry, you're going to sleepy bye land, YOU DIRTY FUCKER!

While unconscious, Rocco applied the handcuffs to his favorite biker friend. He then slapped Biker Barry in the face to help wake him up. Another Officer helped Rocco throw Biker Barry into Rocco's patrol car.

The Sergeant in charge then asked the group of drunken fighters:

"Does anybody else need to go to jail tonight?"

Mumbled replies:

"Uh, no sir. Noooo."

The officers filled out information cards on all the drunks and sent them on their way with a warning not to drive home but to get a sober ride. A couple of the little bar goers disobeyed the Sergeant's directive not to drive home and were quickly snatched up by traffic officers that staked out the bar for drunk drivers. They later joined Biker Barry in jail.

Biker Barry was slumped forward in the rear of Officer Rocco's patrol car. Barry was sufficiently beat up for the night. He knew he was in a bunch of trouble...

"Hey Officer, can I tell you something?"

"**WHAT?**"

"I'm sorry I hit you, I had to. If you took me to jail in front of my bros and I didn't put up a fight, they'd think I was a pussy..."

"Well, did I kick your ass enough so that they know you're not a pussy?"

"Oh yeah!"

"Fuck with me again like that and I'm going to make you one of my permanent personal police projects. **DO YOU UNDERSTAND?**

"Yeah, I'm sorry..."

As he drove to the station to book his best friend into jail, Officer Rocco took out a disinfectant wipe and wiped off his bruised and bleeding knuckles. He had Biker Barry's scooter trash germs all over his hands. He didn't want to get infected with some strange Biker Barry disease. Biker Barry never screwed with Officer Rocco again...

MY DAD IS AN ASSHOLE COP!

When you were growing up, did you think your Dad was an asshole? How about your Mom?

Your Dad was probably the bigger asshole of the two. Dads are usually the ENFORCER of the family. He's DIRTY HARRY for protecting the family brood. Mom does a great job too, but Dads mostly get the infamous rap for being assholes.

DETECTIVE PAYTON

Detective Payton had been on the force for over 15 years. He and his wife had two beautiful daughters.

Payton did the best he could to be a good Father and a good cop. It wasn't always easy, but he performed that balancing act as best he could.

PARANOID PARENTS

When his first child, Gabrielle was born, the world totally changed for Detective Payton. Being a parent carries with it so much responsibility. Payton often thought about the dangers to children in a modern world. He had seen firsthand, tragedies when children are abducted and/or molested. Payton was not going to let that happen to his children. Nope, better safe than sorry: there is no such thing as a "paranoid parent." Parents must always err on the side of caution to ensure the safety of their children, even if their children don't agree with it.

LITTLE GIRLS GROW UP

Detective Payton's "little" girls were growing up. Gabrielle was now 15 years old and cute little girls grow up to be big beautiful girls. That is sometimes an obvious problem for parents that care about their children.

One beautiful summer's day, Gabrielle asked her mother if it would be alright to walk to the store with her friends. Six girls would make the journey. Gabrielle's mother advised Payton of the request.

Payton pondered it for a moment:

Excuse Me? Six cute little 15 year old girls are going to walk by themselves, one mile to the store on a major thoroughfare? I don't think so! That is a scenario for disaster. My little baby is not going on that trip. If anything happened to her I'd never forgive myself. For the rest of my life I would be asking myself, "Why did you make such a stupid decision?" Nope, not happening on my watch!

"You can't go."

"Why not?"

"Because I said so."

"But why, everybody else gets to go!"

"They shouldn't go either. Those other parents must not love their kids. It's not a safe thing to do."

"It'll be safe, there're six of us."

"Excuse me? Six fifteen-year-old girls can take care of themselves against a kidnapper with a gun or a knife? I don't think so."

"But it's not that far."

"It's just far enough for something bad to happen and you're not going!"

"YOU'RE MEAN!"

"O.K., you really want to know why you can't go?"

"YEAH!"

"I think you're old enough to hear this. Right now you are thinking to yourself that your daddy is an asshole. Know what? I AM AN ASSHOLE! God wants me to be an asshole once in a while to look out for your welfare! Your mother and I love you so much that we will not let you engage in unsafe activities.

Let me explain to you what happens all the time to little fifteen-year-old girls that are walking to the store or the mall: Some shitty assholes pull up in a van. They force you into it and kidnap you. They spend the next couple

196

of hours raping you until you are bleeding and can't see straight. The whole time you are thinking to yourself,

'I shouldn't have gone to the store, it wasn't safe, I should have listened to mommy and daddy, I wish they wouldn't have let me go!'

Then your kidnappers slit your throat and dump your body is some stinking field. A couple days later, they go looking for another girl and do it again.

Do you understand what I just told you?"

"Yes Daddy."

"Good, for the crime of raising your voice and arguing with us, you are hereby sentenced to home confinement to be served in your bedroom. You may come out only for a glass of water or to use the bathroom. While in your place of confinement, you can thank God your parents love you and you weren't kidnapped today. When you are older and have your own children, this will all make sense to you. You can thank us later. Your home confinement ends at dinner time and we will, at that time, forget this entire emotional episode in your life ever occurred. You will receive a complete pardon for your actions. Just don't ask to go on anymore walks like that. Also, clean your room up, it's starting to look a little on the trashy side."

"All right."

"Here's a hug, I love you but you have to serve your sentence now…"

Gabrielle got a hug from her Dad. She knew that she had been beat. As she walked to her room, she thought about being kidnapped; that's scary stuff, she was emotionally drained.

Parents have to be assholes once in a while. If more parents were assholes when they're supposed to be, we'd have less kids getting hurt.

And that is how cops are assholes to their kids…

FOOT BAIL

Chasing a suspect on foot is officially termed, "foot pursuit". When an officer notifies their dispatcher that they are in foot pursuit, everyone's adrenaline goes into high gear because some crook has brazenly flipped the bird to the cops by running away instead of submitting to authority.

Law enforcement uses an unofficial term to describe this action of running from the cops. It's referred to as, "foot bail". No need for a bail bondsman to get out of jail after arrest if one has the ability to prevent the cops from arresting you in the first place. Just run away from them...

Some young police officers love chasing suspects on foot. Since childhood, they watched police shows on TV where the cops are always chasing suspects on foot. It's part of being a cop. If you can chase down a crook like they do on TV, you are a full-fledged police officer. Yup, that's what cops do.

But not all suspects that run away are caught. Police are automatically given a handicap when running after a suspect. They have to wear a heavy leather gun belt laden with a pistol, extra magazines of ammunition, a night stick (baton), handcuffs, flashlight, portable radio, keys, tear gas, and maybe a taser. Add to all of that a bullet proof vest and this conglomeration of police equipment can easily weigh twenty or more pounds.

Veteran officers have experienced their share of foot pursuits. They have proven to themselves and their peers that they are bad ass cops and know what they are doing. Several years into their career though, they learn not to run after suspects more than they have to. It's not that they are lazy. They have learned that foot pursuits often involve another problem, destruction of police uniforms. Jumping over fences, walls and other obstacles destroys police uniforms which can be quite expensive to replace. The solution to this problem is to outthink the crook and let them run until too tired to continue, if possible.

During "foot bail", the officer involved in the foot pursuit will usually radio other officers of the suspect's direction of travel. Assisting officers will then attempt to intersect the suspect's path and make an arrest. If everything goes according to plan, the veteran officer will head off the suspect with little or no running on his part. The veteran officer uses his patrol car to drive ahead of the suspect and intersect him when he is tired. The idea is to let the suspect expend his energy to the point of physical exhaustion and eventually give up.

RABBITS

No, we are not talking about cute little fuzzy animals. We're talking about human "rabbits". Rabbits in the wild can run quite fast. Suspects that frequently, if not always, run from the cops are referred to unofficially as, "rabbits". Sometimes, all it takes to get a rabbit to run from a cop is for the cop to make eye contact with them. That's because many rabbits are drug addicts and can go to jail for just being high on drugs. These drug addicts are also notorious thieves and may also be wanted for their latest heist.

BURGLARS

Some burglars specialize breaking into homes. Some prefer commercial buildings.

Cops hate burglars for several reasons. Burglars violate the sanctity of property ownership. What good is owning something if someone is going to break into your house or business and steal it from you? And, the damage caused by burglars when they break into your home or business just adds salt to the wound.

Cops respond to burglary calls and have to see first-hand these violations of property ownership. The cops have to listen to the complaints of the victims and the cops sympathize with them. On top of all that, the cops have to write a long burglary report to document the burglary. Cops don't like writing long reports. If one had to write burglary reports all day, one cannot drive their patrol car around town looking cool. No, burglaries are not good.

Catching a burglar in the act is rare but when it happens, it is a happy day for society. Cops love catching burglars, especially in the act. Burglars are pieces of shit and deserve to go to jail.

STEVIE

As a young boy, Stevie was an agile athlete. He excelled in track and football. He could run so fast, people thought he had wings on his feet. Fellow students were envious of Stevie's athletic abilities. They were sure that Stevie was going to be one of the top state athletes when he entered high school. Maybe go professional?

While growing up, Stevie's parents and teachers warned him about the evils of drug abuse. But, when Stevie got into high school, he was too weak and succumbed to peer pressure. He began to experiment with many of the evil drugs he was warned about. Stevie's high school "friends" introduced him to smoking cigarettes and drinking beer. This was followed by smoking marijuana. This was followed by pills. Stevie was so entrenched in escaping reality through the use of drugs that he never hesitated to start using heroin the day it was offered to him. It soon became a habit. What a waste.

Stevie left high school the beginning of his senior year and worked various manual labor jobs to support himself and his new heroin habit. He learned that he had to shoot up heroin a couple times a day, or he would get sick. His habit became rather expensive and his jobs were not providing enough income to buy his drug of choice. Once again, Stevie's friends came to the rescue and taught him their fundraising techniques.

Stevie learned to steal anything not tied down. He learned how to break into homes and cars and clean them out in record time. Department stores provided racks and racks of new clothing just waiting to be stolen and resold for dope money. But soon, Stevie's lifestyle was interrupted by jail. He had left his fingerprints at a home he broke into and the cops tied him to several other home break-ins. The cops busted Stevie. He tried to blame *My Friend* but the cops and the judge didn't buy it. Stevie was found guilty and went to jail.

Stevie had to spend a year in jail. Stevie met new friends there and soon he was receiving an abundance of knowledge concerning his career in crime. Stevie and friends exchanged information on how to steal that which was not theirs. With such networking, Stevie was well on his way to becoming an official career criminal.

When Stevie was released from jail, he was under the supervision of a probation officer. That meant Stevie had to follow certain "conditions" - like don't steal anything, use drugs, or break any other laws or he would be sent back to jail. One condition of his probation was to attend court ordered drug counseling. The counseling was provided by narcotics anonymous. At first, Stevie didn't want to go to the counseling sessions, but he soon learned to enjoy them. They were group therapy sessions and provided Stevie with valuable information: he learned from fellow probationers who sold the best dope in town. He met new users and dealers. It was like a big family reunion in which one meets family members they had never met before.

By the time he was in his mid-twenties, Stevie was very well known to all the police in his town. He rarely left his home unless he had to go score (buy) some dope or go out to steal to support his habit. During these excursions, he was constantly aware of his surroundings, always looking for the cops. Even though he was a drug user, or "doper", Stevie was still a very fast runner. To the local cops who were always arresting Stevie, he was known as a "rabbit". Stevie would turn into a "rabbit" and take "foot bail" whenever the cops tried to stop him.

LARGE AND SMALL POLICE AGENCIES

Some cities and counties in the United States are so large geographically and population wise that they require more than one police station to provide service to their residents. Take New York City as an example: it is the largest city in the U.S. with over eight million residents, more than twice the size of Los Angeles. New York City consists of more than 300 square miles of land and approximately 165 square miles of water. New York Police Department (NYPD) is the largest and one of the oldest Police Departments in the United States. With such a large area of responsibility, the City of New York needs multiple police stations. These large departments usually have one main headquarters and satellite stations to service other areas of the community. In New York, these satellite stations are referred to as "precincts". NYPD has over 45,000 officers who work out of more than 70 precincts. Sometimes officers will get assigned to one precinct in the beginning of their career and later transfer to another precinct for a variety of reasons.

Other large departments in the country refer to their outlying stations as "substations" and some departments simply refer to their satellite stations as merely, "stations".

Smaller cities and counties usually have only one station for their officers to work out of.

DETECTIVE ERNESTO

Detective Ernesto has been on the job for over

fifteen years. He's worked a couple of years in the jail, a couple of years as a patrolman and the remainder of his career as a detective.

He loves being a detective and figuring out "who done it". He's well liked, can think on his feet and has a good sense of humor. Many of his fellow officers refer to him as a "smartass", but so are they.

Detective Ernesto's department isn't as big as NYPD, but it covers a large geographical area and has quite a few officers within its ranks. The department has over half a dozen substations. Detective Ernesto was promoted to Detective a couple of years back and although he likes his current substation, he sought out a transfer to another substation to work closer to home.

Even though Detective Ernesto will miss his friends at his old station, he will be working with some he hasn't seen in quite a while. He will experience a break in period with the criminal community at his new station: Detective Ernesto doesn't know any of the crooks living in the community of his new substation.

Stevie lives in the area of Detective Ernesto's new station. Stevie doesn't know Detective Ernesto. Detective Ernesto doesn't know Stevie. But they are going to meet and it's going to be so much fun!

As previously mentioned, Detective Ernesto loves being a Detective. He gets to solve crimes, write search warrants to invade the homes of crooks, take back all the shit they stole from society, and then throw the crooks in jail. He has job security because even though many criminals eventually leave their life of crime and retire, someone else just has to fill the void and follow in their footsteps.

Detective Ernesto gets to wear suits to work. He drives to and from work in an undercover police car which looks like any other car on the road. The Department pays for the gas too! Even though this undercover Detective car looks like any other, it is equipped with hidden accessories: a police radio, emergency lights, and a siren. *(In case you were wondering, it is not equipped with a public address microphone to talk to the fucking monkeys.)*

Detective Ernesto had been at his new assignment for only a couple of days. One of his fellow Detectives had a new residential burglary case against Stevie and obtained a felony arrest warrant for him. That meant Stevie was arrestable at any time. The Detective handling the case made up "Wanted Flyers" with Stevie's photograph, physical description, addresses of hangouts, list of associates, prior crimes and the new arrest warrant information. These flyers were circulated to all the patrol officers and detectives at the station. All the cops at the station knew Stevie except for one; and that was Detective Ernesto.

Detective Ernesto's fellow detectives brought him up to speed on who Stevie was and what he represented to the community: a low life thieving piece of shit doper. Stevie was one of their best customers.

Once he was in possession of Stevie's "Wanted Flyer", Detective Ernesto kept a folded copy of it in his official detective notebook. Detective Ernesto always kept "Wanted Flyers" in his notebook. You never know when you will run into a wanted suspect.

All detectives have to keep a notebook. The detective notebook is a permanent part of the detective plainclothes uniform. A detective could be on an extended coffee break looking like he's sloughing off, but if he has his notebook in his hand, he is on the job and taking care of business. Don't mess with a detective when they have their detective notebook in their hand. They just may have to write your name in it and you don't want that to happen. The detective notebook was not only used for taking notes, it was used, if necessary, as a "shit list".

Now in possession of Stevie's "Wanted Flyer", Detective Ernesto felt like he knew Stevie a little bit more. Detectives deal with a lot of "Stevies" in their career. It is to the detective's advantage to know as many of the "Stevies" in their town as possible. Knowledge is power. Power to solve crimes and arrest piece of shit burglars.

Several days after the arrest warrant was issued for Stevie, he was walking towards his local park to meet his drug connection.

It was just before noon and a patrol officer spotted Stevie. The patrol officer was driving in the same direction Stevie was walking. At first the patrol officer wasn't sure it was Stevie but as he drove past, the patrol officer looked in his rear-view mirror and recognized him.

Stevie was not aware of the burglary warrant being issued for his arrest. He's committed so many crimes, he can't keep track of them all. Plus, he thinks he is smarter than everyone else and won't get caught. This confidence is little more than wishful thinking on his part. So, when he first saw the police car drive past him, he didn't look directly at it. But, when Stevie saw the patrol car's brake lights come on and the officer making a U-turn, Stevie knew the officer wanted to bust his ass. The brake lights on the police car were like the ears of a German Shepherd perking up right before he bites you. Stevie did what Stevie does best: he turned into a rabbit and took foot bail.

The patrol officer that spotted Stevie immediately got pissed at himself when he saw Stevie run. He knew Stevie was a rabbit and should have just kept on driving and coordinate a containment area to box Stevie in.

No, that doesn't always work either. Stevie is so damn fast I've seen him get past us even when we box him in.

The patrol officer radioed to dispatch that Stevie the rabbit has just taken foot bail. Stevie was headed in a northeasterly direction from the local park. He was wearing blue jeans and a brown plaid long sleeved shirt. Stevie always wore long sleeved shirts because they hid his hypodermic needle track marks.

It really didn't matter how many times in the past Stevie had taken foot bail. Each new foot bail was an adrenalin rush caused by POLICE FEAR. He never got used to the feeling; each time it was terrifying. All he knew was he had to get the hell away from the cops and avoid capture. Capture meant defeat. Capture meant another police interrogation. It meant going back to jail, drug withdrawals, shitty jail food. Just thinking about shitty jail food will make one run faster. Capture by the cops meant everything Stevie hated in life.

While running from the cops Stevie would be praying that the officers chasing him would get tired and stop. On the times he did get away, he would feel extreme relief; it almost felt like a drug high. But, even if he got away, he always had to live with the fear of the reason why the cops were chasing him.

It just so happened that Detective Ernesto was driving to lunch when he overheard the patrol units chasing Stevie. When something like a foot pursuit takes place, all the cops in the area have to help out. And, since Stevie has a felony warrant out for his arrest, the cop who catches him gets unofficial brownie points with his co-workers.

Detective Ernesto is wearing a semi expensive dress suit and shoes. He doesn't want to join in the foot pursuit unless absolutely necessary.

I can't ruin these clothes. They are fucking expensive! Last time I ran after someone I tore my suit coat and scratched the hell out of my dress shoes. Oh yeah, I fucked up my tie too; don't forget about that, and, those little fuckers cost a fortune now. Ridiculous! The department doesn't replace the ruined clothes and that shit is just too expensive!

Nope, let somebody else ruin their clothes…

Five officers were chasing Stevie through neighborhood streets and backyards. Two of the officers were on foot, three were in police cars.

These five officers were not only working together, they were also in competition with one another. Each and every one of these officers wanted to be the one to find little Stevie and shove their B.F.G. into his face and scare the shit out of him. Then they were going to throw his ass on the ground, face down, and slap handcuffs on him.

Yes Stevie, the cops are coming for you and they are not happy you little fucking piece of burglar shit!

Stevie knew this from prior arrests. He hates losing foot races with the cops. They always act like they are better than him.

Better run faster...

Detective Ernesto drove towards the area of the foot pursuit. He came up with a plan.

Let's see if we can have some fun with this. Stevie doesn't know me. I now know him because I was given a wanted flyer with his ugly picture on it. Instead of being a big bad cop, let's do a police service and try to help out poor little 'ole Stevie. He's been running for a couple of minutes now, he's probably getting a little bit tired and needs some help getting away from the cops.

Detective Ernesto came up with a plan.

Hope this works!

Detective Ernesto made sure he had nothing visible in his car that screamed "POLICE". He hid his holy detective notebook underneath his car seat. His gun and badge were on his trouser belt and hidden by his suit coat. He thought for a second:

The radio. Turn off the fucking police radio or it could ruin the whole deal...Now, turn on the FM radio; not too loud, not too low. Just normal volume. Take your tie off and throw it under the seat too. Be careful not to get dirt on it. Dry cleaning is too fucking expensive these days. Now, unbutton the top button of your dress shirt. Good. Maybe two buttons? Now, act like you're not a cop...

Detective Ernesto drove down a side street where he logically thought Stevie would show up. Sure enough, Stevie came running from a side yard of a home and out onto the sidewalk. He was running towards Detective Ernesto. Detective Ernesto rolled down the passenger window of his car and drove straight towards Stevie. He slammed on the brakes when he came alongside Stevie. Detective Ernesto yelled,

"Hey man, you need a ride? I saw the cops all over the place. Get in!"

The expression on Stevie's face went from one of fear and exhaustion to extreme relief. He jumped into the front passenger seat of Detective Ernesto's unmarked police car.

"Get down man! Bend forward and put your hands over your head. I'll get you 'outa here. I know what it's like dealing with those cops. Stay hidden and we'll drive right past them and they won't know a thing. Just close your eyes and leave the driving to me. Everything will be o.k. Just stay down there for a couple of minutes and we'll have you out of here and away from those fuckers."

"Thanks man, I really appreciate it. I don't know what the fuck they want with me, they're always harassing me for no reason. They fuck with me all the time. It's police harassment."

"I know man, I know. I'm going to have to drive out of here slowly, so they don't stop me for speeding. I could get in a lot of shit for helping you out man so keep your head down."

"O.K., I will."

Detective Ernesto made sure all of his car windows were rolled up. Now the only thing Stevie could hear was the sound of the FM radio.

We don't want Stevie accidentally overhearing a police radio from outside the car either. That would ruin everything.

While Detective Ernesto and Stevie were talking, one of the patrol officers chasing Stevie emerged from the same side yard Stevie had. Detective Ernesto slowly drove towards the patrol officer. Detective Ernesto and the officer made eye contact. The patrol officer recognized Detective Ernesto.

Detective Ernesto placed his finger over his mouth in the universal quiet sign. The patrol officer looked at him quizzically. Detective Ernesto slowly drove past the officer and pointed at Stevie who was bent forward, eyes closed, and hiding in Detective

Ernesto's front passenger seat. The officer rubber necked towards the passenger seat and saw it was Stevie. The officer got a big, crazy grin on his face. Detective Ernesto then pointed towards the station and the patrol officer nodded that he understood.

Detective Ernesto's new station was only a mile away from where Stevie's foot bail took place. As he drove to the station, Detective Ernesto told Stevie a bunch of bullshit. This bullshitting was almost as good as tricking Stevie into jumping into Detective Ernesto's undercover police car.

Fun, Fun, Fun!!!

Detective Ernesto bragged to Stevie about how, in his younger years, he was always stealing cars and running from the cops. One time, he was even on the local news channel for one of those long freeway police pursuits! He had four highway patrol officers chasing him and they wouldn't have caught him if he wasn't so drunk and crashed his stolen car.

God, I'm good. I like that story I just made up!

Detective Ernesto sold drugs for a while but gave that up. He wouldn't get much jail time for stealing cars but for selling drugs, they almost always want to throw your ass in jail or prison for a long time. And that's not fun. But prison is better than jail. Jail sucks. Detective Ernesto asked,

"So what did you do?"

"Nothin' man. I was just walking down the street. Fucking pigs are always chasing me for no reason."

"Yeah, I know what you mean. You can't trust those pigs."

"Every time they see me, they want to arrest me for some bullshit. Lots a times I didn't do it either. It's usually some other dude."

"Some Dude?"

"Yeah, you can't trust them. Sneaky fuckers. Keep your head down, there are still some of those assholes driving around."

"O.K."

Detective Ernesto now told Stevie about how he decided that identity theft was the way to go. He's been doing it for several years now and it's really easy. No messy car pursuits involved with identity theft. Nope, just sit at a computer most of the day; call a couple of old people, con them out of their personal information and hello, big bank account balances to me!!! Yup, identity theft. That's the way to go...Once in a while though he sells some pot to some friends.

Man, I'm good! Hey Stevie, are you getting all this shit? If I do say so myself, I am one fantastic fucking bull-shitter! I am making this bullshit up right off the cuff. I am so good; I deserve an academy award. This shit is not scripted!!! Try to outdo that Hollywood! No memorizing lines here. This is real life shit and we are having FUN! I love being a detective! I could not do any of this fantastic bullshit if I was wearing a uniform. And, on top of it, I'm getting paid to have all this fun! Where else can you do this kind of fun stuff? I deserve an academy award for this shit. They should make a movie out of this one day. And, I deserve bullshitter pay too; or, at least a couple cases of beer. This is one of my best performances. Chief, here I am, get my commendation ready! I believe I am truly the Detective Bullshitter of the Year!

At this point, Detective Ernesto has two black and white patrol cars following him to the station.

As Detective Ernesto pulled into the station driveway, he told Stevie that they were going to a good spot to drop him off and it was one of Detective Ernesto's favorite hangouts.

Now, that part is not a lie! I drink coffee and hang out at the station a lot, and, on payday it is my favorite place!

Detective Ernesto drove up to the back door of the police station where he was greeted by two uniformed officers who were waiting for Stevie.

Detective Ernesto stopped his car adjacent to the back door of the station. He put the car in park and rolled down the passenger window. He told Stevie,

"O.K., it's safe, you can get up now."

Stevie opened his eyes and sat up. At the same time the two uniformed officers and Detective Ernesto yelled,

"SURPRIIIIISE!"

Poor Stevie, he felt like shit warmed over. He put his head in his hands and bent forward. He was crying.

No, no, noooooo!!!!!!!! *Shit!* *I've been fooled. It was too good to be true.* *Fuck, fuck, fuck! FUCKING COPS!!!!*

The uniformed officers opened Stevie's door pulled him out, pressed him against Ernesto's car, and slapped handcuffs on him like they do in the movies. Stevie was quiet, his head hanging down as the officers led him into the station.

As Stevie was being led into the police station, Detective Ernesto still sitting in his car, yelled out to Stevie through the passenger window,

"Bye Stevie. Nice meeting you! Whenever you want, you just call Detective Ernesto for a ride now, you hear? Alright bro, gotta go have lunch, I'm late. I was on my way to lunch when I heard you needed a ride. I thought it was more important to help out a friend in need. I know, I know bro, don't cry, it's o.k. Don't thank me, it's no problem. That's what friends are for Stevie, bye..."

I LOVE BEING A DETECTIVE!

Detective Ernesto left the station and met up with a couple of other Detectives for lunch. Their spirits were high. Stevie was back in jail and everyone had fun putting him there.

THE COMMAND POST

After work, Detective Ernesto headed for the

216

local cop bar, THE COMMAND POST. The "Post" wasn't a particularly fancy place. It was a dark but cozy establishment. It was located in the corner of a strip mall and the sign above it displayed its name "THE COMMAND POST" in small block fluorescent green letters. It didn't need advertising. It had the same repeat customers except for a few out of towners that didn't know where they wanted to drink and accidentally picked "THE POST." Once inside, nobody wanted to leave.

Everyone in town knew the "Post" was a cop bar. They also knew you don't go there to drink unless you were going to behave yourself. There were never any problems at the "Post". Hell, the place was always full of gun toting off duty cops. Sometimes it was full of on duty cops having lunch or dinner. Only a fool would go in there and cause trouble.

The POST was also a place of community assistance. Oftentimes, citizens would go there to pick the brains of cops concerning a problem they had. The problems would range from "How do I register my car" to "My neighbor is an asshole and what do I do?" After a couple of beers, most people had answers to their questions without having to go through a prerecorded police message on the phone.

Instead of calling the cops for information and having to wait on the phone for an hour, I can go and have a beer with them and get a straight answer. This is the best deal in town!

RETIRED SERGEANT ROCCO

THE COMMAND POST was owned and

operated by retired Police Sergeant Rocco. It was *The* place for cops to go after work to unwind. Retired cops also frequented the Post to visit old friends.

Sergeant Rocco wasn't that tall, he was only about 5' 7" but he was stout as a fire plug and just as tough. If you had a couple of extra minutes, Sergeant Rocco would tell you how great it was to grow up in Washington Heights in upper Manhattan. He sported a high and tight Marine Corps haircut and a devil dog tattoo on his forearm.

Sergeant Rocco would always brag that when a criminal would resist arrest, he would give the suspect a couple of "civil rights" with his right fist and then give him a couple of "civil lefts" with his left fist. Sergeant Rocco was famous for his ability to fell even the tallest of suspects. Yup, Sergeant Rocco was good backup. But now, he's retired and operates the one place in town for cops to have some rest and relaxation after work. Now, Sergeant Rocco gives back up to his fellow officers by finding them a safe ride home if they had too much to drink.

The "Post" was originally licensed as a restaurant when Sergeant Rocco bought it, so he was forced to serve food. Any good bar worth its salt had to serve some kind of food to keep the customers coming back. So, Sergeant Rocco came up with his world-famous signature "187 Burger". The only real food on the menu.

"187" is the penal code section for murder and Sergeant Rocco wanted to serve a burger that was murderously good. The "187" was one half pound of 100% Angus beef with a slab of cheese, bacon, an onion ring, lettuce, tomato, zesty pickle chips and even pineapple and egg if you wanted it. It was so big that the buns for the "187" were specially made for it by a bakery down the street. The buns wouldn't fall apart when you ate the "187" and Sergeant Rocco claimed you could roll "Code 3" (lights and siren) and the burger would not fall apart.

Sergeant Rocco also served the "Attempt 187" burger. A one quarter pound kids burger with fries and a drink for when his cop friends brought their kids into the Post. Kids ate for free. Sergeant Rocco's order. He was a big softy inside and all the kids called him "Uncle Rocco." Maybe it has something to do with the free root beer floats he also gave the kids.

The Post also had several TV monitors mounted high on the walls. You could watch your favorite sports teams or you could sit at the bar and watch Sergeant Rocco's TV monitor: the monitor that played five movies continuously: BREAKER MORANT, THE SAND PEBBLES, THE SANDS OF IWO JIMA, PATTON, and THE BRIDGES AT TOKO RI. Yup, you could watch sports figures get paid millions of dollars or watch war heroes die in combat.

DETECTIVE ERNESTO'S AFTER WORK PARTY

At the end of shift, Detective Ernesto's fellow detectives met him down at the Post and bought him celebratory ice-cold beers for his superior detective tactics employed against Stevie. Sergeant Rocco threw in a free round of drinks for the entire bar when he heard of the fancy police work Detective Ernesto had performed. Sergeant Rocco matter of factly told Detective Ernesto,

219

"That's the way I would have done it."

Everyone cheered Detective Ernesto! Everyone cheered Retired Sergeant Rocco!

The mood at the Post was off the charts. Everyone was having a great time. After a couple of hours, it appeared that no other patrons were going to show up at the POST. Detective Ernesto and crew continued drinking and bullshitting.

And then, it happened, at about 11:30: The Chief walked in. He had a serious look on his face and was holding a Manilla envelope in his hand. Sergeant Rocco was behind the bar. The Chief greeted Sergeant Rocco:

"Evening Rocco, how are things?"

"Pretty good Chief. The boys are having a victory celebration over there for Ernesto's fancy police work today. Sounded like a lot of fun and one for the books. You want a drink?"

"Not yet Rocco, I have to talk to Ernesto about something serious."

The Chief waived a Manilla envelope at Rocco.

"I'm going to give Ernesto a write up. When you see him reading it, bring over some drinks for the boys on my tab and bring me a Code Three please."

"Sure thing Chief."

A "Code Three" was one of Sergeant Rocco's signature drinks at the Post. It consisted of a triple vodka (or a little bit more, Sergeant Rocco never measured and that is just one thing his customers liked about him), twice that amount of club soda, some rocks and a split of lime. The "Code Three" was an emergency "lights and siren take the edge off" drink. It was served in a large tumbler glass. Sergeant Rocco only poured quality vodka. He refused to serve cheap alcohol at his headquarters. He didn't want to leave anyone with a hangover due to cheap alcohol.

Some people have to work in the morning. I'm not going to send them out of here with hangover booze in their system!

With a serious look on his face, the Chief walked over to Ernesto's table.

"Evening Chief, will you join us?"

"Maybe. Ernesto, you really did something good today but you went way outside the box and could have potentially gotten yourself hurt. Your first week at your new station and you pull a stunt like that?"

Ernesto's table went quiet. All of a sudden, nobody was enjoying themselves and then, everybody thought about what the Chief said:

Shit, the Chief is totally right. If Ernesto had gotten hurt, he wouldn't have a leg to stand on as far as following proper police protocol. He went way outside the box and could have gotten hurt. Then again, if Stevie was stupid enough to try anything with Ernesto, he would have unleashed some serious shit on

221

himself! But, the Chief is not an asshole and he is right…

The Chief continued,

"I thought about it and I had to make a hard decision about your actions today, I can't let this go and I had to write you up. I'm sorry to deliver it to you in front of your friends, but I won't be in the office tomorrow"

And with that the Chief handed the Manilla envelope to Ernesto.

Ernesto took the envelope and just had to pull out his write up to see what was written on it and find out just how bad he fucked up.

The write up was a PERFORMANCE COMMENDATION and not a reprimand.

"Shit Chief, you had me going!"

"I know, but I had to mess with you just a little bit. Welcome aboard!"

The two shook hands and Sergeant Rocco was spot on with more drinks.

"The commendation I just gave you is a copy because I know you sloppy fuckers are going to spill beer all over it. You can pick up the original tomorrow from my secretary."

The mood in the bar immediately got back up to the high level it was before the Chief arrived and everyone drank happily ever after…

Two patrol officers scuffed their spit shined shoes while chasing Stevie.

Detective Ernesto's tie got dirty from being placed underneath his car seat. The tie needed dry cleaning. Detective Ernesto didn't give a shit though because he had too much fun!

Detective Ernesto is now retired and still a bullshitter.

Nobody knows what happened to Stevie...

THE MEAN SCARY DUDE

A.K.A.: "M.S.D."

Years after the hippo, Bwana, and fucking monkey stories, Officer Dean received reassignment to the detective bureau. He had been in that job for many years when Detective Jim was assigned to the same bureau. Detective Dean was a good mentor and taught Detective Jim how to investigate crimes, write search warrants, conduct suspect interviews, and drink coffee to an acceptable detective level. Detectives are required to drink more coffee than patrol personnel.

Detective Dean was rarely seen without his favorite coffee cup in hand. It was his life blood.

One day, a fellow detective took Detective Dean's favorite coffee cup and hid it in a cupboard in the station break room. That was a big mistake because Detective Dean unleashed his wrath on everyone for a whole week until the guilty party returned the prized coffee cup. Don't mess with Detective Dean or his beloved coffee cup!

GOOD COP – BAD COP

As previously mentioned, a common interview technique for police interrogations is for two detectives to play an interview game commonly known as, "Good Cop – Bad Cop". This involves one detective acting like mister hardass (the Bad Cop) and the other detective being nice (the Good Cop). Naturally, that would make a suspect hate the Bad

Cop and hopefully like the Good Cop. The suspect would be grilled by the Bad Cop and then the Bad Cop would leave the interview room in a fit of anger and frustration if the suspect didn't cop out (admit to their crimes). The Good Cop would then use this intermission to hopefully sweet talk the suspect into a confession.

Sometimes it works, sometimes it doesn't.

When Detective Jim and his seasoned partner, Detective Dean interviewed suspects, Detective Jim was always the Good Cop. That's because Detective Jim's detective partner looked mean. If one detective looks "meaner" than the other, there's nothing anyone can do about it. The mean looking detective is always the bad cop.

During one of their interviews, Detective Jim and Detective Dean were interviewing two young car burglars. The young burglars were individually interviewed by both detectives. Detective Jim and his partner did not have to play Good Cop – Bad Cop because both young criminals had been caught in the act of breaking into a car and the arresting officers found property on them that came from several other cars that had been broken into. The young crooks didn't see much sense in lying about what they had done. They were new at this game, sung like parakeets and cooperated with the detective interrogation. No need to bring out the Good Cop – Bad Cop board game.

After their interview, the young criminals were placed together in a single interview room. They did not know they were being secretly recorded.

Our young thieves openly discussed their crimes again and spoke about a couple of additional facts they forgot to mention during their interviews. They then started talking about the detectives that interviewed them:

> "Hey, I think we need to go to school, and get a degree, and become cops, then we can do this stuff and not get caught."

> "Yeah, we can be like detective Jim, he's cool but I hope I don't ever have to speak to that MEAN SCARY DUDE again!"

And that was it. One interview with a label that fit and Detective Dean now had a new name, "THE MEAN SCARY DUDE", or "M.S.D." for short.

The Mean Scary Dude's fellow detectives loved the new label placed on him because it was ironic in a way: The Mean Scary Dude looked mean and scary but really wasn't. The Mean Scary Dude would give you the shirt off his back if you needed it. But, if you are a crook, just one mean, scary look from him and you would probably confess.

THE MEAN SCARY DUDE IS GETTING READY TO RETIRE

Detective Dean is starting to get up there in years and he's getting ready for retirement. He's got over thirty years on the force and it's time to hang up the gun and badge and spend some time with his family.

The Mean Scary Dude was just weeks away from retirement. One hot summer day at approximately 10:30 in the morning, Detective Dean and Detective Jim are at their desks, working on their cases in the comfortable air-conditioned detective bay.

The detective bay is equipped with an overhead speaker system so the detectives can monitor patrol radio communications. This radio scanner is kept on just in case the detectives are needed to respond to the field for an emergency.

All of a sudden, a radio call goes out to some patrol officers of a residential burglary in progress with multiple suspects. The patrol officers arrived at the scene and three suspects took foot bail.

Detectives Dean and Jim rush outside where Detective Jim fires up his detective car. Detective Dean jumps into the passenger seat of Detective Jim's car and the crime fighting duo speed away towards the area of the residential burglary, wishing for good luck in the hopes of catching at least one of the burglars.

One of the responding patrol units catches one of the burglars that took foot bail. This burglar is extremely scared to say the least. The patrol officer read the suspect his Miranda rights and the suspect gave up the names of his two confederates.

Another patrol unit advised he was following one of the running suspects into a hilly area of the city. Detective Jim drove towards the area that both he and Detective Dean were very familiar with.

Remember the story about "Foot Bail" and Detective Ernesto? The story where the cops let the suspect expend his energy when running and the cops head him off? And, the cops don't get their uniforms or Detective attire all messed up and damaged? Detective Dean forgot all that because he is close to retirement and wants to have one last run for the money and to show all those new cops on the beat that Detective Dean is one mean ass kicker!

Detective Dean demanded that Detective Jim stop the car and drop him off to chase after the suspect on foot: into 100 plus degree heat and in hilly, thick brush covered terrain.

Detective Jim asked Detective Dean if he really needed to do that.

Remember Detective Dean, we are experienced Detectives and don't run after anybody more than we need to. We head them off with our detective unit. We catch them when they are tired and want to give up the chase.

Detective Dean insisted that he was the kick ass Detective of the day and insisted that he be dropped off to chase the burglary suspect on foot.

I don't think that's a good idea Detective Dean. It's hot out and you don't really know exactly where in the hills the suspect is. This could turn into a bad thing.

Detective Jim dropped off Detective Dean and told him that he would drive the car around to the

228

other side of the hilly area where Detective Dean would hopefully intersect the suspect.

Detective Dean spots the suspect running through the hilly area and takes off after him. Detective Jim calmly drives his air-conditioned detective car to the other side of the hilly area where Detective Dean should show up. Detective Dean never shows up.

Detective Jim is called over to the location where the first burglar was captured. Detective Jim interviews the suspect and learns the names of the other two suspects. The other two suspects are named Tim and Greg.

A patrol officer radios in he has caught Greg. Good news, two down, one to go! Detective Jim spoke with Greg and obtained Tim's full name and cell phone number.

Tim is the suspect the Mean Scary Dude is chasing.

Detective Jim, now separated from the Mean Scary Dude, directs a patrol unit to go find him and and make sure he's okay.

It's over a hundred degrees out and that fool, bless his heart, just had to play macho man and run after a twenty-year-old. What the fuck is he trying to prove? I just hope he doesn't get heat stroke. His wife will kill me if that happens!

Driving like crazy, a patrol officer finally located Detective Dean. The Mean Scary Dude was covered in sweat and bent over at the waist, barfing his guts out. He loosened his tie after he was finished barfing and asked the patrol officer if the suspect was located. The officer told Detective Dean the suspect got away. Officer Dean then told the patrol officer he was having a bad day and to please drive him back to the station.

At this point, Detective Jim is driving back to the station without his partner. But he knows his partner was rescued by a patrol unit, is safe, and is on his way back to the station. What Detective Jim does have is the name and phone number of "Tim", the suspect who got away.

Meanwhile, the Mean Scary Dude is still out in the field. M.S.D. was hot and had heat exhaustion. The patrol officer that rescued him had to stop his car on the way back to the station and let M.S.D. out to barf again. Then, they had to stop at a fire station to borrow a water hose to clean M.S.D.'s shoes. He was stinking up the patrol car. The patrol officer was very helpful in hosing off M.S.D.'s dress shoes, the toes of which were vomit covered.

This is not supposed to happen to the M.S.D.! He's the Man! He's the Veteran! He's the one and only Mean Scary Dude Bad Ass Motherfucker!

Once at the station, Detective Jim thinks of an off the wall plan: Call Tim up and ask him to come into the station voluntarily. It sometimes works. Many cops think that they can't talk a suspect into turning himself in because suspects hate cops. That is oftentimes true but if the cop is a good bullshitter and knows how to talk to people, suspects will sometimes turn themselves in. Detective Jim considers himself a good bullshitter and wants to give it a go.

It's worked before. Why can't it work now? Just because Tim is an asshole burglar doesn't mean he won't listen to reason and surrender himself. If you don't ask, you don't receive...

Detective Jim calls Tim's cellphone and introduces himself. He explains to Tim that he understands the terrible time he is having right now. He also explains to Tim that it is in his best interest to turn himself in to the police station as soon as possible because there are a bunch of crazy ass cops looking for him and they are not in a good mood. Also, it will look favorably for Tim if he turns himself in. Tim agrees except that he wants half an hour to get something cold to drink and catch his breath. Detective Jim thinks that's a great idea and reminds Tim that they have a deal.

I cannot believe this shit! What a payday! Fucking Foot Bail Tim has agreed to come into the station after half the force has been chasing him in 100 plus degree heat? Shit, the M.S.D. is going to be pissed at himself for trying to play Clint Eastwood!

Tim arrives at the station and Detective Jim takes him to his favorite interview room. That's right, lucky interview room number four. Detective Jim goes over to his desk to get a pad of paper to write notes on and in walks the walking dead: The Mean Scary Dude.

His hair is messed up, he looks like he is sick, like the flu or something. His white dress shirt is dirty, untucked and half unbuttoned. His tie is missing. His dress pants are covered in dirt from running through bushes and his shoes look like they haven't been shined in ages, partially because they haven't been shined in ages. In short, The Mean Scary Dude looks like shit warmed over. He walks over to his chair, sits down and says,

"We gotta get Tim."

"I know Dean. I have some good news"

"What's that?"

"Well, we didn't catch Tim, but I spoke to him on the phone. You're not gonna believe this but I called him up and asked him to turn himself in and he's now sitting in interview room four."

"You're fucking kidding me. Don't fuck with me, I'm too tired."

"I'm not Dean, he's here. Why don't you go home and get cleaned up?"

"I can't believe I went through all that and he turns himself in. Shit... I'm going to the bathroom to wash off my face again, fuck!."

Tim copped out to Detective Jim. Many of his coworkers couldn't believe Tim turned himself in after so much running around and foot bail in the field.

The Mean Scary Dude became the brunt of many a joke for running after Tim in 100 plus degree heat and subsequently barfing his guts out. Some younger female Detectives got together and made a special name badge for the Mean Scary Dude; they made him wear the special name badge during his remaining weeks at work before his retirement. The Mean Scary Dude had a good sense of humor about it and wore the name badge. It read as follows:

Hi, my name is Detective Dean,

If found roaming the streets,

please return me to the police station

or call 911

STREET JUSTICE COUNTRY STYLE

To prosecute a criminal in court, the police need to have enough evidence to convince a judge and jury that a crime occurred and that the defendant committed it. The police need probable cause (a reasonable belief that a person committed a crime) to make an arrest. For prosecution, the courts need supporting or corroborating evidence. Good cases with lots of evidence usually are prosecuted. Cases with little evidence usually are not prosecuted. Each case is different.

Society tolerates a certain amount of crime but sometimes people get fed up with the crime in their community. They get tired of being robbed, raped, and plundered by shitheads. Some people revert to street justice as their cure for the disease of crime.

BILLY THE THIEF

Billy lives in a large rural valley. The valley is mostly farmland surrounded by beautiful pine covered mountains. The valley and surrounding mountains are home to some fulltime residents but also visitors that take advantage of one of the many available vacation cabins. The valley doesn't have any stores or gas stations. If you want to go shopping, you've got about a twenty-mile drive to the nearest store.

Billy grew up in the valley. He quit high school his second year and was unsuccessful at holding down a job because he was lazy.

Billy soon became a kleptomaniac. And he was good at it. The valley where Billy the Thief lived consisted of over 100 square miles of land and had a higher population of cattle than people. Because the area was remote and had such a low population, there was only one cop in the valley, a resident Deputy Sheriff.

DEPUTY DARREN AND HIS WIFE SUZIE

Deputy Darren lived in the Sheriff's substation located in Billy the Thief's valley. Deputy Darren's wife Susie was his dispatcher. This was because the Sheriff's headquarters was far away from the valley and could not communicate with Deputy Darren when he was patrolling in his off-road police vehicle. The Sheriff's Department installed a repeater radio tower to communicate with Dispatcher Suzie who in turn communicated with her husband when he was out performing his official Deputy Sheriff duties in the secluded valley.

Susie had to take a special radio dispatcher class before she and Deputy Darren were assigned to the remote substation. She was a part time employee of the County and received a small stipend for her duties. Suzie had to always monitor the radio whenever her husband was in the field. She was her husband's lifeline with Sheriff's headquarters. Suzie took care of the household chores and had a radio monitor in every room of their modest substation home.

Deputy Darren and Susie were full-fledged members of their valley community. They knew most of the valley residents and were friends with them. The valley residents were very covetous of their resident deputy. They considered him, *their deputy, their property,* just as if he were their favorite watch dog. The valley residents want peace and harmony in their community, and they want their deputy to make sure it stays that way. It was one big happy valley family. Deputy Darren was so close to the residents of the valley that several times some of them would call him over to help fix their plumbing problems, maybe work on their car or any other problem that would arise. Like a Good Neighbor, Deputy Darren was always there.

The valley residents were not at all hesitant to assist Deputy Darren when needed and on more than one occasion, Deputy Darren would deputize them and make them part time emergency cops. Deputy Darren even held unofficial classes on arresting suspects and handcuffing techniques. He didn't want any of his family members getting hurt. Family comes first...

Billy the Thief stole everything he could get his hands on. He loved unoccupied farmhouses and barns. There he could find hand tools, guns, maybe some jewelry, possibly some cash, and the fridge usually had some good homemade snacks inside just in case you worked up an appetite ripping off your neighbors.

Billy broke into cars and removed the radios, cigarettes, cell phones, loose change, and whatever else needed stealing. If he had time, he'd also steal the vehicle's gasoline. Billy discovered that vacation cabins sometimes possessed new flat screens TV's and other appliances he could sell. Why should you have to go to work to buy things when your community provides for all your needs?

One day, Billy was driving his dilapidated foreign sedan and was stopped by Deputy Darren for having a brake light out. The backseat of the car was full of tools just stolen from a barn of one of the local ranches. Deputy Darren was suspicious of all the tools in the backseat because little Billy didn't appear as if he had been working all day. Also, for about the last year or so, Deputy Darren had been taking many burglary reports in the valley. He was fully aware of what was being stolen and tools were always at the top of the list.

Billy the Thief gave Deputy Darren a beautiful concocted story about how the tools belonged to him. He had inherited them from his dead Uncle in a nearby county and he was merely taking them home to sort through them. Billy was really cool because Billy did not consider himself a thief. Stealing was a normal behavior to him.

Deputy Darren knew he couldn't take the tools from Billy without probable cause but his suspicions remained. Deputy Darren was at least going to write Billy a ticket for the burned-out brake light and take photographs of the tools.

PROPER ALIGNMENT OF THE HEAVENLY BODIES

Sometimes the sun, moon, and stars are aligned perfectly and law enforcement is blessed by the heavens.

As Deputy Darren was writing Billy a ticket, Susie radioed him and advised a barn burglary had just occurred not far from where Deputy Darren stopped Billy. Normally, Susie would wait until after her husband finished with the traffic stop before advising him of the barn burglary but something in her gut told her to let her husband know right away.

Billy the Thief thought the rancher was away during the burglary, otherwise, Billy wouldn't have tried stealing anything. The last thing Billy wanted was for a rancher to stick a 12-gauge shotgun up his ass. Billy didn't take any unnecessary chances; being in a rural area, he didn't want to get caught stealing from an angry rancher and having him play a game of the "Three S's" on him: "Shoot, Shovel, and Shut Up", a rural version of street justice: Shoot the bastard, get a shovel and bury him, then shut your mouth. Simple as one, two, three…

The rancher Billy had ripped off had been away from his barn for only five minutes, just down the road, checking on his irrigation system. When he returned to his barn, all of his favorite tools were missing from his workbench. This was the second time Mister Rancher's tools were stolen and he was pissed. He immediately called Suzie to report the theft.

Deputy Darren told Susie to have the rancher respond to the location of the traffic stop and for the rancher to bring his "kit". What Deputy Darren meant by "kit", is a sidearm, flashlight, and anything else he may want to bring. Deputy Darren knew the rancher and they were friends. Deputy Darren had used this rancher for back up on several occasions. The rancher was trustworthy, full of energy and very helpful when in a jam. Besides that, the rancher and Deputy Darren fished together in the rancher's private pond. They had a special bond.

The rancher showed up at the traffic stop and parked his four-wheel drive pickup truck behind Deputy Darren's patrol car. Deputy Darren told the rancher he was deputized, and he can't get pissed and kick the shit out of Billy if the tools on the backseat of Billy's car were his. However, if once the tools on the backseat are identified, Mister Rancher was authorized to slap the cuffs on Billy the Thief. This should be a small amount of satisfaction for the Rancher and make him feel better about getting ripped off. It doesn't happen very often but once in a while a victim gets a bit of satisfaction.

The Rancher identified his tools, told Billy to get out of the car and slapped the cuffs on him. The Rancher then patted Billy down for hidden weapons and threw him into the backseat of the patrol car. As the Rancher was shoving Billy into the back of the patrol car he whispered into Billy's ear,

"You're going away for a long time. You better not come back here."

Billy knew exactly what the Rancher meant. If Billy returned to the valley, he was going to be a victim of the three "S's".

Deputy Darren asked Billy the Thief if he wanted his car towed or left parked on the side of the road. Billy opted to leave it parked on the side of the road. Billy the Thief then went to jail for one count of burglary.

Both Deputy Darren and Mister Rancher knew they had caught the thief responsible for most of the thefts in the valley. They were excited.

Deputy Darren gave big kudos to his wife when he got home later that night. If it were not for her gut feeling, Billy the Thief might have gotten away that day; but, it wasn't in the stars…

Deputy Darren was on the warpath. He knew Billy the Thief was his guy doing all the crime in the valley. Deputy Darren was going to do everything possible to screw up Billy the Thief's life. Halfway to jail, Deputy Darren had another deputy from headquarters meet him. Deputy Darren transferred Billy the Thief to the other deputy's patrol car and the other deputy took Billy to jail. This freed up Deputy Darren to continue to attempt to locate more stolen property from Billy's home.

Deputy Darren then went to Billy the Thief's home and met with Billy's mother. She was aghast that her poor little Billy was out stealing. And, from neighbors too! She cried when she learned her poor little Billy was on his way to jail!

Deputy Darren wanted to play it safe and get a warrant for Billy's Mom's house. Billy the Thief was responsible for so many thefts that Sheriff's Headquarters sent out a Detective to write a search warrant for Billy's house. After a judge signed the search warrant, Deputy Darren and some eager deputized ranchers found additional stolen property at Billy's place. Billy was linked to many additional burglaries and thefts.

Deputy Darren called the jail and added five more counts of burglary to Billy's paperwork.

Things were not looking good for Billy the Thief.

Now the story should probably end here but it doesn't. Remember the location where all the crimes occurred is secluded and only Deputy Darren patrols it. Deputy Darren will probably be writing reports all night long at his substation because the main crook in the valley is sleeping safely in jail.

Mr. Rancher was so happy that Billy the Thief was caught, he couldn't resist calling up his buddies and meeting down at the valley bar. Mister Rancher loved telling his friends the story about how everything came together and how he got to slap the cuffs on that bastard, Billy the Thief! What a good night! Before you knew it, almost everybody in the valley was calling each other and letting everyone know about the arrest of Billy the Thief. This is big valley news! Somewhere in the conversations, the farmer mentioned that little Billy's car was left on the side of the road…

BIG VALLEY FUN

Dusk came to the valley around eight thirty that night. Billy The Thief's car was still parked where Deputy Darren had left it. About a half hour later, the first pickup truck arrived at the location of Billy's car.

241

The pickup truck was a mammoth four-wheel drive extra cab pickup. It was painted in camouflage and sported heavy duty front and rear bumpers, front end winch, spotlights on both sides, and finished off with an American flag sticker on the rear window. This four-wheel drive beast would have made the American military jealous.

It was so easy. No one was around, it was almost dark, and the four men in the truck had already downed five or six beers a piece. Everyone was celebrating and in the mood. Magic was in the air. The perfect setting for blowing the shit out of Billy the Thief's car.

What happened next was tantamount to one of the best Hollywood shooting scenes. The pickup truck was parked with engine running directly across the road from Billy's car. The four men got out. All carried semi-automatic military style rifles.

The gunfire was loud and echoed across the valley. It was the sound of success. The men shot, reloaded and shot again at little Billy's car. Time for a short pause with a return to the truck for a pull or two on their cold beers. Ahhh, that was refreshing. About a hundred more rounds fired into Billy's car and they were happy with their artwork. The driver's side of little Billy's car looked like Swiss cheese on steroids. The side windows, driver's side fenders and tires were nicely destroyed. The shooters didn't shoot the front, back, or passenger's side of the car. To do so would be impolite because, there would be others. You just can't hog all the fun...Each of the men picked out a wheel on Billy's car and urinated on it. That felt good; icing on the cake. They then drove back to the bar and informed their friends there that someone had shot up Billy the Thief's car. It was just terrible! Such a blatant display of violence in the Valley. What is this world coming to?

After the hit squad left Billy's car, a small sedan showed up. It was a mother-daughter team. They parked their car and got out. Momma had a sledgehammer and daughter had a framing hammer. Momma stated,

"Looks like someone beat us here. At least they were polite enough to leave a little canvass for us to draw on."

Country folks, hmmm, always thinkin' bout their neighbors!"

The daughter stated,

"Go ahead Momma, you go first. He broke down your front door and stole your DVD player."

Momma took her sledgehammer, hung it in the air and let all of her anger go. She started working on the hood, front grill and headlights. The daughter took her hammer and turned all the rear light assemblies into a pulverized mess. She then went to work on the rear window and told her Mother:

"Momma, these rear windows aren't that easy to break! Guess I'm gonna have a little workout here. Have to give it a little extra for that fuckshit Billy!"

The daughter did some pounding on the trunk area and was satisfied the rear end of the car was a total loss. Momma did the same with the front hood and windshield. Momma stated:

"You know child, this just makes me feel a lot better about everything."

"Me too Momma, this was a good idea, it's good therapy."

Satisfied with their version of street justice, they left.

More trucks and cars showed up at the location of Billy the Thief's luxury ride. The passenger side of Billy's car received the attention it deserved and received the appropriate amount of bullet holes in it to make it match the driver's side. Billy's car had multiple urine stains on all four wheels. With all windows smashed out, all body parts in unusable condition, and tires flattened, the car was now considered properly anointed. Almost...

There was one group of residents that hated Billy with a passion, but they did not show up on the first night of fun. They wanted to do their handy work in total secrecy. Billy not only pissed off the law-abiding members of the community, he pissed off the local pot growers. Billy had ripped them off too and they hated him for all the pot he stole from their homes and sheds. They never called Deputy Darren to report their thefts for obvious reasons.

The night after the community blew the shit out of Billy the Thief's car, the local pot growers showed up. They then doused the car in gasoline and set it on fire. After the fire went out, they spray painted a pretty green marijuana leaf on the driver's side of

Billy's car. Underneath the marijuana leaf they spray painted "FUCK YOU". One of the pot growers took a photo of the car while it was burning and later mailed it to Billy the Thief while he was in jail. Just a little message...

Billy the Thief did not have a lot of prior arrests on his record. He could possibly get off with a light sentence and the members of the valley community were not going to let that happen. The inhabitants of the valley pay close attention to politics and the elections of the Sheriff, District Attorney, and Judges. They let the word get out that little Billy better go to prison for a long time or there would be hell to pay come election time. Because little Billy had burglarized numerous homes, he got a one-way ticket to state prison for three years when everything was taken into account. Billy the Thief did not return to the valley after his prison sentence was completed because he feared the citizens might be inclined to use more severe measures of street justice, like "The Three S's."

While in prison, Billy The Thief received a card in the mail. It was a "You're Invited" card. It read,

"Dear Billy,

Hope you like your new home sunshine. We found out your release date and have planned a special coming home party for you. All your friends will be here! We're going to have so much fun! We can hardly wait. You must be excited too! We're going to have a bar-b-que, drinks, and play some games. Remember our favorite game Billy? The one where we dig a deep hole? We heard you really like that game. We can all hardly wait to play it with you.

Come home soon Billy.

Love, *Hope you sleep good tonight baby cakes.*

    Your Valley Friends"

And that, is "STREET JUSTICE COUNTRY STYLE."

GIVE 'EM TO ME!

VACATION TIME

Officer Dale and friends work for a Southern California Police agency. They haven't had a decent vacation in a long time, and they need to have some fun getaway time. They need to get away from the hustle and bustle of overpopulated southern California and enjoy the peace and quiet of the mountains and forests.

After weeks of planning and preparation, Officer Dale and seven fellow officers pile into two vehicles and head to the Sierra Nevada Mountains to do some serious camping, fishing, and beer drinking.

It's always a good feeling to put on the 'ole civilian clothes and not have to act and feel like a cop on duty. Yes, one needs to relax and pretend to be like a regular person and enjoy life once in a while. No radio calls, no dirty street people to handle, no harassment by supervisors you don't like, and best of all, NO DAWN SHIFT! Just thinking about leaving the stinking city is relaxing.

It only takes our group of vacationing cops a four- or five-hour drive to find themselves in God's Country. High Mountains painted with pine tree forests, blue skies, no smog, flowing rivers, lakes, train tunnels, a multitude of old dirt roads, some of which were used by the first settlers of California, and old gold rush towns. The group of cops are hit upside the head by the beauty they are experiencing and find themselves asking,

Just why in the hell didn't we do this sooner?

The sun is starting to set. The off duty two car cop vacation caravan meanders up a two-lane mountain road and find themselves on the top of the mountain. Tall pines line both sides of the road. The off-duty cop caravan automatically pulls into a large vacant dirt parking lot of a very old wooden building. This is a very special building. It appears to have been built in the early 1900's and is as rustic as rustic can be. It's almost as big as a barn and the old brown wood sides give it that appeal. The gable roof is high and covered with brown corrugated metal, accented by patches of green moss and pine needles. There are no windows in the front just a huge wooden door with a 1960's neon sign that reads, "Mountaintop Bar". This bar is so old, it even has a hitching post and waterer for your horse if that is your mode of transportation. This bar has such country western character, the famous western writer Louis L'amour should have written a story about it. Maybe he did.

The vacation cops get out of their cars and know that this bar is a gift from heaven. The day is just starting to come to a close and what a better way to end it than to have a couple of cold country western beers? Especially beers served in an official country western bar.

The group walks in the front door and cannot believe their luck. The bar is authentic. It's semi dark inside, sawdust covered wood floors, a working juke box from the 1960's along one wall, the American Flag on the opposite wall, three pool tables, an old fashioned wood bar with a seating capacity for at least twenty customers, and best of all, no other customers to interfere with the fun that is about to take place.

Behind the bar is a man in his fifties. The bartender is tall, large build, semi-rugged looking, a serious expression on his face. He's leaning on the bar with his hands outstretched on the inner railing and is waiting for the group to approach him.

Officer Dale walks up to the bar and wonders why the bartender isn't happy to see the group. There are no other customers in the bar and one would think the bartender would be happy to see some paying customers show up and help pay the rent.

Officer Dale greets Mister Bartender with,

"Hello".

Mister Bartender still has a serious look on his face and tells Officer Dale,

"Give 'em to me."

Officer Dale doesn't know what in the heck the bartender is talking about:

"Give you what?"

"Just give 'em to me."

"What?"

"No beer until you give 'em to me."

"We have to pay first?"

"No, give 'em to me or get the hell out of here!"

Now, the whole group of vacationing cops are perplexed and wondering what kind of a crazy bartender they have just ran into.

"Whaddya talkin' about?"

"Damn cops, spot you a mile away. Gimme your guns or get the hell out. Look at my ceiling!"

Officer Dale and compatriots look and up see about fifty bullet holes in the ceiling. Evidently, Mister Bartender has served rowdy off duty cops in the past and the cops just had to play cowboy and fire their guns into the ceiling of the bar in drunken off duty celebration.

"I got a bag right here and you boys put your guns in there and you can have 'em when you leave. Otherwise, get the hell outa here, I ain't fixing my roof again."

One by one, our vacationing cops sheepishly placed their pistols in the bag. At least, they placed their B.F.G.'s in the bag. They kept their back-up pistols hidden and never even thought of bringing them out of their concealed hiding places. This bartender was serious about no gunfire in his bar.

"Now, whad you boys like to drink?

Officer Dale and friends got their beers, fired up the juke box and got some games of pool going. They ordered up some bar food and everybody was having a good time. Mister Bartender questioned the group as to what department and assignments they worked. It turned out that Mister Bartender was a former police sergeant and a really nice guy; at least, once you turned your guns in.

About an hour of fun went by, and a group of motorcyclists with Blue Knight decals on their bikes pulled up to the bar. After a couple of minutes, the group of ten men and women, all dressed in nice looking motorcycle leathers walked in the front door. They were middle aged, clean cut and had a particular look about them.

Officer Dale and partners stopped playing pool when the group walked in. Mister Bartender was behind the bar, arms outstretched to either side, holding the railing of the bar just like he did when Officer Dale and friends had arrived. The motorcyclists walked towards the bar and the leader stated,

"Hello."

Mister Bartender firmly ordered,

"Give 'em to me!"

DETECTIVE SEARCH WARRANT BRIEFING

COP FUNERALS

One of the main things Detective Jim learned in the police academy was how well police departments conduct funerals for cops killed in the line of duty.

The academy instructor for officer safety narrated:

"As law enforcement, we don't do everything right. We try our best but sometimes we fall short. We don't always prevent crimes the way the public would like us to. Once we get a call, we don't always show up on time. We oftentimes may not portray the best image to the public. There are a lot of things we could improve upon and we try every day to do just that. But there is one thing that we do the best and I guarantee you that if you don't pay attention to your officer safety issues, you may one day be the guest of honor at that event. I'm talking about cop funerals. If you don't pay attention to your surroundings and practice your officer survival skills and you get yourself killed for making some stupid mistake, I guarantee you one thing: we will give you the biggest and best funeral anyone could ask for. I'm not talking about all situations. Some are just plain dangerous when you are trying to be a hero. I'm talking about you making a fatal mistake because you did not have situational awareness.

The one thing we do the best, and nobody does it better, is a police department funeral. Cops will come from all parts of the state to take part in your funeral. Some will even come from out of state. We will have miles of police cars with their pretty red and blue lights on in the procession. We will close down the freeways in your honor because it will take hours for the procession to reach your grave site. Dignitaries from around the state will be in attendance to celebrate your death. Hell, the Fire Department will even show up to honor you!

Your coffin will be draped with a pretty red, white and blue American flag. This flag will be bestowed upon your loved ones while they cry and mourn for you at graveside. The whole thing will be on local and national television. You will not be forgotten. Your badge will be retired and placed in a Plexiglas plaque at police headquarters. You will have a beautiful funeral if you mess up. No one will forget it. Do your best never to be the guest of honor at one of these funerals.

Afterwards, the situation leading up to your demise will be analyzed by people that weren't there. They will attempt to determine why you earned yourself a spot in the cop funeral hall of fame. Some will make excuses for the errors you made. And then someone will make a training video of how you screwed up because you got lazy or complacent doing your job! Don't screw up! We don't need any more cop funerals or training videos! Your number one job is to go home at the end of your shift!

I'm not talking about situations where we have to step forward and protect others from harm. I'm talking about you paying attention to your surroundings and never becoming complacent."

The academy class was dead silent. The words sunk in.

Detective Jim thought about this every day he went to work. He didn't want to get wasted by some asshole and then have people say he was a dumb shit for not being careful. He wanted to go home at the end of the day in one piece. He also wanted everyone he worked with to go home in one piece. It was a lot better to have a nice ice-cold beer at the end of the day instead of a funeral.

Don't be a dumb shit. No cop funerals. Always stay alert, stay alive!

DETECTIVE SERGEANT BRAD

Detective Sergeant Brad was new to investigations. He worked as a patrolman and then in the traffic bureau. Later he took the test to get promoted to Sergeant and received that promotion. An opening for a Sergeant's position came up in the Detective Bureau and Sergeant Brad applied and got the job.

The most senior detective under Sergeant Brad was Detective Jim. Detective Jim knew Sergeant Brad did not have any experience in the investigations field and took Sergeant Brad under his wing to get him up to speed on the way things were done. There were many reasons for Detective Jim to do this but the primary reason he did so was to have a supervisor he could work with. A supervisor that would agree with Detective Jim and give him assets when he needed them. Catching crooks was the name of the game and if Detective Sergeant Brad was trained correctly, he would grease the skids for Detective Jim's unique way of investigating crimes.

One of Detective Jim's fellow detectives, Detective Paul, was working a case against a home invasion robbery crew. Detective Paul put together a good case against the home invasion crew and wrote search warrants for several locations. All of the search warrants were to be served at the same time to have the element of surprise and prevent the destruction of evidence. Detective Paul asked Detective Jim to be in charge of one of the search warrant locations. Detective Jim was happy to oblige. It was an honor to assist his friend, Detective Paul. Throughout their career, they had worked patrol, plainclothes, narcotics, and investigations assignments. Being asked to take charge of a search warrant location was a big fat cop compliment. It meant trust and confidence in one's ability.

Real life search warrant service is not like it is on TV. It may take hours to write a search warrant. Then, it has to be read and signed by a judge. Then, the lead investigator has to write up a "game plan" for the execution of the search warrant. The game plan explains the "who, what, when, where, and why" of the search warrant execution. It also includes information about logistics and support personnel. Probably the most important part of the game plan is emergency resources available in case things go to shit and somebody gets hurt. But nobody is supposed to get hurt. If somebody gets hurt, it's a bad day.

On the day the search warrants were to be served, Detective Jim summoned a dozen fellow detectives to take part in it. He assembled them in a briefing room which had a large grease board with a crude drawing of the location to be searched.

Once assembled, Detective Jim passed out the search warrant game plans to all the detectives. The game plan was usually an eight-page document. It had each and every participating detective's assignment clearly listed on it. Four detectives, the entry team would make entry into the building to be searched. The entry team had two members with a battering ram and crowbars for forcing open the front door. Other detectives would take up stations on the outside of the building to make sure no crooks escaped out rear doors or windows. Everyone found inside the location would be handcuffed by the entry team. After the entry team contained the inside of the location and handcuffed anyone found there, the detectives on the perimeter would join those detectives on the inside and one big detective search warrant party would ensue. The place would be searched from top to bottom for evidence of the crime.

Serving a search warrant can be very dangerous. The more violent the crime involved meant the suspects at those locations were potentially more apt to use violence against police.

DETECTIVE JIM'S SEARCH WARRANT BRIEFING

So, Detective Jim is giving his search warrant briefing to his fellow detectives. Detective Sergeant Brad is present because he is the search warrant supervisor. Detective Sergeant Brad trusts Detective Jim's judgement.

Detective Jim gives his fellow detectives a briefing as to the nature of the search warrant, which detectives will make entry into the building to be searched, which detectives will contain the perimeter, etc., etc. The briefing lasts about fifteen minutes or so. After a very short question and answer period, Detective Jim tells his team to assemble in the station parking lot and they will all caravan in their undercover cars to the search warrant location.

Everyone leaves the search warrant briefing room except for Detective Sergeant Brad and Detective Jim. Detective Jim erased his search warrant location diagram off the grease board so it would be usable by the next person that needs it. He finishes his erasing and turns around and there stands Detective Sergeant Brad, holding an official looking clipboard and a serious look on his face. But, Sergeant Brad is just messing with Detective Jim:

"Jim…I need to talk to you about something."

"Yeah, what is it?"

"I was taking notes during your briefing, which I thought was very good but I noticed something."

"Why didn't you bring it up during the question

and answer period?"

"I didn't want to embarrass you."

"What the fuck do you mean?"

Well, during your search warrant briefing, you used the word "fuck" forty-two times."

"So, what's the fucking problem?"

"Well, we have a lot of new detectives and some of them are going on this search warrant and I don't want them following your lead in using the "F" word as often as you do. You are a professional "F" word user and know when and where you can use it but some of these new guys and gals are just not quite at your level and may use it inappropriately."

"You're fucking kidding me right? I just want to make sure no one gets fucking hurt so we can all go home at the end of the day and there's nothing like the "F" word to hammer a point home."

"This search warrant is high risk with bad fucking hombres involved. I have to use scientific language that stresses the importance of officer fucking safety. The only way I know how to do that is to fucking hammer it into their fucking heads that there will be no fucking cop funerals because they weren't fucking vigilant and staying on their fucking toes!"

"Jim, thanks for fucking explaining that to me."

"You're welcome."

All the detectives performed their search warrant duties flawlessly and nobody got fucking hurt...

ROBBERY SCHOOL

Cops are required to attend training on an annual basis to try to stay up to speed on their job. This training varies with basic minimal training classes to advanced officer training. Most classes are held at the police academy or a hotel conference room that is large enough to hold big groups.

One class every cop loves to take is ROBBERY SCHOOL. This is the class about real serious crime and how to take care of it Dirty Harry Style.

As Detective Jim advanced in his career, he was one day awarded the distinction of being able to attend the sacred ROBBERY SCHOOL. He had heard about it from more senior detectives and he was eager to attend.

Now it was Detective Jim's opportunity to meet some icons in the law enforcement community and find out how the Big Boys handle Big Problems.

ROBBERY DETECTIVE JAKE

Robbery Detective Jake is the lead Instructor for the Robbery School curriculum. He is overly qualified. He has been working the robbery division of his department since the dinosaurs became extinct and is an icon in the robbery detective brotherhood. Everybody who works robberies knows Detective Jake.

Standing six foot, six, weighing at least 300 pounds, big, square head that resembles a block of quartz stone with a flowing mane of silver-gray hair that would make Kenny Rogers jealous, Detective Jake commands respect by his very appearance. He looks like he could confront the most modern battle tank and come out the winner!

Detective Jake has command presence and the students in his class are in awe of the legend-man that has made the crime of robbery into a science.

The students are in awe:

Holy shit! Who is this guy? He looks like the hulk's wife had a giant for a baby. He looks like he could arrest half the population of the United States on his coffee break...Holy shit, Detective Jake is Mister 'In Charge.'

Detective Jake introduces himself to the class: he has been working robberies for a large metropolitan police force almost his entire career. He should be retired because of his age but he has four ex-wives to support. He believes some of the problems in his marriages were due to the long hours spent on robbery surveillances and possibly some after hour "debriefings" *(after hours drinking)* with his colleagues. The debriefings were held at the local cop bar and Jake may have gotten home late one too many nights.

Probably a lot of nights.

Detective Jake loves all of his ex-wives. They were such nice gals. For some reason they just couldn't understand Detective Jake's job in robbery. He gave up trying to convince them what a great guy he is. Now, they each receive an alimony check of a remembrance of how good it once was being married to one of the best, if not *the* best robbery detective's in the world. Even though Detective Jake is still fond of his ex-wives, none of them love him. Therefore, he continues to work to afford their alimony checks

Detective Jake is married to the police force first, ex-wives second.

In case you were wondering, Detective Jake likes scotch and can hardly wait for the class to end so he can get his 300-pound ass down to the hotel bar for some first-rate drinking and bullshitting. If you are a wimp and can't drink with Detective Jake until 2:00 in the morning, don't show up. You have to be a stand-up cowboy if you want to drink at Detective Jake's Rodeo.

Despite any flaws, Jake is the depository for all things robbery. If one has any question about the subject of robbery investigations,

"Ask Jake".

DETECTIVE JAKE'S FIRST DAY IN ROBBERY

Detective Jake explains to the robbery class students that he was "accidentally" selected for his assignment in robbery. The person he was replacing had recently retired and his department was frantically trying to find someone to fill the position. Robbery is a dangerous assignment. Detective Jake asked for the assignment because he watched too many episodes of black and white cop movies when he was a kid.

Detective Jake applied for the robbery position and was selected even though he did not have any experience and almost no seniority on his department. Jake was selected for the position because he was big and trainable.

On his first day at work in the robbery division, Detective Jake's senior partner sat him down for a welcome aboard speech:

"Son, working robbery is dangerous business. If you have second thoughts, go back to patrol and no one will think anything bad about your decision. Not that patrol work isn't dangerous in and of itself, it is. But we will be going after extremely bad guys who don't give a fuck about you living or dying. You're not going to be issuing traffic tickets anymore. You are not going to be making the occasional felony arrest. We're are going to target and arrest some really dangerous hombres. The baddest of the bad. Am I painting a picture for you?

I picked you because I believe I can mold you into a top-notch robbery detective. A hardnosed son of a bitch. If I'm wrong, and I don't think I am, you will be going back to patrol. But I don't think I'm wrong. I see something in your eyes that tells me you are cut out for this type of dangerous police work.

You are going to have to be dedicated to your new job and it won't always be easy on your family life. Explain that to your wife now. Don't hold anything back, she has to know what you're getting into.

And, there's one more thing you need to know son: If some shithead gets the drop on you and demands that you give your gun up, you are on your own. Don't even look to me for help. You have to make sure you are never in that position. If you give up your gun, you are going to be dead. Know this now that I will never give up my gun to save your ass. You need to think about that son.

If you make the stupid decision to give up your gun, the shithead will kill you, but I want you to have the comforting knowledge that if you do the stupid thing and give up your gun, and you get killed, I will shoot that motherfucker down and kill him for both of us. I will place a couple of extra bullets in his fucking head because he killed my partner. After your funeral, I will visit your wife and let her know what I did to that motherfucker, so she knows justice was done.

After your funeral, the department will announce a new opening in the robbery division. I will then pick a new partner to take your place and have this same talk with him because you were a stupid shit and let somebody get the drop on you. Don't be stupid. You have two days to think it over"

All right Boss Partner. Thanks for the heads up. I guess I have to get my head in the game to survive.

That night Detective Jake went home and went to bed. He couldn't go to sleep recounting the words of his new partner. His (first) wife asked him why he couldn't go to sleep. He told her about what his new robbery partner said about giving up his gun.

Detective Jake's wife told him to make sure he shoots and kills anyone that tries to hurt him. Simple.

"Don't ever give your gun up honey. Now get some sleep.

Oh, you might want to carry a back-up gun just in case, I saw it on T.V."

ROBBERY STAKEOUT

Detective Jake was a good instructor about the crime of robbery and its many facets. One particular area he expounded upon was the stakeout for serial robberies of a liquor or convenience store:

Detective Jake explained to the class about setting up a perimeter around the store with plainclothes detectives and having a takedown team inside the store.

The takedown team inside the store would naturally be hidden away from the robber and they would brief the store employee what to do if and when the robber showed up:

"Tell the employee, when the robber pulls out his gun and demands money, that you are going to confront the robber with a shotgun. Tell the employee that as soon as he sees you confront the robber; the employee is to hit the floor without looking around; the robber will be focused on you.

Do not tell the store employee, **'Hit the ground as soon as you see me because I am going to kill the motherfucker right there!'** (in front of the cash register), because in the State of

California, that is called premeditated murder and now you can be prosecuted for murder."

The class went silent. No one thought of that.

Thank you, Detective Jake, for keeping us from being prosecuted for murder!

Detective Jake Continued:

"Okay, the robber enters the store, he pulls his gun on the cashier, you come out from your cover, the employee hits the floor. Now, the only two words out of your mouth are, **'FREEZE POLICE!'**. Don't say, **'TRICK OR TREAT MOTHERFUCKER'** or some other stupid shit. It's **'FREEZE POLICE'**. If the robber drops his gun when you tell him to and gets on the floor, you arrest him. If he doesn't freeze and starts to turn towards you with his gun, you do your duty. Any questions? Alright, enough for today. Let's get down to that hotel bar, I'm buying the first round…"

Holy shit, Detective Jake is the real deal!

ROBBERY SCHOOL OFFICER SURVIVAL

Robbery school lasted a whole week. Detective Dinosaur Jake stole the show with all of his insight and wisdom.

The final day was taught by Lieutenant Deleon. He taught officer survival. *Mental* officer survival…He stole the show too:

Lieutenant Deleon was a well-respected Detective from the same department as Detective

Jake. He wanted to instill in the class a survival mode for police work. An attitude of:

"I will survive each and every day of police work. I will never have a fatalistic attitude. I will survive and go home at the end of my shift."

Lieutenant Deleon worked many detective assignments including burglary, narcotics, robbery and homicide. He told the class:

"I have been teaching this class for ten years. On some of the previous class critiques, a few students complained that I used swear words too much in my class. I believe these students were new to police work and never had their asses kicked or faced with life threatening experiences. If any of you cannot stand to hear me use swear words in my class presentation, I do not want to offend you. Please go into the hallway and wait for me to finish the class. After class, I will have you come back into the classroom and give you the class without any swear words. Is that okay? So with that in mind, who would like to leave the class?"

No one left.

The class proceeded:

"Everyone knows how dangerous police work is. You cannot survive with an attitude that any day could be your last at work because you might get killed. You must have a winning attitude, an attitude that each and every day, you will survive and win and go home at the end of your shift. No matter what circumstance you are placed in, you are going to win!

Let me give you an example:

You are about to go to work in the morning. You and your spouse are having a heated argument over something stupid. You are both upset and yelling at each other. But, as you walk out the front door to go to work, your spouse is all lovey-dovey because they don't know if they are going to see you at the end of your shift. They tell you: "Oh honey, I love you, be safe, come back home" and all that other softy shit.

If you fall into that trap, you have already sentenced yourself to loosing at work and getting hurt or killed. You have lost your survival mode. **THAT IS BULLSHIT!"**

Tell them, 'Fuck you, this fucking argument is not fucking finished and we'll finish it when I fucking get home tonight! You are wrong and get ready to carryon where we left off!'

Forget that lovey-dovey horseshit. Tell your spouse to go fuck themselves. Be a survivor."

The class was speechless with this new direct approach towards on the job survival.

"I don't care if some 400-pound motherfucker or some crack head junkie wants to kick my ass and shoot me, I'm coming home at the end of shift. I will survive!

Any questions?"

There were no questions.

No Lieutenant Deleon. We heard you loud and clear. We are now prepared to maintain a winning attitude at work and, win the arguments with our spouses!

"Oh, this is not officially part of the class curriculum but, it's nice to have sex with your spouse after you win the argument. It relaxes them and lets them know they are loved even though they were wrong.

Okay, I believe Detective Jake has introduced all of you to the hotel bar a couple of nights ago with one of his famous 'Debriefings'. Let's all meet there in about fifteen minutes to debrief what we learned today."

Everyone met down at the hotel bar for Lieutenant Deleon's debriefing.

He didn't have to buy himself any drinks that night.

WHAT DID WE LEARN IN ROBBERY SCHOOL?

1. Shoot fuckers that want to take your gun away,

2. Don't get married if you are a Robbery Detective named "Jake",

3. Don't say, "I'm gonna kill the motherfucker right there!" or, "Trick or Treat Motherfucker!",

4. Do say, "FREEZE POLICE!"

5. Do "your job" if you have to,

6. Drink at the bar after class,

7. Be a survivor, if anybody argues with you, tell them to go fuck themselves. Forget lovey dovey horseshit! Don't end an argument until they give in! Be a winner! Always survive!

8. Sex with your spouse after they lose the argument is therapeutic, and

9. Drink at the bar after class.

THE KIDNAPPING OF BIG BIRD

One of Detective Jim's most fun cases was the kidnapping of Big Bird. It was fun mostly because Detective Jim got to give his Sergeant a hard time about it.

Big Bird made a guest appearance at a local shopping mall as part of a children's program sponsored by the city's service organizations.

Hundreds of children showed up at the mall to see Big Bird along with all of the other Sesame Street friends. Big Bird was a big hit with the kids. After the performance, the Big Bird suit was taken off by the actor portraying Big Bird and placed in a large cardboard box on the side of the stage. Then, the unthinkable happened: someone stole Big Bird!

The crime was immediately reported to the police. Detective Jim was sitting at his desk at police headquarters. It was about 2:00 pm in the afternoon and the day had been relatively quiet. Detective Jim mistakenly thought he was going to be able to go home on time for a change. What a stupid thought Detective Jim!

After Big Bird's kidnapping, Detective Sergeant Bob received a phone call from the Detective Bureau Captain: the service organizations that sponsored the Sesame Street event are politically well connected and this theft must receive immediate priority. The criminals responsible for this crime must be caught immediately and Big Bird returned to his rightful owners!

Detective Sergeant Bob walked over to

271

Detective Jim's cubicle:

"Jim, we've got a problem."

"What's that?"

"There was a kid's program down at the mall. They had a bunch of Sesame Street characters down there and after the program, someone stole the Big Bird costume. The program was sponsored by all the city's civic organizations and they're in tight with the City Council members. The City is upset and they want Big Bird found and somebody in jail ASAP!"

You gotta be shitting me! I've been through political shit cases like this before. Some citizen gets excited and calls the city council about a dog shitting on their lawn and everybody gets their undies in a knot. Once again, somebody knows a city council member and now the cops have to dance like marionettes to keep everybody happy. That's alright, been there, done that. I'll do the best I can and hopefully have good results, but I just can't believe some of the priorities around here. I'm supposed to be chasing dangerous crooks like My Friend, Some Dude, Some Guy or a Truck Load of Mexicans!

Also, I'm going to have to fuck with Sergeant Bob a bit on this one, especially since he won't let me go home on time!

Oh, we're going to have fun with this one!

"Sarge, number one, 'WE' don't have a

problem. 'YOU' and the major crimes team has a problem. This is a kidnapping! I only work lowly felony thefts. Big Bird is a celebrity and nationally known. I'm just a dumbshit property crimes detective. You need your "A" Team on this one."

Make those fuckers work the case and I can go home on time for once in my career!

"I don't have the experience for high profile cases that the big boys have. Hey, maybe you should call the FBI? They get involved in almost all celebrity kidnapping cases. Also, there's a chance Big Bird has already been killed by his kidnappers and is laying in a shallow grave somewhere in the woods. Have we received a ransom request?"

I think that will rattle Sergeant Bob enough to get him pissed and keep me entertained a bit... After this is all done, Sergeant Bob will appreciate my humor. I hope...

"And, it's just a costume. It has to be worth over four hundred dollars before I get involved."

"The 'costume' is worth several thousand dollars Jim! And the Chief attends all the City Council meetings, knows the council members by name and he also attends all the service organizations meetings. The Chief wants this case solved!"

"I never get to go home on time. I feel like I'm Spartacus, working in the salt mine. Detective

Jim do this, oh, Detective Jim, nobody else is around, they went home on time, handle that..."

"Just work the fucking case Jim. The patrol officer is bringing the report in right now. Quit giving me a hard time on this. Find fucking Big Bird!"

Jim answered in one of his most sarcastic tones:

"Well, why didn't you say so Sarge? I'll get right on it. It'll be my pleasure."

"Smart Ass! Shit!"

So, Detective Jim gets screwed again in that he doesn't get to go home on time. He'll have to work the case as much as he can into the night and then he can go home, have a couple of beers, and return the following morning to pick up where he left off.

Jim gets the crime report and calls the victim/reporting party (the person who didn't keep an eye on the Big Bird costume when it was stolen). The victim/reporting party, "Mary" tells Jim about the nice event for all the little kiddos and how much fun they had meeting Big Bird in person. Mary is also embarrassed that she didn't keep an eye on a costume worth several thousand dollars. Mary noticed that there were also lots and lots of high school kids at the mall that day. Evidently, they still like Big Bird.

Jim does all the follow up he can for the night. He goes home, cracks open a frosty beer and thinks about the case:

> *Who would steal Big Bird?* *No one saw any terrorist kidnapping teams down at the mall. No reports of My Friend, Some Dude, Some Guy or a Truck Load of Mexicans being in the area. Just a bunch of preschoolers with their Mothers and some high school students at the mall.*

> *I think I know who stole Big Bird but it will have to wait till morning...*

The next day Detective Jim gets into work early. Sergeant Bob wants to know the progress on the Big Bird kidnapping case:

"Jim, what did ya find out?"

"Well, it appears the only people in the area of the kidnapping were Mothers with their preschoolers and a bunch of high school kids. No professional kidnapping teams, no reports of My Friend, Some Dude, Some Guy or a Truck Load of Mexicans in the area. I think I know who kidnapped Big Bird and I'll try to have a name by noon but I need the higher ups off my back. These kidnapping cases are sensitive you know, and I need to focus..."

"Keep me posted..."

Detective Jim thinks Big Bird's kidnapper is a high school student that played a dumb prank. The student is probably a male, sophomore or older, was at the mall with friends, and they talked him into kidnapping Big Bird. This student probably wouldn't have committed the kidnapping if he was alone; he got talked into it by his friends. He's probably a good kid and just did something stupid on the spur of the moment. The suspect now has a large cardboard box containing the Big Bird costume and doesn't know what to do with it. He probably even regrets being so stupid as to having taken it in the first place. Because of that, our suspect is now at school, shooting off his mouth to his friends about the big heist he pulled off (and now regrets). It's bragging and confessing at the same time.

Detective Jim calls Susan, the Vice Principal at the local high school. Susan and Jim are friends. They have worked hand in hand for years to eradicate crime from the community. A good VP knows all the students, who their friends are, etc. They are fellow detectives.

Detective Jim tells Susan about the Big Bird kidnapping case and asks her to put out her feelers with the students. Jim hangs up the phone, confident in Susan's abilities to obtain information from her students.

An hour and a half later, Detective Jim receives a call from Susan:

"We've got him! It's Brad, a junior, average student but not a bad kid. I'm kinda surprised he did it. He was shooting off his mouth to his buddies and a friend of a friend overheard it."

"Is he in school today?"

"Yes, gets out at 3:00 today."

"Can you call him to your office, and I'll be right down?"

"No problem."

"And Susan?"

"Yes?"

"I love you!"

"I'll be waiting Jim."

Detective Jim walks over to the Detective sign out board and signs himself out to the local high school. Barbie, the secretary asks:

"Going out in the field Jim?"

"Yeah, interview at the High School."

"Is this about Big Bird's kidnapping?"

"Top Secret Barbie can't discuss it unless we were in the cone of silence."

'I understand but I have a feeling you are going to interview and arrest the suspect. You have that look on your face."

"What look might that be?"

"Oh, that confident look""

"Bring that fucker to justice Jim! That dirty little atrocity committing son of a bitch!"

"You're funny Barbie. I like your sense of humor!"

277

Susan met Detective Jim outside her office:

"Brad is inside."

"Good. I'm going to have a little fun with this one, just go along with me. And Susan?"

"Yes.."

"Good job again. Millions of little partners will have their Big Bird back today because of you."

"Just doing my job…"

Detective Jim entered Susan's office and found a sheepish Brad sitting in a hard-plastic school chair.

"Brad, I'm Detective Jim with the Police Department. You probably know that by my suit and tie. And, you know why I'm here…"

"I didn't mean to do it, I'm sorry, it was stupid!"

Detective Jim interviewed Brad about the kidnapping of the century. Who Brad was with at the time and exactly what Brad did to perpetrate the crime, which was really quite simple: Brad was at the mall with his friends, Brad saw the Big Bird costume get put into a cardboard box, Brad saw people walk away from the box, Brad's friends said they should take the box, Brad took the box and placed it in the trunk of his car.

With a very serious tone Detective Jim let Brad have it:

"Brad, do you realize what you have done? Do you realize the social implications of taking Big

Bird and denying millions of children in the country of their friend? There are a lot of people angry at you right now Brad: Mothers, Fathers, and countless children. Not to mention the City Council and all the service organizations involved in the Sesame Street presentation that brought so much joy to so many small children. And then Brad gets a brain fart and kidnaps Big Bird! Disgusting Brad, you'll have to live with this the rest of your life, I hope you are sorry?"

"I am."

"Where's Big Bird right now?"

"In the trunk of my car."

"Where's your car?"

"In the school parking lot."

Shit! Big Bird is right here in the school parking lot! We're going to recover Big Bird without the help of major crimes or the FBI! Then, we'll drive up to the station to fingerprint Brad and release him to his parents. He doesn't need to go to juvenile hall. Brad is not a dangerous criminal. He just used bad judgement and we can probably get this whole thing cleaned up and make everybody happy again. But I have to keep scaring the crap out of Brad so he doesn't do anything stupid like this again.

Detective Jim and Brad go to Brad's car and retrieve Big Bird. The three of them drive up to the station in Detective Jim's car.

Once at the station, Brad is placed in an interview room. Detective Jim fingerprints Brad and fills out some reports. Brad is left alone in the interview room a while to stew over his predicament. Detective Jim knows this will help in his rehabilitation and not wanting to get arrested again for something stupid.

While Brad is in the interview room, feeling like shit, Detective Jim goes to the lunchroom to have a victory cup of coffee. Detective Jim takes his cup of coffee out onto the patio. The day is another beautiful sunny California day. It's hot and gorgeous. Jim is savoring his coffee and a fellow detective, Detective Chad, walks out onto the patio. Detective Chad has a sarcastic grin on his face and Detective Jim knows what is coming:

Anus Brain Detective Chad is now going to make fun of me and the Big Bird Kidnapping case. I just know it. I know the look on his face. We're going to have a verbal confrontation again: Chad is going to cut me down in his stupid fashion and I'm going to have to make him look like a dumbshit again. No problem, I'm used to it. Let the battle begin…

Several other fellow Detectives follow Detective Chad out onto the patio to hear the sarcastic exchange that is about to take place:

"Jim, good work on the bird-knapping case! We heard you found Big Bird but it was kind of a chicken shit deal!"

Oh, that was funny Chad!

"No, basic police work Chad. You guys go home on time, I get fucked again. Status quo. Ya know Chad, the Big Bird Kidnapping case should have been assigned to you since you're the only Detective here who still watches Sesame Street."

"Sounds like Sergeant Bob got something stuck in your craw?"

"Real Funny Chad. All the Detectives are laughing at Jim."

"Hey, don't get your tail feathers ruffled Jim!"

"Okay Chad, you win. Thanks for all the funny jokes. For once in my life I don't have a comeback for you. You got me. You made fun of me and everybody is laughing at me. Good job. I told my Mother about your sense of humor and you know what she said?"

"What?"

"FAFAFAFAUUUUUUUUUCK YOU!"

Chad turned around and left the patio. All the Detectives were laughing at him. Chad never learns, he always returns to the scene of the crime of trying to make fun of Detective Jim and loses the battle. Somethings don't change.

Okay, Big Bird is rescued from his kidnapping. Brad is in the interview room and scared shitless, thinking he's going to prison for life, the City Council members and service organization members are going to be happy, the Chief will be happy, Sergeant Bob will be happy, and, I told Chad to go fuck himself (again). This has turned out to be a very productive day! We have reached all of our objectives and we're going to wrap this up!

Brad asked Detective Jim if there was some way he could get out of his predicament.

"Yup Brad, there is. Detective Jim has been doing this for quite some time. Detective Jim, besides being a detective, operates an unofficial program where he helps dumb shits from getting prosecuted for the stupid things they did in life"

Detective Jim has Brad write out a 'Letter of Apology' addressed to all the people he has hurt by his kidnapping of Big Bird. In the letter, Brad states he is truly sorry and admits to his stupid actions and promises not to repeat his crime.

Brad's parents come up to the station to pick him up and his parents tore into him for being so stupid.

So far, so good…

The parents then ask Detective Jim if there is some way their poor judgement kid can forego prosecution. Detective Jim informs them that if the victim of the crime agrees to it, yes, there is. But Detective Jim can file charges anytime within a three-year time period if Brad screws up again. The parents are happy and take Brad home.

Victim/Reporting Party Mary shows up to the station and took possession of the Big Bird costume. Closure for Mary, she is happy. Jim gives Mary a copy of Brad's 'Letter of Apology'. She reads it and asks:

"What do you think?"

"He's not a bad kid. I don't think we should waste court resources on this. He's scared and knows he messed up. I scared him, his parents tore into him, I have three years to file this case if I want to, but he won't do it again. It's up to you."

"Three years?"

"Yes."

"Okay, I'm glad. Give him three years."

"Done. Sign right here please. I already prepared a no prosecution form, but it can be reversed if Brad so much as sneezes wrong."

"You knew this was going to happen?"

"I had a feeling. It happens quite a bit. I think you're doing the right thing."

"Detective Jim, I want to thank you so much for all of your help on this. I can't believe how fast you solved the case "

"Thank you so much but I had help, it was a group effort. If you're that happy, write the Chief a short note telling him how happy you are, he'll be glad to hear from you."

Yes Mary, write the Chief a note stating how happy you are and what a terrific job Detective Jim did! The note will be placed in Detective Jim's personnel file as to what a bitchin' job he did fighting 'crime'. It will be used for Detective Jim's next performance appraisal as a statement of Jim's devotion to duty. It will also counteract any negative complaint some unhappy soul may make against Detective Jim in the future.

The next time somebody calls in to the station to complain about what an asshole Detective Jim is, all Detective Jim has to do is refer his supervisors to his personnel file and all the letters from satisfied customers like Mary. Voila!

Detective Sergeant Bob was happy with the outcome of the Big Bird Kidnapping case. The Chief was off his ass and another tragedy could be put to rest:

"Hey Jim, good job on Big Bird, I knew you could do it."

"Yeah, it's just knowing who to talk to. I had help from I.I.N., my International Intelligence Network that surpasses INTERPOL's abilities. Susan down at the high school saved my ass on this one."

"Well, at least it all came together."

"We were really lucky on this one Sarge: Big Bird was imprisoned in the trunk of the suspect's car for over twenty-four hours without any food and water. He was rescued just in the nick of time."

Sergeant Bob, so used to Jim's sarcasm came right back:

"Well at least you didn't have to give him mouth to beak resuscitation. You don't have the proper training…"

"Sarge, I have to talk to you about a couple of issues."

"What issues?"

"About me solving a high-profile missing person case without the assistance of major crimes or the Federal Bureau of Investigations and the lack of department recognition for a bitchin job done, i.e. commendation for your favorite detective on your investigations team. I know I'm your favorite, you just won't admit it."

"Don't start that shit again!"

"I can't help it; I'm part Irish and I take it with me wherever I go.

"You're full of shit!"

"I know I'm full of shit, but it's good shit!

Well, if no commendation, how about a case of beer, call up the little lady and tell her we're coming home for some adult victory soda pops."

"Jill likes you but you can't come over to the

house, especially when you're drinking."

"What? Why not?"

"You know the kids are under ten years old and she doesn't want them learning how to say the word, "fuck" until they're teenagers. You have a foul mouth Jim."

"Aside from that, you need to throw down with a commendation for your favorite Detective. You have to admit it but I help keep morale up around here."

A smile came across Sergeant Bob's face:

"Let's just say you keep things interesting Jim."

"Another thing Sarge."

"What now?"

"If Bert and Ernie go missing, I don't want a fucking thing to do with that case. I refuse to work it."

"Goodnight Jim!"

"Wait Sarge, seriously, I need to take a couple of vacation days."

"For what? You're not due for a vacation."

"I wanted to do some volunteer work with a detective friend of mine who works for Anaheim Police Department."

"What kind of volunteer work?"

"He needs assistance with an adultery case at Disneyland, he found out that Minnie Mouse is fucking Goofy and he wants to tap into my superior crime fighting abilities to help solve the case..."

"GOOD NIGHT JIM, GO HOME!!!"

A VERY SHITTY DAWN SHIFT

As we have learned in past chapters, the dawn shift is sometimes referred to as a "shitty shift". But, to get through such an undesirable shift an officer needs to do two things: be well rested prior to shift and drink plenty of coffee to get through the shift.

COFFEE AND POLICE WORK

There has been a lot of mention about cops drinking coffee in this book. There have not been any official studies conducted about the relationship between coffee and police work, but any good cop will tell you that coffee plays a critical role in police work. Many a crime has been solved over a cup of coffee at the police station and coffee definitely keeps cops awake during dawn shift. Scientific studies have shown that coffee makes one happy and increases concentration.

Coffee was first popular in Africa and the Arab countries. History records the origins of coffee in Ethiopia, not Starbucks. Coffee later spread to Europe and America. The top five coffee producing countries are Brazil, Vietnam, Columbia, Indonesia, and Ethiopia.

Approximately 2.25 billion cups of coffee are consumed throughout the world each day. Finland, Sweden, and Iceland consume the most coffee per capita but various sources show other countries leading the way.

France, the USA, and Canada drink more coffee as a whole but not per capita.

After tea and beer, coffee is the most consumed beverage in the world.

The top three professions that drink the most coffee are Journalists, Police Officers (big shock there), and Teachers. Police Officers probably drink more coffee than journalists do, but the articles about coffee consumption are not written by cops but by journalists.

OFFICER RAY

Officer Ray is in his early thirties. He went to work one night to face the dreaded dawn shift without being well rested: Mistake #1. Add to that the fact that he did not consume much coffee prior to his shift or during his shift. Officer Ray was driving his police cruiser around his beat half asleep and his shift wasn't even half over: Mistake #2. Officer Ray should have run code three (lights and siren) to the nearest coffee shop, but he didn't. For some stupid reason, he thought he could make it through his shift on minimal sleep and coffee.

Just what in the hell were you thinking Officer Ray?

Part of Officer Ray's beat area included a sewage waste treatment plant on the edge of town. The treatment plant was on an "extra patrol" list which meant Officer Ray had to check up on it from time to time or at least one time during his dawn shift. The "extra patrol" designation was due to teenagers partying at the treatment plant and committing various acts of minor vandalism and littering. Officer Ray didn't really want to have to check up on the treatment plant, it stunk like one could imagine, but if the place got vandalized on his shift and he didn't check up on it, he could possibly get blamed for it and he didn't want that to happen.

Officer Ray's sewage waste treatment plant consisted of four main basins containing sewage that was in various stages of treatment. These four basins were rectangular in shape: about fifty yards long and thirty yards wide. There was a road around the perimeter of the basins but no fence between the basins and the road. The road was higher than the basins and offered a good view of all the shit that was being treated.

I'll just whip on over to the sewage plant, check on it real quick, tell dispatch I checked on it, and then head over to a coffee shop. If I don't get some coffee, I won't make it back to station. Gotta get some coffee...

So, half asleep Officer Ray drove over to the treatment plant. The road around the plant was in the shape of a square and only about three-eighths of a mile long; he should be done in no time. The area was dark, but Officer Ray's patrol car headlights illuminated the area around the plant sufficiently.

Officer Ray was in a hurry, so he was driving a little bit faster than normal. He's done it so many times, he's sick of doing it. He's tired and just wants to go home. While just starting to negotiate the first curve in the treatment plant road, Officer Ray received a radio call of an injury traffic accident and he needed to respond Code 3. This call was on the far end of his beat and it would take him some time to get there. Officer Ray's clip board was lying on the passenger seat beside him and he reached over in the dark to retrieve his pen which was attached to the top of the clipboard (nowadays, most departments have computer screens in the patrol cars and the clipboards are archaic). Officer Ray needed to write down the time of the call and location on his clipboard. He reached over, and while grappling in the dark to locate his pen, it slipped out of his hand and landed on the passenger floorboard. Officer Ray bent over to retrieve the pen while attempting to negotiate the first turn of the sewage treatment plant road. Officer Ray was tired and had a difficult time locating his pen on the floorboard. He could have just retrieved another pen from his shirt pocket but when one is overly tired, one doesn't always think of all the options clearly. Officer Ray kept struggling to find the lost pen in the dark and inadvertently turned his steering wheel a bit too much to the right. Office Ray's patrol car gently slid off the road and into raw sewage basin #1; the basin with the freshest raw sewage.

HELLO SHIT!

Officer Ray's patrol car was in deep shit and it was sinking. He crawled out through his driver's window and received a healthy covering of shit on his uniform, from the chest down. He climbed up onto the roof of his patrol car in an attempt to stay out of as much shit as possible. The police car was full of shit up to the roof.

NOOOO! *I am literally in deep shit!*

SHIT, SHIT, SHIT, I hate this shift! FUCK! What was I doing?

Officer Ray's patrol unit was nowhere near the edge of the sewage basin. If he wanted to make it to shore, he'd have to swim through more shit and he's wasn't going to do that.

Officer Ray has another problem: he has no communication with headquarters; unless he wants to reenter his patrol car, which is full of raw sewage, and attempt to use the radio microphone that is submerged in raw shit and is probably inoperable.

I'll use my portable radio it's on my duty belt!

No Officer Ray, you can't use your portable radio. Remember about an hour ago, you took your portable radio out of your duty belt radio holder and placed the portable radio on your passenger seat because the radio was digging into the side of your abdomen and it was creating some discomfort? Your portable radio is also soaking in shit, inside your shitty patrol car. Yes Officer Ray, police work is a very shitty job!

So now, Officer Ray's patrol car is sunk in a shit hole up to its roof and about ten feet from dry land. Ray is almost completely covered in shit and standing on the roof of his patrol car. He has no way of communicating with his dispatch:

Officer Ray is in Shit Lake without a paddle!

Headquarters tried reaching Officer Ray over the radio but to no avail. After all the emergency calls were handled, the other patrol officers working that night were sent to Ray's patrol beat to search for him and hopefully find him in one piece. The department was in a panic! Officer Ray was missing!

After several hours, another patrol officer found Ray in the middle of Lake Shit. Headquarters was notified that Ray was in one piece, but he smelled like shit. Patrol Officers were able to locate a long plank and place it from the bank of the sewage basin to the roof of Officer Ray's car. Ray walked the plank to freedom. He was hosed off and taken back to the station to end his shitty dawn shift. His shitty patrol car was taken back to the station and "sanitized" for several weeks and put back into service to save valuable taxpayer money. The patrol car was eventually scrapped because every time someone turned the heater on, they vomited.

THE MORAL OF THE STORY

If Officer Ray had been a good cop and drank the required amount of coffee for his shift, none of this shitty stuff would have happened. Drink coffee, it makes you happy and alert. If you don't, you could end up in Shit Lake without a paddle!

A JURY OF YOUR PEERS

Going to court to face charges can be a very stressful event in one's life. However, if someone routinely breaks the law, they become accustomed to courtroom settings and the criminal justice system. Going to court is not necessarily a huge stress, it's just part of the game...

MARK

Mark is in his mid-forties and had spent his fair share of time in court because he just hasn't learned not to drink and drive. Mark just can't plan ahead for his drinking escapades and he always runs out of beer. Then, he has to drive down to the local liquor store and get more beer. When Mark makes these last-minute liquor resupply trips, he is usually twice over the legal drinking limit and forgets how to keep his car travelling in a straight line.

Mark has been arrested four times for driving under the influence of alcohol. He spent a lot of time in jail for the last two offenses. Now, Mark is going to municipal court to face his fifth driving under the influence charge and trying to convince the judge he wasn't that drunk.

Mark has the right to be represented by an attorney, but he believes he can handle the case himself. When someone represents themselves in court, it is called "Pro Per", which is short for "Propria Persona," which is Latin and means "for oneself". A Pro-Per case is handled in court much like a traffic ticket case: The officer will testify and then the defendant testifies. The judge may or may not ask questions of either side and then decides the case.

Mark believes he spent too much time in jail on his other drunk driving cases and it was mostly due to poor representation by the Public Defender's office.

I can do better than those idiots!

Okay Mark, show us how it's done...

Mark had previously advised the court that he waived his right to a jury trial and agreed to let a lone judge decide the matter. This is commonly referred to as a "Court Trial" instead of a "Jury Trial".

JUDGE CRAWFORD

Judge Crawford is a colorful character. He went to law school straight out of college and got a job with the local Public Defender's office. He later ran for an open judge position in the municipal court and won the election. Almost everyone in the criminal justice system liked Judge Crawford; even the cops who usually can't stand defense attorneys. Many cops don't like defense attorneys because of the grilling they oftentimes get on the witness stand. Judge Crawford was probably the perfect person to have on the bench. He was intelligent, logical, and fair. Everyone trusted his judgement. He was as impartial as a person can be and also possessed a sense of humor from time to time while presiding over his courtroom. But judges have to remain professional at all times, so Judge Crawford was careful with his occasional courtroom humor.

Sometimes a case may have some humorous elements, but a judge must always remain professional.

Besides all of Judge Crawford's positive personality traits, he had a dashing appearance. Judge Crawford was tall, had a full mane of combed back white hair and a large bushy white mustache that made him appear like one of those stereotypical civil war generals from the history books. Add to that a deep, resounding voice and a black robe and it was obvious to all in Judge Crawford's courtroom that he was "The Judge".

MARK'S DAY IN COURT

Mark arrived in court for his drunken driving case. The courtroom was packed tight with offenders, officers, witnesses, and attorneys. Mark can barely find a place to sit but finally gets a seat.

The courtroom bailiff calls everyone to attention:

"All rise, the Honorable Judge Crawford presiding."

Judge Crawford enters from the courtroom from his chamber's door and swaggers over to his seat.

"Everyone, please be seated."

Judge Crawford reads through the courtroom calendar to see who has shown up for court and who has failed to show. He issued a couple of bench warrants for defendants that failed to show up and then heard a couple of pretrial motions presented by some of the attorneys' present.

The courtroom clerk proceeded with a mass swearing in of the courtroom for anyone that will be giving testimony. She tells the witnesses to sit down and Judge Crawford takes over.

For some reason on this particular day, Judge Crawford has a lot of Pro Per drunk driving cases. Each defendant so far has been found guilty and instructed to sit in the empty jury box because Judge Crawford has "remanded" them into custody, which means they are going to jail immediately to begin their jail sentence. If someone is found guilty of drunk driving, Judge Crawford always remands them into custody because if they go out and get drunk again and hurt someone in the process, Judge Crawford will appear soft on drunk drivers and get blamed. Judge Crawford is not going to let that happen.

Reelection is coming up and I'm not going to give anyone a reason not to vote for me! Mothers Against Drunk Drivers: I'M YOUR JUDGE!

Judge Crawford has seven guilty male drunk drivers sitting in the jury box, waiting to be carted off to jail. The last driving under the influence case is Mark's.

The patrol officer that arrested Mark testified as to why he stopped Mark: Mark was all over the road, and why he arrested Mark: Mark was blotto drunk and barely able to stand up. The officer gave Mark a breathalyzer test that showed Mark's blood alcohol level at .20 which was over twice the legal limit.

Mark was then allowed to testify on his behalf but he was not required to. Mark remembers how he was screwed over in his other cases, by those attorneys who thought they knew how to represent a defendant but failed miserably at it.

I can do a better job than them! I've been arrested five times! I know what I'm doing!

Sitting in a courtroom, listening to testimony as an observer can sometimes be quite entertaining and Mark did not let anybody down:

TWO OR THREE BEERS

"Your honor, I'd like to tell you what really happened."

"It's your turn, go ahead…"

"Well your honor, it's true I had a couple of beers that day but I really didn't have that many. In fact, I was on my way to the liquor store because I ran out!"

Chuckles erupted from the courtroom audience. The arresting officer is also smiling and fighting off laughter.

"If I had been drinking as much as the officer said I was, why would I have to go to the liquor store to get more beer?"

"Well, Mister Mark, probably because you have a high tolerance built up over the years. Just how many beers did you have that day?"

"Two or three."

Wait, two or three beers? You expect me to believe that? How about two or three six packs of beer? That's more like it Mister Mark.

"Do you remember exactly how many?"

"No sir but I think it was only two or three."

"Okay, let's move on to your driving Mister Mark."

"Well your honor, I'm glad you brought that up. You see I have a steering problem with my car and the front end veers off to the side sometimes."

Yeah Mister Mark, I know all about your car veering off to the side. It veers off to the side when you just happen to be driving when you are blotto drunk!

"The officer said you could barely stand up. Can you tell us about that?"

"Yes your honor, since I was a child I've had this condition in my inner ear where sometimes I can't get my balance."

"Does it get worse when you are drinking?"

"Oh no your honor, in fact if I have a couple of beers, it helps. I was really walking good when the officer stopped me."

"That's not what the officer testified to."

"I know it looks bad your honor, but the officer was wrong. I think the officer was having a bad day and just had to take it out on me."

"Is that right officer?"

"Uh, no your honor, in fact I didn't want to arrest Mister Mark because I was due to get off shift when I saw Mr. Mark driving down the middle of the road and I had to stop him before he hit something or someone."

"What do you say about that Mister Mark?"
"Your honor, I told you I only had two or three beers and that's the truth. My car veers to the side and I have a balance problem in my inner ear. I can drink a lot of beers and not get drunk. In fact, I'm a better driver when I'm drinking, the officer is lying!"

Poor Mark has just dug himself a big hole he cannot get out of. Judge Crawford is chuckling and quite amused. Almost everyone in the courtroom thought Mark was a dumb ass for opening his big mouth. Everyone was enjoying the show including the arresting officer who could barely keep from openly laughing.

Judge Crawford thought about Mark's testimony for a while and asked:

300

"Is that all Mister Mark?"

"Yes sir, I'm not guilty, I'm a good driver when I'm drinking."

"Mister Mark, your blood alcohol level was point-two-zero (.20). That's just a little high."

"I don't think it's that high your honor."

A smile comes over Judge Crawford's face. He looked to his left where the seven guilty drunk drivers were sitting in the jury box and nonchalantly, but with a mildly comical tone, asked them:

"So, what do you guys think?"

Everyone in the courtroom is surprised by this out of the ordinary procedure.

In unison, all the remanded drunk drivers that were sitting in the jury box, lifted their right hand and gave Mark a thumb down. Judge Crawford didn't miss a beat:

"Mister Mark, you have just been found guilty by a jury of your peers and I remand you to the custody of the Sheriff!"

The courtroom busts up. Everyone was laughing except for Mark. The bailiff showed Mark his seat in the jury box with the other guilty drunk drivers and Judge Crawford ordered a brief adjournment to go into his chambers and laugh in private without witnesses…

Sometimes, it is better to keep your mouth shut in court...

LUNCH WITH DAD

SOME SMALL CITY IN THE MOJAVE DESERT

CIRCA 1960

The Mojave Desert is situated mostly in the states of California and Nevada but extends into parts of Arizona and Utah. It is the 21st largest desert in the world. Even though it is a "desert", it has some towns of considerable size within its borders.

JERRY

Jerry was a good kid. He was a well-behaved child and had spent his entire 14 years in a mid-sized town in the Mojave Desert. It really wasn't such a bad place to grow up for a boy: plenty of adventurous hikes and bicycle riding through the desert, which has a lot to offer if one just searches a bit.

Jerry's Dad was a Sergeant on the city police department. Besides the Chief of Police, and one Captain, Jerry's Dad was the senior officer on the department and he basically ran the show.

Oftentimes, Jerry's Mom would fix his father a sack lunch and have Jerry ride his bicycle down to the police station and deliver it to his Dad.

SCARED STRAIGHT POLICE SERGEANT DAD STYLE

One hot summer day, two weeks after Jerry turned 14, Jerry's Mother asked him to ride down to the police station and drop off his Dad's lunch. Jerry liked going to his Dad's work; all the police officers treated him like he was their own.

Jerry thought the world of his Dad. His Dad was a hardnosed cop, but he was the best Father in the Universe. The two were always involved in projects and outdoor activities and Jerry's Dad was always schooling him about life.

Jerry rode his bike down to the police station and walked up to the front desk with his Dad's brown sack lunch like he's done a hundred times before. As he is about to place it on the front desk, the desk officer tells Jerry his Dad wants it delivered in the back, down the hallway where the jail is.

Jerry walked into the jail hallway looking for his dad. The jail had four cells along one wall and there was an arrestee in one of the cells. As Jerry walked by him, he saw the guy was very, very filthy. And not only that, the prisoner was yelling and cursing his head off.

Jerry's Dad rounded a corner and met Jerry in front of one of the empty cells.

"Hi Dad."

Jerry handed off the lunch sack to his Dad.

"Hi son. Thanks for bringing my lunch. Now, get in here."

Jerry's Dad pushed him into the vacant cell

next to the loud arrestee and slammed the heavy bar laden cell door shut before Jerry could say anything. Jerry's Dad matter-of-factly stated:

"This is what happens to you if you make bad decisions in life."

JERRY'S JAIL CELL

Jerry's jail cell wasn't dirty; in fact, it had the odor of strong disinfectant. But it *looked dirty.* The ceiling and walls appeared to have been painted ten years ago. The ceiling was painted off white and had a single dim light bulb encased in a wire mesh screen. The walls were painted in a dark green and looked like they had been chipped and painted over in numerous spots. Adjacent to one wall, there was a hard metal bunk without bedding. The back wall had a metal toilet that appeared like a leftover from the toilet factory. The toilet didn't have a seat like the one at home; the seat of the toilet was molded into the top of it. The front of the jail cell was, of course, heavy iron bars with a heavy iron bar door that bangs shut when closed. The cell floor is bare concrete. The temperature in the cell is *HOT* and the air is stifling. The weather outside the police station is over a hundred degrees and not much cooler inside. The police station and jail are not air conditioned. Jerry's jail cell screamed: "DARK AGES POLICE BRUTALITY!" but there is no one to save him.

What did I do to deserve this? I did all my chores. I don't back talk my parents; Dad would kick my ass if I did. I was minding my own business. Obviously, I did something

305

really bad for my Dad to throw me in here.

Can my Dad actually read my mind? Did he read my mind about something bad I thought of doing but didn't actually do? No, he can't read minds. I must have done something but I don't know what…

Not only was Jerry in jail for something he didn't do, he had a next door neighbor that stunk like shit and who had a very profane vocabulary.

That dirty guy in the cell next to me stinks so much I feel like I need to take a shower!

Jerry does not like his jail cell and is ready to leave, he yells out:

"Daaad!"

Jerry's Dad shows up in front of the jail cell,

"Yes son?"

"I didn't do anything!"

"I know son, but you see, you are starting to get older and in a few years, you are going to be sixteen. You see son, most young men, when they turn sixteen or seventeen, they think they know everything, and they start to make some bad decisions in life. You need to know where bad decisions send you: they send you right here, to jail. From now on, when you think you know everything, I want you to think about this jail cell. I wish I could put every boy your age in here to give him this valuable lesson in life. I'll be back in a while. I have to finish my lunch. Your Mother makes the best lunches!"

And with that, Jerry's Dad walked down the hallway, out of sight.

I hate this jail cell. I want to go home to my room. I love my room. My room is safe. This place isn't safe and it's the ugliest place on earth. I'm never doing anything bad again. I'm sorry! I hate jail!

Jerry had a seat on the metal bunk and contemplated his classroom while his next-door neighbor kept screaming obscenities at imaginary enemies. There was a faint odor of stale beer in the air, no doubt from the screamer. Jerry vowed that he will never be tricked again into entering the jail to deliver his Dad's lunch.

After an hour and a half, Jerry's dad appeared at the cell holding a set of giant keys that obviously unlocked the jail cells,

"Learn anything today?"

"Yes sir. I don't ever want to do anything stupid to make me end up in here."

And with that, Jerry's Dad unlocked the cell, opened the door, and stated,

"Go ahead and go now. Tell your Momma I should be home in time for dinner."

Jerry didn't hesitate to exit the cell and the Police Station. He pedaled as fast as he could to get home. He was scared straight.

Epilogue

Jerry never did anything stupid in his life to get arrested.

DETECTIVE JIM GETS ARRESTED FOR MURDER

LAW ENFORCEMENT STRESS

Some cops will tell you they deal with a lot of stress. Others will say they don't have an issue with on the job stress. It all boils down to the fact that everyone deals with stress differently. Some can handle it; others may have issues with it. Cops have to go through a psychological test before they are hired. But, in the end, we are all human...Sometimes even our finest can have difficulties in life that are too much to handle.

And so it happened on one of Detective Jim's coveted days off, he and his wife were arguing incessantly. The two had been arguing for weeks and even started going to marital counseling. The counseling was just a bitch fest for Jim's wife to ridicule and berate him.

So, on Jim's day off, his wife asked him to drive the two of them to the grocery store. On the way there, his wife started another argument. She just couldn't keep her big mouth shut. Jim just couldn't take it anymore; he was advised over and over again what a piece of shit husband he was...

Jim was at his breaking point. He pulled into a parking spot at the far end of a shopping center. His wife kept bitching and complaining about everything under the sun. Jim had had enough and when his wife looked away, he pulled out his B.F.G. and put a bullet in her left temple. She was now leaning against the passenger door post, very still and very quiet...She was at peace now. You'd think she was just napping if it wasn't for the trickle of blood coming from the bullet hole in her left temple and dripping all the way down her cheek.

There, that should quiet the little bitch down! Arguing is not healthy for a relationship!

Jim sat in his seat, reveling in the quiet. Well, it really wasn't that quiet, he now had a loud ringing in his ears from having shot his wife but it was quiet as far as no more arguing and yelling.

End of problem, no more arguing. Shit, here come the cops; the ones that are working anyway. Someone must have seen what happened and called it in.

Well, it is kinda right out in the open and in full daylight. What do I tell them so they don't think I'm an asshole? I hope it's a male cop who argues with his wife, he might understand...

Jim wasn't really happy with what he had just done but now he had to live with it. And, he had to convince everyone else in the world that what he had just done was the best course of action under the circumstances.

Jim placed his B.F.G. on the dashboard in front of him, in plain sight. He got out of his car and walked about ten feet away from his driver's door. He didn't want to be near the car. He didn't like his car because in it was what's leftover of the woman that would never shut up!

How am I going to explain this to the cops so they don't take me to jail? I know, I'm the victim! I'll play the 'Victim Card'! And, I'm good friends with the Chief! That's it, I'll convince them what a terrible woman she was, how I'm good friends with the Chief, and I'm an all-around great guy! She forced me to do it. Simple!

OFFICER NEW GUY

The department sent over a new cop on this call. The officer and Jim didn't know each other.

That could be good or that could be bad...

Officer New Guy got out of his car with an extremely serious look on his face and went up to Jim.

"Can I see some identification please?"

At this time a second officer, a patrol sergeant, arrived on the scene and stayed back observing Detective Jim and Officer New Guy.

Detective Jim:

"Sure Officer, here's my license, I don't have my other I.D. with me but let me first tell you that I am a very peaceful man and you don't have anything to worry about."

311

"What happened?"

"You know how sometimes things get outta hand and sometimes a woman just won't shut up and she harasses you to the point of exhaustion and you just can't take it anymore?

"You two had an argument?"

"Well yeah, but I'm a peaceful man and I'm a friend of the Chief's, so you don't have a thing to worry about."

"What's wrong with your wife?"

"Oh, that! Well, you see, she was verbally attacking me to the point of no return and I just had to put one in the 'ole "X" ring (Jim pointed at his wife's head) right there and that shut her up."

The "X" ring is the center of a pistol target. It is "dead center". If one can shoot and hit the "X" ring on a target, one is a very good shot with a firearm.

Officer New Guy bent down and looked into Jim's car. He could now see the blood trickling down the side of Jim's wife's head.

"You shot her?"

"Yes, but I'm friends with the Chief and I'm a very peaceful man. You don't have anything to worry about. I just threw one in the 'ole "X" ring to quiet her down and boy did it work."

312

Officer New Guy grabbed his handcuffs and told Detective Jim he was under arrest. He slapped the cuffs on Detective Jim and put him in the backseat of his patrol car.

Sergeant Dean walked up to Officer New Guy and asked him:

"What ya got?"

"I just arrested him for murder; he admitted to shooting her and she looks dead."

Sergeant Dean yelled at Detective Jim,

"You ready to come out now Jim?"

"Yeah, get these damn cuffs off of me, they're killing my wrists and don't forget to lock them next time so your arrestee's hands don't fall off from lack of circulation!"

You see dear readers; Officer Jim was role playing for the newest police recruit class. Sergeant Dean asked him if he would help out by being an "actor" and "role play" for one of the scenarios the police recruits have to be tested on before they can graduate from the police academy.

Detective Jim jumped at the chance to act out and role play:

O.K., let me get this straight Sarge: you want me to dress in comfortable clothes, drink free coffee, bullshit the new police recruits, and I

*get paid for my performances? Hell yes, count
me in Sarge! You've come to the right guy for
the job! Better than having a bad shooting
dream. I'll get to fine tune my bullshitting skills!
I'll bring my B.S.'er's badge! Sign me up!*

Sergeant Dean asked Officer New Guy:

"Why did you take so long to arrest him?"

"When I first pulled up, it looked like she was
just sleeping in the car and then I saw the
blood. And the guy kept talking and talking…"

"He's a pretty good talker isn't he?"

"Yeah."

"Jim, you have any comments?"

"Yeah, you almost took too long to hook me up
(To "hook" somebody up is slang for
handcuffing them), but once you realized what
was going on, you did the right thing. Try to
be a little bit more observant, but overall, you
did a good job."

Detective Jim and Officer New Guy shook
hands. Officer New Guy drove away to another
hypothetical police call to test his abilities.

Detective Jim's "wife" woke up from her death
nap and joined Sergeant Dean and Detective Jim.
Detective Jim's wife was a female police officer who
also volunteered to help out with the role playing.

Even though she didn't have a speaking part, it isn't easy getting shot so many times in one day!

Husband Jim:

"Honey, I'm sorry I had to shoot your ass again but if you would just learn to shut the fuck up when I tell you to, this kinda thing wouldn't happen!"

All three of them were having a good laugh.

Jim's Deceased Wife:

"Yeah Jim, you keep this shit up and I won't share my coffee with you, fucker!"

"You little brat! You've really crossed the line this time! I'm going to have to shoot you again!"

The three laughed some more, had a couple sips of coffee and got ready for the next murder scene role playing.

Detective Jim had to murder his wife about twenty times during the role playing scenarios. While lying still, supposedly dead, Detective Jim's "dead" wife had a hard time containing her laughter while listening to Jim's storytelling to the police cadets about what a nice guy he was, how "peaceful" he was, and what a "good friend of the Chief's" he was. He got to fine tune his bullshitter skills to the point that three of the police recruits didn't arrest him for murder. Jim confused them and they failed their test. Now that's some good story telling.

Aren't you glad Detective Jim didn't really get arrested for murder?

Author's Note: Don't try this at home!

THE GREAT STAGECOACH HEIST!

Circa late 1980's

DETECTIVE MACK

Detective Mack worked felony theft crimes. He usually wore a suit and tie to work and primarily dealt with residential, commercial and vehicle burglaries, grand thefts, and sometimes a major fraud case or two. Detective Mack had been on the force about a dozen years and he was a very conscientious investigator. When Detective Mack presented a case to the District Attorney's Office for filing, it was usually a masterpiece of detective workmanship. He also was not afraid to go outside the box to solve a case. If a case needed unusual (but lawful) methods, so be it.

DISTRICT ATTORNEY WADE

The District Attorney's Office prosecutes crimes in court, reviews search warrants before they are presented to judges for their signature and is also involved in some criminal investigations.

Deputy District Attorney Wade was in charge of overseeing various misdemeanor and felony cases in his office. He had been with the District Attorney's office for over ten years and had been in law enforcement before that. He came from a big family of cops, firemen and prosecutors. Deputy District Attorney Wade was well respected by his superiors, peers, and subordinates. Oftentimes he went the extra mile to help out cops with their search warrants and cases that needed to be filed in the District Attorney's Office. He became friends with many officers and also had a fringe benefit for his friends that visited him: a personal coffee pot with the strongest French Roast Coffee in the District Attorney's Office! Win – Win! He also possessed a good sense of humor and also liked to have fun on the job, if he could. The District Attorney's Office is not a "fun" place. It is a very serious place with serious responsibilities. However, sometimes there is a case that turns out to be "fun" and is long remembered for bringing some lightheartedness to the office. Detective Mack provided District Attorney Wade with just such a case.

One day, Detective Mack was sitting at his desk, minding his own business and his Sergeant gave him a stack of new cases to investigate. Most of the cases did not have much in the way of suspect leads. One case did have a very solid lead. It was a stolen stagecoach case and the stagecoach was worth tens of thousands of dollars, more than many cars at that time.

You gotta be kidding me. A stagecoach? Who in the hell steals a stagecoach, let alone, who owns a stagecoach?

WELLS FARGO AND COMPANY

Wells Fargo and Company was founded in 1852. The company operated "Ocean to Ocean" to help fulfill the banking and transportation needs of the growing United States. When the transcontinental railroad was completed, Wells Fargo utilized the rail system and their stagecoaches took over where the rails ended.

The Wells Fargo stagecoaches were built in Concord, New Hampshire and were known as the Six Horse Concord Coach. They weighed approximately 2,500 pounds and had an original price tag of approximately $1,100.00. Today, some coaches are worth upwards of $50,000.00.

Some of the coaches are still around today and they can be seen in museums and parades.

It just so happened that a successful southern California doctor, Dr. Adams, was an old west history buff and one day decided to buy himself an official stagecoach from the 1800's. This stagecoach was oftentimes loaned out for various parades. Dr. Adams was so generous, he loaned it to another prominent member of the community, his friend, Jack. Jack said he wanted to use the stagecoach in a parade. The parade was held and afterwards, Jack said the stagecoach was "missing" and he didn't know what happened to it.

Dr. Adams didn't believe Jack's story about the stagecoach all of a sudden going "missing". Dr. Adams did some research and discovered that Jack owned a vacant lot of land close to the city. When Dr. Adams visited the property, he found his stagecoach parked there. However, the stagecoach was surrounded by a fence and a heavy, locked gate. Dr. Adams backed off and filed a police report for the theft of his stagecoach.

Upon receiving the stolen stagecoach report, Detective Mack phoned Dr. Adams and went over the whole story with him. Detective Mack set up a secret recorded phone call between Dr. Adams and his friend, Jack. The two talked about the stagecoach and Jack again repeated that the coach went missing after Jack used it in a parade. That was all the information Detective Mack needed and the phone call was ended.

Oh little Jack! You've been caught in a big fat lie! Now we're going to recover the stagecoach and you're going to be facing a nice fat felony theft charge.

The next day, Detective Mack left his suit and tie at home. He put on some blue jeans and a long sleeved work shirt and went to the area of the vacant lot where the stagecoach was being stored. Detective Mack took along a pair of binoculars to view the stagecoach from afar. He didn't want Jack to detect his presence and then remove the stagecoach before it could be seized.

Detective Mack crept through some bushes on an adjoining piece of land. Through his binoculars, he could clearly see the stagecoach inside the fenced area. Detective Mack knew that he would need a search warrant to seize the stagecoach. That would entail Detective Mack getting fellow detectives to stake out the area while Detective Mack returned to the station to write a search warrant, drive it over to the District Attorney's Office, then have it signed by a judge and then return to the vacant lot to seize the stagecoach. All of that protocol could take up to half a day or more. (Nowadays, some police departments can type up their search warrants on their smartphones and have them approved electronically).

As Detective Mack studied the stagecoach through his binoculars, he noticed something odd about it: the stagecoach had a tow bar attached to the front of it. Dr. Adams never mentioned this in his police report.

Detective Mack phoned Dr. Adams and asked him if he attached a tow bar to the stagecoach. Dr. Adams told Detective Mack that Jack must have added the tow bar because the stagecoach never had one. Detective Mack knew that if the stagecoach qualified as a "vehicle" under the California vehicle code, he could seize it without a search warrant and save a lot of time.

Detective Mack stayed hidden in his bushes and called District Attorney Wade on his cellphone:

"Hey Wade, this is Mack, I'm in the Rio Robles Valley area and I'm in the bushes staked out on a stolen stagecoach and I got a question."

District Attorney Wade had been enjoying a cup of his favorite French roast coffee...

"Wait, you gotta what?"

"I'm staked out on a stagecoach that was stolen, it's worth a lot of money, it's in a lot surrounded by a fence and I have a search and seizure question."

"Mack, what year is this? Is this a joke?"

"No, I'm serious, I've got the stagecoach under observation and I want to seize it before the thief returns and moves it to another location."

"This better not be a joke Mack. If you're recording this and it's a joke buddy you're going to regret it."

"I'm not kidding Wade, this is no joke. I'm on surveillance in the bush. A doctor is a history buff and he bought himself an official stagecoach from the old west days. The coach is used in parades and his friend stole it from him. It's worth tens of thousands of dollars. I need your opinion on the law, that's why I called you."

"O.K., what do you need help with?"

"The stagecoach has a tow bar attached to the front of it. The tow bar was added by the thief but that's beside the point. I need your professional opinion on whether the stagecoach now qualifies as a vehicle under the vehicle code and if I can seize it without a search warrant because it's now a vehicle?"

"Alright Mack, let me research this and I'll call you right back. One question; is this a *real* stagecoach from the 1800's or is it a reproduction?"

"It's an authentic stagecoach from the 1800's"

"O.K. let me research it and I'll get right back to you. And Mack?"

"Yeah?"

Now was District Attorney Wade's chance to start having some fun:

"Keep a good eye out for Indians and stage robbers, I heard they like to hit stages for the cash boxes, keep your Winchester lever action handy partner, I don't want you gettin' bushwhacked!"

"I need your help."

"Call you right back."

District Attorney Wade cannot believe that he is now involved in a stolen stagecoach case.

This stuff is unbelievable! Who owns a stagecoach? Wow! I now get to have some fun at work because of an unusual case. Detective Mack is going down in history as part of THE GREAT STAGECOACH HEIST!

Wade digs out his copy of the vehicle code. He then gets on his computer and reads a couple of appellate court cases concerning search and seizure of stolen vehicles and what does and does not qualify as a "vehicle" under the law. This is where District Attorney Wade shines: helping out fellow D.A.'s and cops in need. It's what he's famous for (besides his French Roast Coffee). Wade calls Mack back:

"Mack?"

"Yeah Wade, what did ya find out?"

"Well, it appears that since someone attached a tow bar to the stagecoach, it now qualifies as a "vehicle" and you don't have to obtain a search warrant. I need to know how you plan on seizing it though?"

"Why?"

"You can't seize the stagecoach without first forming a posse. You have to properly deputize all the posse members and, all the posse members must be on horseback. I found some case law that stated that is the proper way to recover stolen stagecoaches."

"Oh, you're messing with me now."

Wade is having the time of his life:

"Not my intention. Also, after the stagecoach is seized, you have to buy all the posse members whiskey down at the local saloon. These are not my rules, they are tradition and we won't file charges if you ignore proper posse protocol."

"I can tell you guys are going to be making fun of me for quite a while on this one."

"And Mack?"

"Yeah?"

"If the thief shows up while you are recovering the stagecoach, you and the posse members are not allowed to hang 'em high on the way to the station. That's only for horse thieven'"

"Anymore advice smartass?"

"Yup, I went on the internet and found out there's still an active warrant for the arrest of Black Bart, the notorious stagecoach robber. If you see him, might as well bring him in too. Also, I want to personally review this case when you're done. If anyone else at your station has, say, cattle or horse rustling' cases, bring them all to me. I'm getting into this old west crime stuff!"

"I'll call you, Wade, after we recover the stagecoach."

"Good job. I'll be here in the courthouse with Judge Roy Bean."

They both hang up.

Mack can't believe it, the joking has begun and he's going to hear it for a long, long, time…

Detective Mack asked his police dispatcher to have a tow truck respond to his location:

"Station One, Five David Three, request an on call tow to my location."

"Five David Three advise type of vehicle?"

Mack knows what is now going to take place on the radio: no one is going to believe that he needs a tow truck for a stagecoach. They're all going to think it's a big joke.

"Station One, Five David Three, I am recovering an 1850's stagecoach and I need a flatbed tow truck.

"Five David Three 10-9?" or,

Are you kidding? A stagecoach? We never send tow trucks to tow stagecoaches. Did someone steal a police radio and is playing a prank on us?

"Station One, Five David Three, I need a flatbed tow truck for a recovered stolen stagecoach. I have a report number if you want to look it up. Again, this is not a joke."

"Five David Three, 10-4."

Almost all the officers monitoring the radio traffic between Mack and dispatch started clicking their microphones. One of the officers had Detective Mack switch to a side band on the radio:

"Five David Three, Two Adam One"

"Go ahead for Five David Three"

"Yeah, if you haven't formed a posse yet, I'm available to assist"

"You're late, I've already heard that joke and just about every other one, good-bye"

A flat bed tow truck eventually arrived and removed the stagecoach from the property.

Detective Mack left his business card on the gate to Jack's property with a note for Jack to call him. Jack called Detective Mack who invited him up to the station for an interview.

Jack was indignant that his "rights" were violated by Mack trespassing on his property and being accused of stealing his friend's stagecoach. The whole thing was just a big misunderstanding! That is, it was a misunderstanding until Detective Mack played the recording of the secret phone call. Mack arrested Jack for the stagecoach theft. Jack eventually pled guilty to the crime.

Since that time, whenever Detective Mack and District Attorney Wade saw each other, they had to talk and laugh about the Great Stagecoach Heist!

ANYMORE QUESTIONS FOR THIS WITNESS?

CRIMINAL JUSTICE SYSTEM HATRED

Basically, the criminal justice system can be said to consist of the courts (judges, prosecutors, and defense attorneys), law enforcement, and last but not least, the accused, or criminals.

There is some obvious hatred within the system. Not all participants are "haters" but there are some members of each of the above groups that do hate one another.

Some criminals hate cops. Some cops hate criminals. Some cops hate defense attorneys and some defense attorneys hate cops. Some prosecuting attorneys hate defense attorneys and vice a versa.

Many members of the criminal justice system try not to hate. They understand why the criminal justice system exists in the first place and to work within it without unnecessary hate.

Some cops realize defense attorneys are just defending their clients and giving them their constitutionally guaranteed "day in court." Some defense attorneys realize the cops are just doing their job too.

There are some defense attorneys that believe all cops are liars because they experienced, or thought they experienced, a cop that either lied in a police report or during testimony in court. And, it has happened, but that is not a valid reason to paint law enforcement with such a broad brush of negativity. Additionally, some attorneys, both prosecuting and defense, believe they are a higher life form because they spent more years in college than most of the grunt cops on the street.

DETECTIVE RALPH

Detective Ralph is a fifteen-year veteran. He is considered one of the best detectives on his department. He is conscientious and always tries to perform the best he can. Besides his fellow officers, he networks well with the District Attorneys, Defense Attorneys, and just about everyone he has contact with as long as they will meet him halfway. Detective Ralph has frequently drank from District Attorney Wade's Fountain of French Roast. The two are good friends.

Detective Ralph prides himself on his honesty and does not appreciate anyone questioning it. He also doesn't like "hot shot" attorneys that are disrespectful and think their shit doesn't stink.

> *Don't think you're better than me just because I didn't take the bar exam. I have to think on my feet everyday so don't lock horns with me! Respect goes two ways…*

Detective Ralph ends up testifying in court quite frequently. Most of these appearances are for "preliminary hearings". A preliminary hearing is held before a trial in a felony case to ascertain if there is enough probable cause (reason) for the defendant to be tried for the offense alleged by the police and district attorney's office. The preliminary hearing is kind of like a "mini trial".

In California, police officers with more than five years' experience are allowed to testify in preliminary hearings for other officers involved in a particular case. This officer testifies from the police reports the other officers wrote. This allows the courts to speed things up a bit without the need to drag a bunch of police officers into court.

Detective Ralph had a felony theft case assigned to him. He received a subpoena to show up in court for the preliminary hearing and he did so. Deputy District Attorney Paula was assigned to the case. She was a bulldog in court and extremely focused. Paula and Detective Ralph were work friends because they had so many cases together.

The defense attorney, Mr. Stevens, was from out of the county and unknown to everyone in court. He was from the big city and because of that very fact; he thought he was a higher life form then everyone else in the courtroom. Mr. Stevens proved to everyone in the courtroom just how superior he was.

Deputy District Attorney Paula called Detective Ralph to testify. He was sworn in by the court clerk and took a seat at the witness stand. Detective Ralph testified to the reports written by the patrol officers and himself. The defense then got a chance to ask questions of Detective Ralph.

Mr. Stevens started off,

"Now Detective Ralph, you say you've been working for the police department for over fifteen years?"

"Yes Sir."

"And approximately how many times have you testified in court?"

"Hundreds."

"Do you always tell the truth?"

"Yes."

At this point, Detective Ralph knows that Mr. Stevens is going to try and set him up to make him out to look like a liar. There are different ways of doing this, the most common is to try to confuse the witness and call their credibility into question. Mr. Stevens continued:

"You testified that on the day in question, the defendant was wearing blue jeans and a white shirt. Is that correct?

"Yes."

"Blue jeans and a white shirt?"

"Yes."

"Your honor, may I approach the witness?"

"You may."

Mr. Stevens walked up to the witness stand with a paper in his hand. He had a smug look on his face. D.A. Paula didn't know what Stevens was trying to pull. Detective Ralph was waiting to see what kind of crap Stevens was trying to drag him into. Stevens handed Detective Ralph a page from a police report.

"What I've just handed you is page five of the police report. In paragraph two, line one, please read that to the court."

Detective Ralph knew exactly what was going on and he was ready to play his part. He put on the best performance he could:

"Paragraph two, line one, the suspect was running westbound through the alley, he was wearing a blue sweatshirt and black pants."

Oh shit! It appeared that Detective Ralph was all screwed up and testified incorrectly. Everyone was staring at him. The suspect sitting at the defense table was smiling ear to ear in the hopes of being set free because of a police screw up. Stevens had that look on his face that said, *"I got you now bastard!"* District Attorney Paula didn't quite know what to do. The court reporter and court clerk were looking at Detective Ralph with that, *"You poor guy"* look. Stevens continued,

"Please read that again, louder, for the court to hear..."

"The suspect was running westbound through the alley, he was wearing a blue sweatshirt and black pants."

"And you testified earlier that the suspect was wearing blue jeans and a white shirt?"

Detective Ralph humbly answered,

"Yes Sir."

Detective Ralph had that worried look on his face like maybe his career was over. Stevens continued,

"So Detective Ralph, you lied in court today, didn't you?"

"No sir."

At this point, Stevens got loud and arrogant:

"Yes you did! You testified he was wearing different clothing. What else in that police report I handed you are you lying about?!"

At this point, it was Detective Ralph's turn. He took a moment for a breath. Everyone in the courtroom was waiting to see what possible saving grace comeback he could have. Detective Ralph took a long purposeful, pregnant pause. He bent forward, toward the witness stand microphone and in a voice just a bit louder than he usually used in court, he looked Stevens in the eye and slowly, methodically, stated,

333

"Mr. Stevens, I did not lie to you. Everything I have testified to here today is the truth."

"How can you say you truthfully testified when you don't even know what clothing the suspect was wearing?"

All eyes were on Detective Ralph. Everyone was wondering how he could possibly get so confused and ruin his career like he was doing...

"Mr. Stevens, the police report you handed me was a report of a different crime in another jurisdiction, involving officers, witnesses and suspects I've never heard of!"

Hey Stevens, you are a real bombastic dumb ass! You think you are a big city lawyer but you just made a big city fool out of yourself!

A look of astonishment and embarrassment came over Mr. Stevens' face. He was speechless just staring at the report in Detective Ralph's hands. Stevens walked over and grabbed the report from Detective Ralph's hand and took it back to the defense table. He compared it to some other papers on the table. Stevens' head was bent down as if he had just been beat. The courtroom was quiet. Almost everyone in the courtroom was happy that Mister Big City Attorney had just made an ass out of himself.

The judge asked in a mildly sarcastic tone,

"Anymore questions for this witness Mister Stevens?"

"No your honor, the defense rests."

"Good, we'll take a ten minute recess then."

The judge had to rush into chambers with the court clerk and reporter. They could barely contain their laughter. District Attorney Paula was chuckling to herself. She and Detective Ralph went out into the hallway:

"Ralph, that was fantastic. For a second I didn't know what was going on."

"For a second, I didn't either. As soon as I saw he handed me a report from a different agency, I knew he screwed up and I did everything I could to help him look like the foolish fool he is. I think I helped him quite a bit."

"Yes, sometimes it's better to keep your mouth shut in court!"

POLICE DEPARTMENT ANIMAL FARM

DAWN SHIFT BOREDOM

Dawn Shift has a period of time around 3:00 am when sometimes, there are no police calls for service; only crickets and frogs are out serenading the populace to sleep. This is the dawn shift "Dead Time" and it is oftentimes hard to stay awake. Yes, sometimes, *My Friend, Some Dude, and Some Guy* are out capering because they are on a methamphetamine high and can't sleep, but oftentimes, even they are holed up in their dirty filthy stinking apartment (or wherever they live) and they are not out in public. Crickets and frogs rule the night...

During the dead time of dawn shift, the patrol officers are trying to stay focused on staying awake. They think about work, their families, and friends. Things they like and dislike about work, life in general; anything to help stay awake.

Many years before this story took place, there was a scary train in the city and lions and monkeys that needed to be awakened. But that is now all ancient history. The old entertainment is gone forever.

But is it really? Does fun just leave all of a sudden? No, fun is in the heart. Fun is a mental attitude! If one has the proper attitude, FUN LIVES FOREVER!

OFFICER WILL

Officer Will had been on the department about five years. He was a good cop, very diligent. He grew up in the country, went to college and joined the service. After getting out of the service, he joined the big city police department. He loved police work, like many of his fellow officers. It wasn't just a job; it was a calling for him.

And then it happened one dawn shift at 3:30 am. Officer Will thought of a brilliant plan to help motivate his fellow officers to think about something fun to do instead of fighting sleep on dawn shift. It was bound to happen. No one could prevent it:

I'm going to pull a really good prank on the radio. Right now, nothing is happening. The police radio band is completely quiet. WE ALL NEED TO WAKE UP AND ENJOY DAWN SHIFT! Yes, we can make dawn shift enjoyable at least for a couple of minutes and bond together as one big happy dawn shift family! We're all screwed by working this shift but we have to come together! We must have fun!

If this works, we will all get motivated to the point of total awakeness, go down to the nearest coffee shop, refuel on coffee and go kick some dawn shift ass on My Friend, Some Dude, and Some Guy! Or, at least stay awake...

As previously mentioned, Officer Will grew up in the country, or suburbs of California. His parents were from the Midwest and since the family had a reasonable size piece of property, Officer Will's Mother wanted to raise chickens. Officer Will had a brother and the two of them raised a flock of twenty Rhode Island Red hens while they were growing up. Their chickens were prize winners in their neighborhood and Will's Mother got high neighbor points for giving them giant brown farm raised chicken eggs.

Officer Will's chickens were spoiled, free range, anti- hormone, organic, beautiful egg laying machines. Officer Will and his brother spent so much time with their chickens that they could talk to them in chicken language and the chickens would talk back!

Now, years later, Officer Will is going to use his chicken as a second language to help motivate his dawn shift crew.

Yes, now's the time, we have to do this!

It was 3:30 am. Everything was quiet on dawn shift. The radio was silent. Officer Will was a little bit scared but he told himself:

THOU SHALT HAVE FUN!

Officer Will let it go over the police radio:

"Praaaaaaack-praaaack-praaaack-praaack-praaaack!

**PRAAAACK-PRAAAAAK-PRAAAAK   -
PRAAAAAAAACK!"**

*There, I've done it. Let's see what happens.
Maybe my brothers and sisters on duty will
shine me on, maybe not... I did it for our own
good. Let's see what happens...*

A couple of mikes clicked and then it came:

"BBBBBBaaaaaaaaaaaaaaaaaaa!
BBBBBBaaaaaaaaaaaaaaaaaaa!"

*Good, we've at least we've got the dawn shift
sheep talking to us!*

And then:

"MOOOOOOOOOOHHHHHH,
MOOOOOOOOOOHHHHHH!!!"

The dawn shift cow is with us too!

And then the radio broke open: the dawn shift
pig snorted, the dawn shift duck quacked, the dawn
shift horse whinnied, the dawn shift cat meowed, the
dawn shift elephant trumpeted and then the dawn
shift guard dog began barking in approval . It was
one big beautiful dawn shift Animal Farm!

We're Alive! We're Awake! We're having fun!

All dawn shift family members were talking to
one another in one big happy Dawn Shift Animal
Farm Family Reunion! Who could ask for more fun?

339

The fun continued for at least three minutes because many of the dawn shift animals were having such a good time! Officer Will was so happy his family was spending quality dawn shift time together! What a beautiful dawn shift!

Back at headquarters, the watch commander, Captain Brake, couldn't stand it:

How could grown adults act in such a fashion? And they're cops! We have to be professional at all times! The FCC is going to fine us for illegal use of the police radio band and it's on my watch!

I've got some news for you Captain Brake; the FCC doesn't give a shit about us having a little bit of dawn shift camaraderie over the radio. They are sleeping nice and tight in their beds like normal people. And, if they do have a recording of the Police Department Animal Farm communications, they will probably just laugh their asses off because whether you like it or not, it is funnier than hell!

Every night when the dawn shift was quiet at 3:30 am, the dawn shift animal farm animals spoke to one another; it was a nightly activity and everyone working the dawn shift looked forward to speaking with their fellow officers in their special animal languages that helped them stay awake and entertain themselves.

Captain Brake couldn't stand it. He didn't really have any friends. He was not a "people

340

person". His officers would have felt sorry for him except he was always trying to find fault with them; he thought it was his duty to reprimand the troops instead of commending them. Such is life, some people are that way.

Go screw yourself Captain Brake, no Christmas card for you!

After about five dawn shifts of Dawn Shift Animal Farm reunions over the radio, Captain Brake had had enough. He attended a dawn shift briefing before the officers went out on patrol. Normally the briefings are only held by the patrol sergeant (who was thoroughly amused by the Dawn Shift Animal Farm reunions).

The dawn shift sergeant gave his briefing and then Captain Brake interjected:

"There's been a lot of barnyard talk on the radio and it's not acceptable. We know who some of you are that are doing it and if it doesn't stop there is going to be some discipline handed out. It's not professional."

While saying this, Captain Brake looked at several officers at the briefing with a suspicious eye. One of those officers was Officer Will. Will knew he was a prime suspect because, he was Suspect Number One and totally guilty!

After Captain Brake finished chastising the patrol officers, Officer Will thought:

Now is the time to really have some fun with Captain Brake:

With a most genuine and serious tone, Will stated,

"Captain, I'm glad you are finally down here at briefing and bringing this subject up. I for one am embarrassed at whoever is doing all of this unprofessional barnyard talk because it brings discredit upon all of us. It's not professional. I hope it finally stops!"

Officer Will's fellow officers were biting their tongues.

Will is such a smartass and he may have just gotten himself off the suspect list!

Captain Brake looked at Officer Will with a look that said, *"Oh, you're not one of my suspects".* Officer Will's friends knew exactly what Officer Will was doing, shifting the blame and acting innocent.

After dawn shift briefing, all the officers went out into the police department parking lot to check out their patrol units. In the parking lot, Officer Will spoke to a couple of his buddies that were also members of the Dawn Shift Animal Farm Conspiracy:

"Did you hear that shit from Captain Brake?"

"Yeah, we did."

"You know what we have to do, right?"

"Yup, give it to him extra hard tonight."

"O.K., when the magical hour arrives, I'll see you at the animal farm!"

That dawn shift, when 3:30 am arrived, the dawn shift animal farm erupted into a five-minute chorus of animal talk. All the animals had extra comments to give to one another. All of the animals knew that it was driving Captain Brake crazy and they just had to chat a bit longer on the radio.

It was later learned from the dispatchers at the station that Captain Brake almost lost it mentally, he just couldn't stand the fun his officers were having. He should have just relaxed, enjoyed the dawn shift animal farm talk over the radio and eaten some fresh organic, free range eggs for breakfast!

Sorry Captain Brake but we're going to have fun whether you like it or not!

"Praaaaaaack-praaaack-praaaack-praaack!

PRAAAACK-PRAAAAAK-PRAAAAK - PRAAAAAAAACK!"

DOGSHIT SEARCH WARRANTS

Detective Dan and Detective Pierce had been working in the detective bureau a couple of years. Prior to that, the two really didn't know each other. They worked on different detective teams but became quick friends because both of them liked to joke around, tell stories, drink coffee, and generally have fun at work, if they could.

One night, the friendship between the two was cemented. Pierce had to stay at work a little late and was getting ready to leave. Dan was feverishly working on a case and was stressed out to the max.

Pierce asked Dan,

"Hey what's got you all stressed out?"

"I've got two in custody (two suspects to process), reports up the ass and an evidence report that will take me all night to write."

"Where in the hell are the rest of your team members? They should be helping you out."

"They didn't want to stay and help out"

Dan was pissed…

"That's bullshit, how much evidence do you have to process?"

"A bunch, I've got boxes of it, I'll be up all night with this shit!"

"OK, if I process all your evidence, will that take a load off of you?"

"You don't have to; you're not even on my team."

"Give me the evidence. I'll book it all into property for you."

"You will?"

"On one condition, we get to have a coffee break before diving in."

"You got it partner."

After their coffee break, Pierce took all of Dan's evidence, photographed it, labeled it, documented it on an evidence report and booked it into evidence, taking a big stress off Dan. All the work took about a third of the time if Dan had been working alone. So, Pierce saved Dan's ass and Dan never forgot it.

Dan and Pierce became close brothers; their kids played on the same sports teams and they frequently socialized off duty. They were best friends. Life was good.

Dan was a very diligent detective and ended up writing his fair share of search warrants for the homes of his burglary suspects. Serving search warrants requires multiple officers for safety and searching. Dan always asked Pierce to help on his search warrants. Pierce was happy to oblige.

DOGSHIT IN THE BOOT TREADS

Dan's detective team mates always helped out on his search warrants. Because they were his teammates, they were put on the entry team. This meant they went in the front door of the house to be searched. Everyone else on the search warrant team was positioned on the perimeter: they watched the sides and backyard of the house while the entry team went in the front door.

On the first search warrant Pierce helped Dan with; Pierce was assigned to the backyard team. Pierce didn't care that much that he didn't get to be on the entry team. Sometimes it was the officers in the backyard that saw the action because someone would take foot bail out the back of the house and the backyard officers would get to screw their B.F.G.'s into the suspect's face and prone their ass out!

The personnel in the backyard are sometimes required to move around a lot to keep a good eye on the back of the house and maybe also a side window or two. It helps to be quick on your feet. Pierce performed this function quite well. To ensure he always had good traction with the ground, he wore military combat boots with big lug soles. Many of the backyards at the search warrant locations had overgrown grass and trash lying around. Some crooks just don't care what their backyards looks like.

So, on the first search warrant Pierce helped out on, the entry team knocked down the front door of the house and made entry. While this is going on, Pierce was in the backyard with another officer,

B.F.G.'s drawn, and the two are moving from side to side on the backyard lawn, keeping a good eye on the back of the house. Someone from the entry team came out the back-sliding door and announced the house was secure and ready to be searched.

At this point, all the officers on the perimeter will search the back and side yards and then go inside the house to search there too.

Detective Pierce stepped off the lawn and onto the rear patio of the house to help out with the searching. He discovered, he can't go into the house quite yet because he stepped in a big pile of dogshit and it is all over the sole of his left boot. And, it stinks a lot, like fresh dogshit. There isn't any dog around, but Detective Pierce has dogshit stuck in his boot treads.

Detective Pierce was kind of a dogshit expert. He grew up with a large German Shepherd and knows what dogshit is. Pierce also knows, due to his training and experience that the dogshit he stepped in was less than a day old and it stinks to high heaven.

So, Pierce was pissed because he stepped in dogshit and had to clean it off his boot before he could go into the house to help conduct the search. Detective Dan came outside and stated,

"Hey, I got a search assignment for ya."

"That's great Dan, I'll be right there after I get the fucking dogshit off my boot!"

Pierce lifted his left boot so Dan could see the bottom was covered with dogshit.

Dan started laughing. He thought it was funny,

"Well, at least you didn't get it on both boots!'

"Fuck you! I'll be in as soon as I clean off my boot."

Note: Dan and Pierce are good friends, they are always telling one another to "fuck off." It's common language for the two and foul language doesn't hurt their friendship, it just makes it stronger.

Pierce found a hose and rinsed off his boot. He got a stick and cleaned out all the boot treads. After a second rinsing, he went into the house to help out with the searching.

DÉJÀ VU

About a month later, Dan had another search warrant to serve:

"Hey buddy, I've got to search another house tomorrow, different case, can you help me out?"

"Yeah, but there better not be any dogshit in the backyard like last time!"

"Hey Bro, you know I don't have any control over that. I need somebody reliable in the backyard again."

348

"I'm your man."

The next day the search warrant was served. The entry team barreled through the front door of the house. Pierce was doing his usual thing on the lawn in the backyard and saw a suspect coming out a back window. Pierce got on his portable radio and told the troops he's got one adult rabbit taking foot bail. For some reason, our little escapee doesn't see Pierce and almost ran into him. Detective Pierce promptly threw him on the ground and screwed his BFG into the guys back and cuffed him.

Pierce was joined by two other perimeter officers. He stayed on top of his little track star until the interior of the house was secure.

Dan exited the house through the rear sliding door and walked up to Pierce and his arrestee. Dan looked at the arrestee and the sarcasm started:

"Joey! What the heck are you doing man? Always trying to run away from me. Dude, I thought we were good friends! I'm very disappointed Joey, it seems like our friendship doesn't mean anything to you..."

Dan had another officer take Joey back inside the house.

"Good job Pierce, I knew I could count on you!"

"At least I got to have some fun and meet one of your close friends!"

349

The two laughed. Dan continued:

"Well, let's get into the house and start searching so we can get the heck out of here before lunch."

Dan led. He and Pierce started walking towards the house. As soon as Pierce stepped onto the rear patio, he felt it: DOGSHIT ON THE BOOTS AGAIN!

"Oh shit! I've got fucking dogshit on my boot again! Damn your search warrants Dan; all of them are dogshit search warrants, this sucks!"

Dan just has to be a smart ass and screw with his friend,

"Well, at least it's on your right boot this time, last time it was on your left boot."

"Dan?"

"What?"

"Fuck you again! I'll be in after the usual hosing off of the dogshit ceremony has concluded!"

Later, back at the station, Pierce was telling the entire detective bureau that all of Dan's search warrants are in "dogshit country" and be prepared for the worse.

ENTRY TEAM HERE I COME!

A couple of months later, Dan had another search warrant planned and he approached Pierce to help out:

"Hey Bro, can you help me out on another search warrant? I've got you on the entry team and your dogshit days are through!"

"Finally, a promotion for having spent my time in dogshit hell!"

"Yup, no more backyard dogshit for you my man!"

Pierce was glad to be on the entry team; he wouldn't miss having to clean any more dogshit off his boots. Being on the entry team is also a big adrenaline rush because it is dangerous. One never knows what they will engage on the other side of the front door.

On the day the search warrant was served, Pierce and three other detectives hit the front door, slapped the cuffs on a couple of suspects and secured the house in less than two minutes.

That wasn't bad at all. Nice clean entry, no foot bail, two subjects hand cuffed, and best of all, NO DOGSHIT ON THE BOOTS! This is going to be a good search warrant day!

Things are going great. Detective Dan made assignments for the rooms to be searched. Detective

Pierce was assigned one of the bedrooms and he started searching it. The room was untidy but somewhat clean; Pierce had seen worse. Some houses are so dirty you feel like you need a shower as soon as you set foot inside them. This one didn't appear too dirty.

Pierce started searching the bed area first: he searched under the bed, the mattresses and then the bedding. The bedspread was oversize and flowed over the sides of the bed so you couldn't see the floor area near the bed, Pierce walked over to one side of the bed and felt something soft underneath his boot. He lifted up the bedspread:

> *I stepped in fucking dogshit! They have dogshit on the floor in the fucking bedroom! I'm on the entry team. The entry team doesn't step in dogshit! What the fuck is this shit? Every time I go on one of Dan's fucking search warrants I step in dogshit! I'll bet if I was assigned to search the fucking attic, I'd step in dogshit up there too! I can't believe this shit!*

"FUCK!"

Dan heard Pierce and walked into the bedroom.

"What's wrong Bro?"

"Look."

Dan busted up laughing, he couldn't help himself. His best friend, who temporarily hates him, stepped in dogshit for the third time in a row. Nobody is going to forget this.

"Stop laughing fucker, it isn't funny."

Dan, talking and laughing at the same time:

"Oh yes it is, I can't believe this. Hey, everybody, Pierce stepped in dog shit again!"

"YOU FUCKING RAT!"

The whole search warrant team filed into the bedroom one at a time, to pay their disrespect:

"At least you're not up shit creek…"

"It's O.K. Bro, it'll wash right off, ha-ha.",

"Bro, it's a dirty job but somebody has to do it.",

"Hey, could be worse, could be elephant shit."

"Look at it this way, Pierce, you really know your shit!"

"It's alright Pierce, shit happens."

And on and on the comments went. When they were all finished, Pierce asked them a question in a very calm voice:

"Hey guys could you do me a small favor?"

"Yeah, what is it?'

"Could all of you please go outside for a moment and play a game of hide and go fuck yourselves? I'd really appreciate it"

There was no reply. The search warrant team deserved the remark and they just laughed it off.

From that day forward, Detective Pierce was known as the Dogshit Search Warrant Detective because of his vast experience. Detective Pierce was often consulted on various search warrant locations because of his dogshit expertise. He would always provide the Dog Shit Probability Factor for new detectives and their search warrants because, he had his shit together!

Detective Pierce even made a new unauthorized police report form entitled the "DOGSHIT ACTIVITY REPORT", or, "D.A.R." for short.

Detectives Dan and Pierce are now retired but still best friends. Dan still brings up the dogshit search warrants every time they see each other. That's because Dan is still a smartass.

Pierce still tells him to "Fuck Off!"

THE DIFFERENCE BETWEEN POLICE OFFICERS, DEPUTY SHERIFF'S, STATE POLICE AND OTHER LAW ENFORCEMENT OFFICERS/AGENTS

It's time for some more classroom training. Many people wonder what the difference is between Police Officers, Sheriff's Deputies, State Police, and other law enforcement officers/agents.

Law enforcement agencies exist at the federal, state, and local (County and City) levels.

Let's take a look at how a state is divided into local governments. We will use California as an example:

California has 58 counties. Each County is responsible for its own law enforcement. The County Law Enforcement Office entity is known as the Sheriff's Office (Department). Each County Sheriff's Department is responsible for enforcing the law and keeping the peace in the unincorporated area of the County. The Sheriff's Department is also responsible for operating a county jail to house, *"My Friend, Some Dude, and Some Guy."*

An "incorporated" area of the County is a "City". When a group of citizens come together to control a specific geographical area within a county, they can "incorporate" and form a city. This gives the city residents more control over their community desires. When a city is born, they are now responsible for their own fire and police protection;

355

they have to form their own fire department and police department (and many more services too). For an example, let's look at the County of Los Angeles and the City of Glendale:

Los Angeles is one of the 58 counties in California. Within the boundaries of Los Angeles County, is a city known as the City of Glendale. Police services within the county are provided by the Los Angeles County Sheriff's Department. The Glendale Police Department provides police services within the boundaries of the City of Glendale.

Some states have parishes or townships instead of counties. Some counties in the country call their County Law Enforcement Officers, "County Police." Some jurisdictions have "Constables" which may or may not have the same powers as Police Officers and Deputy Sheriff's.

Los Angeles County contains 88 cities, 42 of these cities contract with the Los County Sheriff's Department for police services to save money because the Sheriff's Department has a vast infrastructure. What this means is that a city like Malibu, California saves money by not having to establish its own Police Department. So, if you are driving through the city of Malibu, California, you may see a Sheriff's car labeled, "SHERIFF – PROUDLY SERVING MALIBU" or something close to that.

The Los Angeles Sheriff's Department is the largest Sheriff's Department in the United States with over 18,000 employees. They provide services for over 153 communities, 300 county facilities, 177 county parks, the Los Angeles Transportation Authority, city rail lines, ten community colleges, golf courses, and 16 hospitals.

So, Counties have Sheriff's Departments and Cities have Police Departments. Police Officers and Deputy Sheriffs are both empowered by the State of California.

At the state level, many states have a "State Police" and/or "Highway Patrol". Usually the Highway Patrol does just that, they patrol state highways and freeways. They help you when you are stranded, take an accident report when you crash, and give you a ticket when you get caught going too much over the speed limit. Some states not only have a "Highway Patrol" but may have a "State Police" instead that may provide highway enforcement, various forensic services, investigative or security functions.

State governments usually have a "Department of Justice" (or some other name) with investigative, support, and enforcement units for narcotic enforcement, firearms, gambling, forensic services (C.S.I.), Native American Affairs Unit, criminal intelligence unit, victim services unit, and various fraud units, etc. Most of these officers at the state level are known as "Agents". Besides the Department of Justice, a state may have other units with law enforcement powers like a fish and wildlife department.

Originally, Police and Sheriff's Officers were designated as "Peace Officers" because they are supposed to keep the peace, i.e. – Break up family fights, remove drunks from bars, etc. They are still referred to as peace officers. Agents at the state level are also defined by law as "Peace Officers" but their duties usually do not include keeping the peace in your community. They are specialized units to enforce the law, i.e. – combat the scourge of drugs, take guns away from bad guys, keep gambling under control, etc. State Agents usually don't engage in breaking up bar fights.

WHAT ABOUT MARSHAL DILLON?

Town Marshals, in the old days, basically performed the same duties as a town Sheriff. There are still Marshals in some jurisdictions.

Marshals at the County level may be involved in courtroom security (bailiffs), serving subpoenas, levies against property, warrant service, and evictions.

At least one State, Connecticut, still has State Marshals for certain civil processes.

On the Federal Level, there is the U.S. Marshals Service. It is the oldest federal law enforcement agency and has existed since 1789. The agency consists of approximately 3,752 Deputy Marshals and Criminal Investigators. Their duties include protection of federal judges, operating a witness protection/security program, transportation of federal prisoners, and the apprehension of federal fugitives.

Other duties include asset forfeiture and maintaining a Special Operations Group for responding to emergency situations.

There are numerous law enforcement agencies at the federal level that mirror and surpass the ones at the state level. Most enforcement officers at the federal level hold the title of "Agent" and also will not normally engage in breaking up bar fights and keeping the peace in your community; not their job.

The most well-known federal law enforcement agencies are the Federal Bureau of Investigation (F.B.I.) the Drug Enforcement Agency (D.E.A.), and the Bureau of Alcohol, Tobacco, and Firearms (B.A.T.F. or A.T.F.). Their job is to enforce laws at the federal level. They also will not show up to help break up the bar fights in your town. They deal with violations of federal law.

The F.B.I. has over 13,000 agents and 20,000 support personnel. The F.B.I.'s forensic laboratory is considered the biggest and best of all crime labs in the world. It is located at Quantico, Virginia.

The D.E.A. has over 5,000 agents. They investigate federal drug violations, violent drug gangs, and seize assets from violators. Like the F.B.I., the D.E.A. will not show up to break up the bar fights in your town. They do get to dress in plainclothes and look cool though.

The A.T.F. investigates illegal trafficking of alcohol and tobacco products, firearms/explosives violations, and arsons/bombings. The ATF employs over 5,000 personnel which include approximately 2,600 agents.

As of 2018, there were more than 700,000 law enforcement officers in the United States.

All of the agencies listed above can join forces and form a "Task Force", for say, drug smuggling, money laundering, catch a serial killer, catch a kidnapper, or any other reason.

Hopefully you now have a better understanding of the differences between the various law enforcement agencies in the United States. Remember, there is always an exception to the rule so you may live in an area where some of the above information does not apply.

THE GREAT CHICKEN MASSACRE

In many areas of the United States there are communities bordering cities that are part of the city but have a country feel to them because they are zoned differently from the rest of the inner city. These are areas that are in effect "country" but within the "city limits".

Bordering one such city is a housing tract that was designated as a "Ranch Community". These communities usually feature ranch style homes on approximately one acre of land (a nice big lot) and if you buy there, you won't be sorry. You can board your horse (we discussed the horse cult earlier in this book) and have many other farm animals you desire as long as your animals don't disturb the neighbors.

The community features wide streets and instead of sidewalks, a horse trail. Yes, a beautiful trail to ride your horse on. Bicycles and pedestrians have to yield the right of way to horses on these trails. Not too much to ask for.

Regardless of whether one lives in the country, the city, or in a ranch community, one is responsible for one's animals. There is something called a "leash law". That law basically states that one has to keep a "leash" on one's animals. That means that one's animals are not allowed to go roaming on other people's properties. The only exception to this law is cats because they are so independent, they don't listen to anybody unless you have food. Yes, cats get a pass on the law, no one can control cats.

OFFICER DARIO

Officer Dario has been on the Police Department for only two years. He's not yet a "veteran" but he has handled a lot of calls and has a solid footing for taking care of problems. Sometimes he gets calls to go kick some serious ass. But once in a while he gets a call requiring some special peace keeping skills, a call where everyone wants to kill each other but they need some guidance in homicide prevention. Officer Dario tries to handle calls as if his family and friends were involved:

My family and community need protecting. I'm working this job because I want to be of service to my community. That's what I signed up to do. That's what I'm going to do. If I need to kick the shit out of some scumbag, I will. If I need to just keep the peace, I'll do that.

Officer Dario received a call of a neighborhood dispute: Neighbor's dogs killed neighbor's chickens.

What? Dogs killing chickens? How about a call of Some Guy, My Friend, or Some Dude robbing a bank or burglarizing a home or something really big? I don't want to deal with dogs and chickens!

CHICKENS AND DOGS IN THE UNITED STATES

There are almost 395 million chickens in the United States. The dog population in the U.S is approximately 77 million; add to that approximately 300,000 coyotes and 18,000 wolves, that brings the number up to 77,318,000 canines that are prone to eating chicken for dinner. For you cat lovers out there, the population of American cats is approximately 58 million.

CHICKEN PEOPLE

The chicken people immigrated to the United States from a northern European country known for order and discipline. They were very good citizens and loved their new country. They were overjoyed when they bought their retirement dream home in the ranch community. They basically kept to themselves and enjoyed a quiet retired lifestyle. America is good!

Chicken People have only chickens. No horses, dogs, cats or any other animals, only chickens. They love their chickens, they are egg laying machines! One Saturday afternoon, their prize winning hens were foraging for insects in their front yard; as long as their chickens stay on their own property, there is no leash law violation, no problem, their chickens stayed on their property. Even if the chickens strayed onto someone else's property, no one would probably care. Chickens are generally clean up artists eating bugs and seeds to make themselves happy.

DOG PEOPLE

Across the street from the Chicken People are the Dog People. The Dog People consisted of middle-aged Mrs. and Mrs. Dog and two children, a daughter and a son. They are third generation Americans and their ancestors emigrated from Italy.

The Dog People were very family oriented, living the good life in the ranch community. Dog People owned a horse, which is properly corralled, and two big beautiful pure-bred adult Akita dogs which are contained in their yard by a four foot high fence.

Chicken People and Dog People didn't know each other. They basically stayed to themselves.

On the day in question, the full-grown Akita "puppies" saw the big beautiful birds foraging across the street; they jumped their short fence and gave chase to the lovely chickens. The end result was: three killed, two wounded, and several others traumatized for the rest of their adult chicken life. It was a nasty scene, feathers, and such everywhere...

The Chicken People saw the attack of the evil Akitas and sprang into action, they were livid that their beautiful babies were attacked. With much yelling and commotion, the Chicken People were able to lock up the evil Akitas in their front courtyard. The chicken killing Akita dogs were imprisoned behind wrought iron gates and padlocked in!

The Dog People heard yelling and screaming coming from across the street. The neighbors were yelling at their "little puppies" and doing something terrible to them!

How dare you lock up our precious little puppies!

Mr. Dog saw that the neighbors across the street were yelling and screaming at his dogs and the neighbors were locking his dogs up for no reason. Mr. Dog had no idea what his little puppies had done; he just thought the neighbors were mistreating his animals. He called for his teenage son to help him and the two of them ran across the street to rescue the dogs.

When Mr. Dog got to his neighbors front courtyard, he was getting yelled at by Mrs. Chicken. He couldn't understand what she was yelling about except that she was really pissed. Mr. Dog said he wanted his dogs back and he only got yelled at more.

EVERYBODY IS PISSED!

"My chickens are dead! I hate your dogs!"

"I want my dogs! Give them to me now!"

Mr. and Mrs. Chicken aren't using their words effectively to explain the situation to Mr. Dog. Mr. Dog thinks his puppies have been hijacked. Mr. Dog tells his son to go back home and get a hacksaw.

Really, you think you can kidnap my dogs? I will saw your house down!

Dog Son returned with a hack saw and Mr. Dog started sawing away at the gate which held his puppies captive. Mr. Chicken grabbed a garden hose and started hosing down Mr. Dog. Mr. Dog then took his hacksaw and lashed out with it and scraped Mr. Chicken's forearm with the hacksaw blade. There you have it: assault. It could be stretched into "Assault with a Deadly Weapon", a felony crime.

That's all the Chicken People needed to call the cops. Officer Dario received the call of THE GREAT CHICKEN MASSACRE.

It's 1:00 o'clock in the afternoon on a Saturday and nothing of this sort is supposed to happen.

Saturdays are supposed to be quiet, you know, a weekend day of rest and all that. Maybe some work around the house, nice dinner afterwards. But no, we're going to have a clash of cultures that don't want to communicate with one another. Really? Who gets a call with The Chicken People and the Dog People? Is this a joke? I'm supposed to be chasing "My Friend, Some Dude, and Some Guy!"

The whole ordeal was a shit story, but taught Officer Dario some valuable lessons in how to handle people and resolve their problems without beating the shit out of everyone. He can't beat the shit out of anybody unless they are extremely out of control. The chicken and dog people are supposedly good members of society, pay taxes and live in a good neighborhood. They are *Normal People.*

Officer Dario arrived at the chicken house with his big "posse box" (an oversized metal clipboard which contains reports and notepads). He just had a feeling he was going to have to take a very long report which he does not want to write. He'd rather be out chasing *"My Friend, Some Dude, and Some Guy!"*

The Chicken People's home was immaculate, super clean. Mrs. Chicken jumped into a tirade of vengeful hate against the Dog People. She told Officer Dario how the evil Akitas killed, wounded, and traumatized her beloved hens. She had to get a lot of shit off her chest and thank God the Police Department sent over a therapist: Officer Dario.

Dario listened to the long tirade. Mr. Chicken had a look on his face that said,

Yup, that's the way it happened and if you don't interrupt her, we'll both be better for it.

Dario knew that Mrs. Chicken needed to expel her hatred and be done with it. She kept yelling at Officer Dario as if the whole ordeal was his fault. He just let her vent.

Here we go again: some upstanding citizen has been harmed by an evil event and they are taking it out on me. If Mrs. Chicken was a dirtball I'd just tell he to shut the "F" up! But no, I have to let her vent and finish her tirade.

Dario asked Mrs. Chicken if she had anything else to add. She reiterated her hatred for Dog People. Officer Dario said he understood and explained that if he was to take a report, he needed to concentrate and she had to calm down so he could write his report. Mrs. Chicken was quiet most of the time; every once in a while, when Officer Dario would ask a question to complete his report, Mrs. Chicken would spew off with more dog hatred. At these moments, Officer Dario would stop writing and just wait for Mrs. Chicken to finish her tirade. Dario sat at the chicken people's dinette table and wrote and wrote and wrote, all the time wishing he had never been sent to this call.

Dario finished the report of the Great Chicken Massacre. He explained to the Chicken People he was going across the street to interview Mr. Dog about his involvement. Mrs. Chicken was ecstatic. Finally, the dirty Dog lovers would pay!

Mrs. Chicken was pissed, and she wanted Mr. Dog's head on a platter!

Officer Dario empathized with Mrs. Chicken. Dario's family had raised chickens and also a big mean guard dog. He knew the propensity for dogs to sometimes go on a killing spree. It looked like the Dog People were screwed on this one because of the leash law violation. He also knew that there would be no happy resolution until after everybody calms down and releases their anger.

We'll just have to go over to the Dog People's home and get their side of the story...

Officer Dario walked across the street to the Dog People's Home. Mrs. Dog answered the door and invited him inside.

Mrs. Dog explained that her husband had an "unexpected, 'emergency', golf game" and was unavailable to be interviewed as part of the GREAT CHICKEN MASSACRE.

I kinda don't blame him. He screwed up just a little bit. Hope he has a nice game of golf...He's probably screwing up the back nine, worried he's headed for jail or something like that. I'm sure his golfing buddies are counselling him as we speak. Hope the Nineteenth hole is good!

THE TRAP

At this point in time, Officer Dario is now inside the Dog Family's home and is having a really big problem: he can't concentrate! Mrs. Dog is cooking homemade spaghetti sauce and the delicious aroma fills her home; it smells so felony delicious it reminds him of one of his favorite childhood memories: his Mother cooking homemade spaghetti sauce and garlic bread with all the garlic and oregano aromas filling the home while his older sisters practiced their accordion and piano by playing beautiful Italian pieces. There is accordion music in the dog home but it is coming from the radio. Mrs. Dog has set a trap for Officer Dario!

They planned this...Homemade spaghetti sauce, garlic, oregano, homemade garlic bread, beautiful Italian accordion music, next thing you know, she's going to try to shove a glass of wine into my hands. What more would anyone want?

Am I in the Twilight Zone? What the hell is happening? This is an Italian trap to throw me off guard! The Dog People are supposed to be terrible people and they are taking me back to

369

one of my favorite childhood memories of all time, and, I'm hungrier than shit! This is not fair! The dog home feels warm and cozy... I have to be professional...

Got Wine?

Mrs. Dog:

"Officer, I understand that something bad happened and I don't know what to think. Everyone is so upset."

"I need to talk to your husband, can you call him on the phone so I can talk to him?

Mrs. Dog dialed her husband and handed the phone to Officer Dario:

"Officer, you wanted to talk to me?"

"Yes sir, we need to talk about what happened today."

"Things got out of hand, I lost my cool. Can we talk about this tomorrow? I'm trying to cool down. Do you think you can work something out?'

Yeah, you're probably going to need a whole night to calm your hot headed Italian ass down...

"Right now, Mrs. Chicken wants to kill you, so, I'll come back tomorrow and we'll talk about it and see what we can do. Just stay away from each other."

"Thanks, I really appreciate it and I'm sorry about this."

"We'll try to handle it tomorrow. Sleep on it."

Yeah, Mr. Dog is going to get a whole bunch of solid sleep tonight, thinking about how he screwed up with that hacksaw move of his...

Officer Dario told Mrs. Dog,

"Thank you Ma'am, I'll come back tomorrow morning, first thing on my shift and we'll see what we can do"

"Would you like to stay for dinner?"

Really? Stay for dinner? I could get fired for that! The Chicken People would hate me and know something was up. No, you Italians are trying to trick me into a glass of wine, then two, then a delicious homemade spaghetti dinner. Afterwards, we have more wine and talk about the good 'ole days and all that.

God, the garlic and oregano aromas are killing me. I have to get outta here. Is my Mother hiding in your home? If she's here, I'll stay. I only trust her right now. If my Mother isn't here, I can't stay. I won't fall for your delicious Italian Goodness! I'm stronger than that! I've been through the police academy and they trained us not to take bribes!

At least somebody in this equation is treating me nice for a change. I like the Dog People's home a lot more than the Chicken People's.

Got Wine?

"I would love to but I can't. You sent me back to many a fond memory and it is torture. We'll try to work this out tomorrow. Because of what I have been told today about the events that transpired, I could arrest your husband, but, something tells me not to. I'll be back tomorrow."

"Thank you Officer."

"You're welcome, see you tomorrow."

And thanks a lot for torturing me with the home full of delicious spaghetti sauce and garlic bread aromas. You tried to bribe me didn't you? That's against the law and you could go to jail for that!

Got wine?

It was the end of Dario's shift and as he drove back to the station. He thought about family, good wine, homemade spaghetti, good wine, Italian music, good wine, family again, good wine, all the good things in life, and more good wine. He was hungry and the more he thought about the dinner he could have had, the more his stomach growled.

I never thought I'd get tortured like this on duty; I should have had backup!

DAY TWO OF CHICKENS AND DOGS

The next day Officer Dario went back over to the Dog Home to interview Mr. Dog. The faint aroma of delicious spaghetti sauce and garlic bread was still in the air but not that strong and Dario, thank God, wasn't hungry. He's glad he's not hungry and has had professional training to withstand Italian bribery!

Officer Dario finally got to meet Mr. Dog after the "emergency golf game" the day before.

Mr. Dog was just an average middle class American business man with an Italian background; a background that occasionally reared its Italian temper when he was crossed.

"Officer, I lost my cool and I know I got a problem with this."

"Technically, you could be arrested right now for a felony, assault with a deadly weapon, the hacksaw."

"I want to fully apologize. Would you please ask them to let me apologize and pay for all damages?"

"I'll go over and talk to them but the wife really hates you."

"I know, but please ask them."

Officer Dario went over to the Chicken People's home:

"Mr. Dog is very sorry for what he has done and wants to make it right. He is very sorry and wants to make amends.

Mrs. Chicken, yelling:

"I don't care! He's terrible and should never have acted that way! His dogs killed our chickens!"

"I agree, and so does he. What I will do then is file for a warrant for him to be prosecuted and he will receive a notice in the mail to appear in court. Is that alright with you?"

Officer Dario didn't want to arrest Mr. Dog if he didn't have to, it just didn't seem like the right thing to do. The Dog People were really good folks...

"Yes it is."

Officer Dario walked back across the street to tell Mr. Dog the bad news. He told Mr. Dog that Mrs. Chicken was prosecuting him and he would be contacted by the District Attorney's Office at a later date.

Dario left the Dog House and walked back to his car; he was approached by Mr. Chicken, who up to this point did not have much say so in the matter:

"Officer, we would like to talk to you inside if you don't mind."

Officer Dario went back into the Chicken People's home.

This shit never ends! Freaking neighbor disputes! Over to the Dog House, then over to the Chicken House, then back over to the freakin' Dog House. These neighbor disputes suck! Chicken and Dog madness!

Mr. Chicken:

"We talked about it and decided that it would be best for all of us, if he apologized and paid for all the damages, we will not prosecute him."

"I spoke with him. He's a good man and just got hot headed, he is ready to apologize and wants to make everything right and he is sorry for the injured chickens and willing to pay for all damages."

Mrs. Chicken, yelling once again:

"He should be! Those were our best chickens!"

"I told him that."

"If he makes a full apology and pays for all damages, we will forgive him. But, he must make a *full apology!*"

Officer Dario knew that a *"full apology"* to Mrs. Chicken will entail Mr. Dog groveling at and kissing her feet, apologizing over and over again until she feels totally vindicated and superior to Mr. Dog.

But, so be it...

Better than getting charged with being a hot-headed Italian and going to jail!

Up to this point, Officer Dario had already written twelve pages of reports on The Great Chicken Massacre. Normally it would seem like a waste of time to write that much and not take somebody to jail. But, this was an unusual situation:

Why screw up somebody's life over one bad incident? Especially when everyone agrees? If we can correct this without the courts, we can make everybody happy and save the system a lot of time and money in the end.

The trick is going to be pulling it off so that nobody pulls back on the agreement. We've got a very head strong Northern European and a hot headed Italian. Let's try to get a little peace in the neighborhood if we can...

Dario went back over to the Dog People's home:

"What happened?'

"Well, you won't believe this, but they are willing to accept your apology and restitution."

"Really?"

"Yes, but we're going to have to practice your apology."

"What do you mean?"

"May I speak frankly?"

"Yeah, go ahead."

"She's going to rip you a new asshole and you're not going to be able to contain your hot-headed Italian self. I know it."

Mr. Dog looked a little embarrassed and pissed at the same time.

"Put your pride away because she is holding all the cards right now and you could go to jail. I know you can't afford that. There's no golfing in jail and the food really sucks. You have to do this and I can help you but you have to practice your apology before going over there."

"You're right, okay, go ahead."

"I'm Mrs. Chicken, go ahead and apologize."

"I'm really sorry for what happened and I apologize, I would also like to pay for any ...."

Mrs. Chicken interrupts Mr. Dog:

"You should have thought about that before! You have bad dogs and that makes you a bad neighbor! You attacked my husband and you're bad!"

At this point, Mr. Dog started getting upset. He was going to reply. The reply was prefaced by him moving his arms in proper Italian communication style.

Officer Dario:

"Okay, two things: One, quit getting pissed, you can't afford to get pissed. Bite your tongue and just be quiet. You don't hold any cards. I'm trying to help you. Don't do or say anything negative. Also, I need you to put your hands in your pockets when you are talking to her. Italians talk with their hands and it's like verbal Italian Ninja Karate chops when you talk with your hands; that's going to turn her off completely. You can't do that. Are you okay with that?

"It's real hard Officer. You're right; I'm emotional and not used to this."

"I know it's hard. You're a real man but you have to put up with this shit or she is going to send your ass to jail and no more golfing for a month! We all know that she's going to be a royal bitch to you and you are going to have to stand there, bite your tongue, and take it. The good news is, it will only last for a couple of minutes and then it's over. Just look at the ground and bite your tongue. Can we do that?

"Yes, I can."

"Can we go over there and you apologize?"

"Yeah."

"Okay, when it gets hard, and it is going to get hard, look at me and I'm going to look at the ground. That's when you shut up and just look at the ground. No jail, you get to golf next week if we do this right, okay?"

"Okay."

Mr. Dog and Officer Dario walked over to the Chicken House. Mr. and Mrs. Chicken invited them inside. Officer Dario told Mr. and Mrs. Chicken that Mr. Dog would like to apologize for everything that had occurred.

Head towards the ground, Mr. Dog gave a nice apology, stating that his dogs got out and he was sorry for having put everyone through the recent negative events.

But, before Mr. Dog could finish his apology, Mrs. Chicken ripped into him about what a terrible, disgusting person he was. Into her third insult, Mr.

Dog raised his head to tell her to go "fuck herself" but his eyes met with Officer's Dario's. Dario nodded his head towards the ground in a sign of, *"Not time to be Italian, look at the ground."* Mr. Dog humbly sent his eyes to the ground, doing the right thing. Mr. Chicken only looked on, he said nothing.

Mrs. Chicken ended her ass chewing and felt like queen of the neighborhood. At the end of it, Mr. Dog thanked the Chicken People and walked home, relieved the apology torture was over.

Mr. Dog thanked Officer Dario for helping him apologize:

"I don't think I could have done that without you. Thank you so much!"

"I'm glad I could help out. You have a really nice family and I hope everything returns to normal for you."

And with that, Officer Dario left the scene of The Great Chicken Massacre.

Epilogue

Mr. and Mrs. Dog gladly paid for all damages. They put up a six-foot-high fence around their property to contain their pretty chicken killing Akita puppies.

Officer Dario was happy knowing the Chicken People were content with having received their apology and getting paid for all damages. He was also happy knowing that Dog People could now proceed with having a normal life without anyone going to jail. Life has problems, sometimes we can fix them.

Officer Dario could have arrested Mrs. Dog for trying to bribe him with the delicious felony spaghetti dinner, but he didn't arrest her because he knew his Mother would have killed him for that.

Since the Great Chicken Massacre, whenever Officer Dario smelled the aroma of homemade spaghetti sauce and garlic bread, he thought of the Dog People and how they perfectly mimicked his Mother's cooking. He wished he could have stayed for dinner and enjoyed the good family love and cooking he had as a child.

Family is good…

Got Wine?

SOME DAYS, NOTHING GOES RIGHT

FAMILY DISTURBANCES

Many cops handle so many calls involving family disturbances; they become unofficial expert family counselors. Family disturbances range from two people having a shouting match and bothering the neighbors to extreme violence with injuries or death.

OFFICER BOB

Officer Bob had been on the force about six years; everybody liked him. He could handle any call thrown at him and had a talent for diffusing situations with his calm voice. Officer Bob had a great sense of humor and could always find some kind of comedy in almost everything he did.

JACK AND JILL

Jack and Jill had been high school sweethearts. After high school, they both chose the vocation of nursing and they were good at it. They were both later hired by the same hospital which was convenient for the two. Shortly thereafter, they married, bought a beautiful single story home in a residential neighborhood and lived at the end of a quiet cul-de-sac.

Jack and Jill had a great relationship except for the fact that Jill had a physical condition that made intimacy challenging. After several years, because of Jill's physical issue, she agreed to let Jack have a girlfriend on the side as long as he did not get emotionally attached to his girlfriend.

For several years, the aforementioned relationship worked out for Jack and Jill. They would go on vacation and it seemed like everything was working fine. So fine, that Jack was allowed to bring his girlfriend along on the vacations.

Whooh Jack, this is not a family show anymore...

Over the years, Jack had many a girlfriend and then he started to keep the same one. He was becoming emotionally attached to her and Jill became depressed. Jill told Jack he needed to break up with his latest girlfriend and he refused. Jill became more depressed, so much so that she became suicidal.

One Saturday morning, Jack was trying to sleep in. The weather was hot and he was sleeping nude on the master bedroom waterbed, face down. Jill came into the room:

'I need you to drive me to the hospital."

"For what?"

"I'm depressed and want to check myself in for depression."

"I don't have time."

"Well then, I'm going to kill myself."

"How are you going to do that?"

"With the gun. Where's it at?"

"It's in the box on the closet shelf. Do it in the kitchen on the tile so you don't get blood all over the carpet, it'll be easier to clean up the tile."

Jack tried to go back to sleep.

Jill retrieved the pistol from the bedroom closet and took it into the kitchen. She wrote three farewell letters: one to her parents, one to her sister, and one to her husband. She then took the pistol, placed it against her head, and "click," nothing.

Jill woke Jack up:

"The gun didn't go off, somethings wrong with it."

Jack woke up, grabbed the gun from Jill and racked a bullet into the chamber. He then pushed the safety on. He matter of factly told Jill,

"You didn't put a bullet in the chamber retard."

Jill just stood there for a moment. Jack continued:

"If you're going to do this, just do it."

Jill went into the kitchen, her feelings hurt by Jack calling her a "retard". She was crying and sniffling as she walked back into the master bedroom. Jack was once again asleep on his belly. Jill took the pistol off 'safe' pointed it at Jack's head and stated through her sniffling,

"I'm not a retard!"

And with that, Jill pulled the trigger,

"KABOOM!"

Jill had been shaking a lot and she did not hit Jack squarely in the head. In fact, she barely hit him; the bullet slightly nicked the carotid artery in his neck. (We all have two carotid arteries in our neck on each side of the windpipe. The arteries carry blood to the brain and carotid artery punctures are usually fatal.)

Jack was now wide awake and blood was getting everywhere. Jill squeezed off another round and hit Jack in the right tri-cep. Naked Jack ran into the master bathroom which had a door leading to the backyard. He tried to get out the door but couldn't. It had a deadbolt lock on it and required a key to open; the key was missing.

Good news for Jack though, the bathroom door leading to the outside and freedom was equipped with a doggie door. Jack lunged through the doggie door but had a problem: his hips got stuck in the doggie door. His upper torso was through the doggie door but his legs and buttocks were still inside the bathroom and here comes Jill, sniffling and crying.

What do you think Jill did next? If you think Jill shot Jack in the ass, you're right!

Jill took aim and hit Jack squarely in the right buttocks. This last bullet actually propelled Jack through the doggie door. Jack ran as best he could and hid in the far end of the backyard.

Don't ever call me a retard again Jack!

At this point, Jill is confused and frustrated. She also knows she is in deep shit for shooting Jack. Jack may die and she still has to kill herself too. For some reason, she now thinks that suicide by car crash is the way to go. She goes into the garage, gets in her car and drives away, leaving the garage door open.

Jack hears Jill drive away. His body was covered with blood and it lubricated his torso enough to help him crawl back into the house through the doggie door. That's a good thing because there was no one in the back yard to shoot Jack in the ass to propel him through the doggie door. Jack stumbles into the kitchen, grabs a cordless phone, and calls his mother,

"Jill shot me!"

"She what?"

"Jill shot me and I'm bleeding really bad."

"Hang up and call 911! I'll call them too!"

Jack calls 911 and Officer Bob was sent to handle the call. The Police Department also dispatched Officer Dylan to help out. Both Officers have about the same amount of experience on the force. After calling 911, Jack stumbles into the laundry room leading to the garage, sits down and waits for help to arrive. Blood is everywhere. Paramedics are also on the way.

Maybe I shouldn't have called Jill a retard?

Officers Bob and Dylan arrive at Jack and Jill's home. With B.F.G.'s drawn they enter the house through the open garage and find Jack in the laundry room. Blood is everywhere. It's obvious Jack isn't armed because he's still naked, he's just covered in blood. Officer Bob tells Jack to keep pressure on his neck wound and that paramedics are on the way. Jack states no one else is in the house.

Even though Jack told the officers that no one else is present in the blood splattered house, they have to make sure. They don't know Jack and they can only confirm the house is clear of other subjects by checking the house themselves. One never knows, *"My Friend, Some Dude, or Some Guy"* could be armed and waiting in any one of the rooms.

Officers Bob and Dylan entered the house proper from the laundry room and found themselves in the front hallway. Down the hallway to the left were the kitchen and living room; down the hallway to the right was the front door foyer and bedrooms. Officer Bob covered the bedroom hallway while Officer Dylan cleared the kitchen and living room. The kitchen looks like somebody took a gallon of red paint and flicked it all over the walls with a paintbrush.

Dylan rejoined Bob and the two began to proceed down the hallway leading to the front door foyer and the bedrooms. This hallway was covered in blood and there were bloody handprints all over the walls, it was a horror movie mess. Officer Bob was in the lead and they took about two steps and were stopped in their tracks by the most blood curdling piercing screech from hell they had ever heard! This blood curdling screech was so severe, that both officers instinctively got hurled backwards to avoid getting wasted from some horror movie demon. Officer Dylan's reflexes threw him backwards, back into the laundry room and into a paramedic that arrived to treat Jack.

After recovering, Officer Bob cautiously peered into the front foyer, B.F.G. ready, pressure on the trigger, and ready to waste the evil threat. Bob can't believe his eyes:

It's a fucking two foot tall Cockatoo! Son of a bitch! God they're scary!

The Cockatoo was in a corner in the foyer in a five foot high cage. Obviously, it needed some attention.

"Dylan, get back in here, it's only a bird!"

"Yeah, well it sounded like the worst horror show I've ever heard."

Bob and Dylan cleared the bedrooms. The master bedroom, master bath and doggie door have blood everywhere. Bloody handprints are on all the walls as if someone was faux painting the house.

With the house cleared, Officer Bob returned to the laundry room where Jack was being treated for his injuries by the fire department. Bob was thinking:

I am so glad the nice fire department paramedics showed up to treat Jack for all of his injuries. They're doing a real fine job. And I don't have to get that bloody shit all over my uniform!

I like firemen…

While Jack was being treated, Officer Bob got a basic story from him as to what had happened. During this interview, an emergency call went out over Officer Bob's portable radio: an injury accident involving an overturned vehicle on the freeway. Police, Ambulance, and Fire are responding CODE THREE! The make and model of the car was broadcasted. The location of the accident is about a mile away from Jack and Jill's home. Everybody heard the call, including Jack:

"That sounds like my wife's car."

It turned out it was Jill's car that overturned on the freeway. She had left home after shooting Jack for calling her a retard and decided to end her life by crashing into a concrete freeway overpass support. If things went well, it shouldn't be painful at all.

Jill got on the freeway. She knew which freeway overpass support she wanted to crash into. It's the one in the middle of the freeway on the way to work, she sees it every day and it is her favorite freeway overpass support. Jill accelerated to 100 miles per hour and aimed for the overpass support.

It should be over soon...

Jill was finally going to be successful in her suicide attempt. She aimed her car at her favorite overpass support and was ready to smash into it. Then, at the last second, she chickened out and pulled the wheel to one side. Her car flipped over and flew into the opposing traffic lanes and ended up in a ditch on the other side of the freeway. Luckily, traffic was light at that time and she didn't take anybody else out with her; only Jill was injured.

Jill received a lump on her forehead the size of a baseball and was transported to the local hospital. She was treated in a nice big emergency room bed and was required to sit upright and hold an icepack on the baseball that had grown out of the side of her forehead.

Jack also got a nice big bed at the hospital but he had to lie on his stomach because Jill shot him in the ass.

Officer Bob arrived at the hospital. He entered Jill's room, pulled up a chair next to her. He took her hands in his, looked her in the eyes and with the most sympathetic voice he asked Jill:

"Ever had one of those days where nothing goes right?"

That opened Jill's floodgates and total sobbing ensued:

"Yes, today!"

She grabbed Officer Bob in a big bear hug and wouldn't let go. She sobbed and sobbed and sobbed...

Some days, nothing goes right...

Epilogue

Jill was originally prosecuted for attempted murder. The charge was later reduced to assault with a deadly weapon. Jack testified at her hearings and trial on her behalf and pleaded with the court to be lenient with Jill. Jill ended up only spending a short time in jail.

Jack was prosecuted for assisting someone in a suicide and got some jail time too.

The Fire Department did a bang up job at the Jack and Jill house and the traffic accident scene: No cops got their uniforms dirty!

MR. TOAD'S WILD RIDE

Detective Pierce was assigned to work auto theft cases. He was sent to auto theft school and learned as much as he could about auto thefts and how to investigate them. Pierce was assigned to drive a plainclothes van because he needed tools from time to time to inspect stolen cars.

Most motor vehicles have "secret numbers" hidden throughout the vehicle. If a car is stolen and the thieves change or obliterate the "secret numbers", there still may be one left that a Detective can locate and identify the vehicle by. Really good auto thieves know the location of the "secret numbers" because they strip cars for parts and find them.

Two of the cases assigned to Pierce were a pair of luxury cars stolen from an auto dealership in town. A suspect went into the dealership and test drove two new cars, a Jaguar and a Yukon Denali. The suspect was very well dressed, acted professional, and paid for both vehicles with a cashier's check. He and *"Some Guy"* then drove the cars off the lot, never to be seen again. The next day, the dealership found out the cashier's check was counterfeit.

Damnit, "Some Guy" strikes again!

Detective Pierce just had his undercover detective van serviced by the police mechanics. The mechanics gave the car a tune up, changed the oil, and installed new brakes on all four wheels because:

"Pierce, your brakes were shot! You drive your van too hard. You're safe now!"

So, Detective Pierce's undercover van has new brakes that have not yet been broken in. When one receives new brakes on one's car, one should drive easy on them for a couple of hundred miles to break them in gradually.

His undercover van, just having been serviced by the cop mechanics was waiting in the cop car parking lot for Detective Pierce's first drive with new brakes. Pierce was sitting at his desk, minding his own business, enjoying his second cup of morning coffee. Everything was quiet and he might get some work done for a change. And then, his phone rang:

It was the auto dealership that gave away the Jaguar and Yukon Denali to *"Some Guy"* and his well-dressed associate. The dealership had been called from the vehicle manufacturer in Detroit. The Yukon Denali, a "luxury vehicle" had a factory installed stolen vehicle tracking device on it and the vehicle was on a freeway in Los Angeles.

Pierce, go get our stolen car. That's your job! Drop your coffee and get our car that we gave away to "Some Guy" and his friend! Screw your quiet morning coffee dude, we need our car back! Hurry up you lazy coffee drinker!

You guys dress up nicely and go to work for the auto dealership. You don't really "work", you sell cars to rich people. You don't dig ditches, you don't do any physical labor. You just sell expensive cars to rich customers and you "think" you work. You get greedy when someone shows up with a cashier's check and you don't even call the bank to verify it. Now, you know where your stolen car is and you want it back 'right now!' You screwed up and expect me to drop everything I'm doing and get back your expensive property that you foolishly gave away.

Well, that is what I'm paid to do...

Detective Pierce called the tracking center in Detroit and told them he'd be on the road in a couple of minutes; he would call them back.

I'm taking my fucking coffee with me. They are not depriving me of that. And, even though they are spoiled little car salesmen, this could turn out to be some fun. I've never had anything like this happen and I think it's going to turn out to be interesting...If we get their expensive little car back, we better be getting some invites to the annual car dealership Christmas party!

Knowing it would be nice to have backup available, Detective Pierce wanted Detective John to go with him because Detective John was a hard charging son of a gun. Detective John was also enjoying his second cup of coffee when Detective Pierce approached him:

"John, I've got a moving stolen (stolen car) down in L.A. and I'm in contact with a tracking center in Detroit. I need someone to go with me, can you go?"

Detective John had that look on his face that said,

What? Are you kidding? I barely got to work. But, it sounds important...

"Yeah, let me get my bag."

"Bring your jacket and raid vest (bullet proof vest to wear over the detective garb) just in case. I don't know how nasty it may get. Also, grab a full cup of coffee, it's in L.A. and we have a ways to drive."

"Be right there."

And with that, Detective Pierce and Detective John put on their bullet proof vests and a police windbreaker over that. The windbreaker had a badge on the chest and "POLICE" in big bold letters on the back. The jacket screamed "POLICE" if anybody would have a doubt who they were. They piled into Pierce's van and headed for the freeway.

Pierce started hauling ass down the freeway:

No highway patrol with us, that's good, we don't want to make the highway patrol stop us and have to explain we are in hot pursuit of My Friend, Some Dude or Some Guy. The highway patrol hates it when they stop a car for going over a hundred miles an hour and it turns

395

out to be cops chasing bad guys and they don't get to write one of their favorite tickets! We don't want to put them through that mental anguish!

Detective John called his watch commander and told him where they are going and what they would attempt to do. He asked the watch commander to notify the Highway Patrol and Los Angeles Police Department of the situation. The watch commander did so. Pierce and John got to finish their coffee on the drive down to Los Angeles.

At least we got to finish our brew. That's good!

John was on the cell phone with "Cathy", the dispatcher in Detroit that was tracking the Denali. She's a really nice gal and loves her job. Cathy is going to hopefully help Pierce and John intersect the suspect vehicle. She tells John that he needs to take California Highway 134 Eastbound towards Interstate 5, that's where the stolen vehicle is currently driving.

Pierce is driving hard. He's dodging in and out of traffic, slamming on the brakes, accelerating hard…

That's the way it's done in the movies. This is real life and I'm going to catch that vehicle thief!

The brakes on Pierce's van are starting to squeak. They haven't been broken in yet. They are getting abused. Detective Pierce is a car brake abuser!

Cathy advised the stolen Denali got on the Interstate 10 westbound. Pierce floored his detective van…

"John, we're going to catch that son of a bitch and you gotta admit it, this shit is fun! I'm driving like mad, but I know my limits and that of my van, but I'm going to push it brother and we're going to have some fucking fun screaming all over these fucking freeways whether you like it or not! And I know you like this shit too!"

"Wouldn't have it any other way Pierce as long as you don't crash Brother!"

"I won't. Let's get it on!"

John turned on the van's FM radio:

Let's haul ass with some appropriate music to help out!

John found a station playing a most appropriate Steppenwolf song. Pierce changes the lyrics and, he doesn't have a bad singing voice:

"Get your van a runnin'…

Head out on the highway…

Lookin' for adventure…

And whatever comes our way…

Yeah Captain gonna make it happen…

397

Lock and Load in a gun embrace…

Fire all of our guns at once and –

Explode this case..."

And with that, Pierce hammered down on the gas pedal and back up to over 100 miles per hour. Life is good when you are a cop, doing the right thing, and having fun getting paid to speed!

> *They pay me to speed on the freeway! I love this job!*

"*I like smoke and lightning …*

Heavy metal thunder…

Racin' on the freeway…

And the feelin' that I'm under…

Yeah Captain gonna make it happen…

Lock and Load in a gun embrace…

Fire all of our guns at once and gonna solve this case…"

Pierce is pushing his van hard, rapid accelerating, hard braking, and dodging in and out of traffic:

> *Stay the hell out of the fast lane you slow fuckers! What idiots! Don't get in the fast lane unless you're going fast! What dumbshits!*

"Like a true Alpha child…

We were born, born to be wild…

We can drive so high…

I neverrrr, wanna die…"

"John, are you having a good time, because I'm having a really good felony fun time?"

"Yeah as long as you don't crash!"

"Doin' the best I can Brother, not driving over my capabilities."

"Thanks!"

"Your singing isn't that bad."

"I practice in the shower Bro!"

They made it to the Interstate 10 and Cathy informed them the stolen Denali got off the freeway. Pierce slammed on the brakes and cut off a bunch of cars. The off ramp had so many cars on it that it looked like a parking lot. The off ramp was controlled by a traffic light. Pierce came to a stop and the strong odor of overheated brakes permeated the van. They were boxed in and couldn't get around the other cars. They still had a red traffic light. The Denali was nowhere in sight and Cathy advised it was getting farther and farther away.

Way to go Pierce! You haven't caught any bad guys and you burned up the new brake pads on your van! The police mechanics are going to want to kill you when you get back to the station; if you ever make it back to the station with all your shitty driving and such. You're so lucky you haven't been involved in a five car pileup with your aggressive driving! Better watch it…

So, Pierce was behind four stopped cars near the top of the freeway off ramp:

"John, I'm going to throw it in park to keep my foot off the brake and maybe help cool the brakes down."

"I think it's too late for that."

John looked out his passenger window towards the right front wheel, smoke is billowing from it:

"We have a minor issue; the right front wheel looks like it is going to catch on fire."

"Pour some water on it!"

"I don't have any water!"

"Then get out there and piss on it!"

"I'm not going to piss on it!"

"Check my bag, I may have a bottle of water in there."

John got a bottle of water out of Pierce's bag and gets out of the van. Traffic was starting to inch forward and Pierce was holding up traffic.

"Hurry up!"

"I am damnit!"

John poured the whole bottle of water onto the right front wheel. A column of burnt brake odor steam rose from the wheel.

"Get in we gotta go!"

John piled back into the van and away they went.

Cathy guided them through city streets. She explained the tracking system was only good within 100 yards. In a crowded city, that could seem like a mile away. Pierce and John were on the freeway, off the freeway, down a couple of side streets, back on the freeway, repeat, repeat, repeat. Still no Denali in sight.

Shit!

Cathy had the ability to make the stolen Denali's horn go off. She activated the horn from time to time. Pierce and John heard the horn off in the distance but couldn't see the stolen Denali. There were just too many streets and too many cars on the road. And, they didn't even know where the hell they were! They didn't know L.A. streets to save to their lives. This went on for hours.

Thank God we started with a full tank of gas...

The Denali got back onto the Interstate 10 westbound, to the Interstate 110 Southbound, to the Interstate 105 eastbound, to the Interstate 710 southbound to the Interstate 405 northbound. Cathy continued to guide our lost cops.

Pierce was driving the van hard. He tried to stay off his smoking brakes as much as possible.

"John, thanks for coming along bro, I really appreciate it."

"Yeah, well let's catch this guy! Ya know, this is kinda fun! Beats sitting at a desk!"

The Denali got off the Interstate 405 and drove to the community of Venice Beach and was on the surface streets. Detective John was letting his dispatcher know where they were and please have LAPD respond to the area to assist in the stop of the stolen Denali. Cathy was doing a great job giving directions to Pierce and John. John had Cathy on speaker phone and Pierce advised her:

"Hey Cathy?"

"Yes?"

"Have you done a lot of these?"

"I've done a couple."

"Okay, I just want to let you know, I think we may get to box this guy in, these streets are really tight and we see him now not too far in front of us. We're going to keep you on the phone just in case there is trouble during the stop. If you hear gunfire, get an ambulance or two sent our way. And Cathy, during the stop, if you hear a little bit of colorful language, it's so that we can properly communicate with the suspects as to the gravity of the situation and they need to cooperate so nobody gets hurt. Do you follow?"

Cathy laughed,

"Yeah, I know what you mean."

Many of the side streets in Venice Beach are effectively single lane because the streets are narrow, and cars are parked on both sides of the streets. The driving is really tight. The Denali found an open spot to park on the right side of the street. Pierce advised John:

"He's parking. I think we can box him in Bro. When he's in his parking slot, I'll drop you off behind the Denali and you go to the passenger side. I'll box him by pulling right up next to him. Be careful Bro."

John doesn't reply. He doesn't have to. He knows what to do.

The Denali parked, barely fitting in between two other cars. Pierce dropped off John who ran around to the passenger side of the Denali. Pierce rolled both of his van's windows down and pulled up alongside the Denali; Pierce was exactly parallel to the Denali and saw the driver for the first time: Male subject, clean cut, looks about thirty years old. Pierce pulled out his B.F.G. and pointed it across his passenger seat at Denali Man's head. Both front windows of the Denali were rolled down. Detective John was on the passenger side of the Denali, also pointing his B.F.G. at the suspect's head.

At this time, Detective Pierce is breaking one of the cardinal rules of officer safety. Pierce doesn't have any real cover in case the suspect has a B.F.G. of his own and decides to use it.

Pierce and Detective John initiated what Pierce likes to refer to as an "Improvised Felony Stop". "Improvised Felony Stops" are not sanctioned by the Police Department. If Pierce got shot and killed during his "Improvised Felony Stop", Police Tactical Instructors across the country will band together and make a video of Detective Pierce's "Improvised Felony Stop" screw up. They will teach the world of Policemen throughout the planet that Detective Pierce was Detective dumbshit of the year and one should never follow in his footsteps. But, according to Pierce at the time:

I don't give a shit. If this guy so much as flinches the wrong way, I'm going to unload my whole magazine into his fucking head! Besides, John will kill the bastard if he kills me...

Pierce yelled at the suspect:

"Put your hands on top of your fucking head!"

Denali Man did so.

John yelled at Denali Man,

"Put your hands on the steering wheel asshole!"

Denali Man started to do so but Pierce yelled again for Denali Man to put his hands back on his fucking head or he will get his shit blown away!

Denali Man kept his hands raised with his fingers spread. He looked at Pierce with a look that says:

Uh, I don't know what the fuck to do! Both of you are yelling at me and I don't want to be a police accident!

It happens all the time, cops get into their B.F.G. moment with so much adrenaline involved that there is sometimes a *failure to communicate...*

At this time, John is looking at Pierce with a *What the Fuck Pierce?* look.

"Take it John."

John takes control of the stop and is ordering Denali Man out the front passenger door. Pierce exits his van and runs around to John's location. Denali

Man is proned out and handcuffed. Mr. Toad's Wild Ride is officially over.

During the Improvised Felony Stop, Cathy at Mission Control was left on speaker phone just in case a shooting occurred. Cathy's partner was on another phone with L.A.P.D. giving them blow by blow updates. Cathy and her partner heard all of the cop profanity. L.A.P.D. is not on scene.

Pierce got on the phone with Cathy:

"Cathy?"

"Yeah Pierce?"

"That wasn't too bad was it?"

"Nope, I've heard worse. I'm just glad you boys are O.K."

"Me too and our suspect is shook up but nobody is hurt. Thank you so much to you and your partner, you two did a bang up job. I'm going to let your supervisor know."

"Well thank you. You and John have a great rest of your afternoon."

"Thank you Cathy, take care."

"You too, bye."

Then five L.A.P.D. patrol units surrounded Pierce, John, and Denali Man. L.A.P.D. had their

B.F.G.'s out. Pierce raised his hand in the air and showed the cavalry four fingers. Displaying four fingers is cop sign language for "Code Four" or, "No further assistance needed", or, "Everything is good!".

An L.A.P.D. Sergeant approached Pierce:

"Why the hell didn't you tell us you were down here?"

"We did. We called at 10:30 this morning and our dispatch center and Detroit Michigan has been on the line with your dispatch center for the last four hours."

"You did?"

"Yeah, your dispatch knew where we were the entire time we've been trying to catch this guy."

The Sergeant's attitude changed:

"Oh. What can we help you with?"

O.K., now we're on the same team again. Glad we can all be friends!

"We need to borrow your station for a suspect interview and maybe park our recovered stolen vehicle there too. Can one of your people escort us because we are lost down here?"

"Sure thing."

Pierce confirmed the Vehicle Identification Number on the Denali was the same one given away by the dealership. L.A.P.D. took Denali Man to their local station followed by Detective John, driving Pierce's van and Detective Pierce brought up the rear, driving the Denali.

Holy shit Batman! This car is styling! What luxury!

Once at the station, Pierce searched the Denali. It was real clean inside. Pierce found a bunch of paperwork in the console and he took it. L.A.P.D. placed Denali Man in an interview room.

Pierce and John entered the interview room to conduct the suspect interview and the first words out of the Denali's Man's mouth were:

"I didn't steal that car, I bought it last week."

Holy Crap, we might have an innocent purchaser on our hands. Thank God he didn't do anything stupid and we didn't have to shoot him.

Denali Man waived his rights faster than fast and stated he bought the car from *"A Guy"*, the week before.

Denali Man's story washed clean. He had proof he put $5,000.00 down on the Denali and was to make payments to a shady financing firm. He knew he was getting a good deal on the Denali and couldn't pass it up. He always wanted a Denali and now he lost over $5,000.00 on his dream vehicle.

If the deal is too good to be true, it probably is...

Pierce explained to Denali Man that if the real crooks ever get caught, he may get his money back. Pierce also explained that the use of extraordinary language during the stop was to ensure effective communication and cooperation so no one got hurt, A.K.A., No *Police Accidents* occurred.

Denali Man replied:

"Officers, thank you for the way you treated me. I really appreciate it. My brother is a Sergeant on the Los Angeles Sheriff's Department and I'm going to tell him how well you treated me."

What Denali Man said between the lines in his statement was,

"Thank you for not beating the shit out of me because you thought I was a bad guy!"

Pierce replied back:

"We were here to make an arrest and recover a stolen vehicle, you gave us no reason to go ninja on you, you complied with our commands and everything turned out O.K., except you got conned out of some money."

Everyone shook hands.

Hit the Like button and follow us on Twitter!

Denali Man called for a ride home.

Pierce and John drove back to their station to the odor of burned out brake pads.

Once back at the station, Detective Pierce had to turn his van back into the police car maintenance shop. He felt really bad about ruining the new brakes on his van. He parked it, bought a couple of cold sodas as a bribe for the mechanics and told them the truth:

"I fucked up the new brakes on the van. They are total shit!"

Pierce sensed the mechanics wanted to kill him and he spent half an hour telling the mechanics about the four hour long Mr. Toad's Wild Ride throughout the freeways and side streets of Los Angeles; he jokingly stated that if Detective John had pissed on the brakes when he was told to, the brakes could have been saved. The mechanics just looked at each other with the look that said:

Another masterful Detective Pierce bullshit story!

Pierce eventually won over the mechanics. They did not want to kill him anymore. Good thing because Pierce and the mechanics had been friends for many years and he wanted to keep it that way.

Epilogue

The assholes that stole the cars from the dealership eventually got caught for all of their scams but Denali Man never received any restitution because the well-dressed thief and *Some Guy* spent all of their ill-gotten gains on women and booze.

Officer Pierce and Officer John did not get invited to the annual Car Dealership Christmas party:

Spoiled, Ungrateful Bastards!

WILLY DALTON OFF RAMP

Officers Jack and Pete were working a two man dawn shift car. Normally, the department didn't have two man patrol cars but on this particular night, too many cops showed up for work. Departments will sometimes schedule more officers than needed for a particular shift; that way if someone calls in sick, or whatever, no need to look for someone to work overtime. There is an extra officer available on the schedule. So, instead of taking out two separate patrol cars, Officers Jack and Pete decided to team up with Pete driving.

Jack and Pete searched their beat area for *My Friend, Some Dude, and Some Guy.* They were nowhere to be found. They cruised the surface streets, the freeways, nothing. Silent night, quiet night. People just weren't out. No burglaries in progress, no traffic accidents, no drunks walking the streets, no family fights, nothing.

Somebody should have told us it was going to be quiet and that My Friend, Some Dude, and Some Guy weren't working tonight...

After filling up with coffee, Jack and Pete got back in their patrol car and kept cruising their beat. A neighboring beat officer radioed he was stopping a car on the freeway.

We're bored as hell buddy and you're going to get a two man felony back up car whether you like it or not...

Pete got on the empty freeway and picked the speed up to over 80 mph. He stayed in the slow lane because the freeway was empty, no cars in sight.

The overhead red and blue rotating lights from their beat partner could be seen about a mile ahead. Pete continued at 80 miles per hour. About 300 yards from their beat partner's traffic stop, Jack and Pete saw two dim red eyes directly in front of them:

"Holy shit, it's a car!"

They couldn't see the car that well because that stretch of freeway had burned out freeway lights and the car appeared to be a piece of junk painted some kind of dirty brownish/gray color that made it blend in with the road surface. The car was only travelling at about 30 miles per hour and Pete slammed on the brakes and swerved to the left, barely missing the car. Pete ended up doing a 360 degree spin out in the fast lanes. He recovered and brought their patrol unit behind the slow moving junk car and stopped it right behind their beat partner's patrol car.

Shit! That was close!

Pete approached the driver while Jack kept an eye on him from the passenger side of the car. Jack also kept an eye on their beat partner who did not indicate any problems with his traffic stop.

The driver of the piece of junk car was in his 60's. He had red watery eyes but there was no odor of alcohol about him. The car was full of deep sea fishing poles. Pete had the driver step to the rear of his car so they could talk about his extremely dim tail lights. The driver had a small amount of difficulty walking to the back of his car.

He could have been drinking or he could just be old and has trouble walking, we'll see.

Jack, Pete and the driver were standing behind the junk car they had just stopped. Jack and Pete were examining the car with their high intensity flashlights. They couldn't tell what kind of vehicle they stopped.

JOHNNY CASH
ONE PIECE AT A TIME

In 1976, Johnny Cash recorded a song entitled: ONE PIECE AT A TIME.

The character in the song went to Detroit and worked there, assembling Cadillacs. He couldn't afford one himself so he devised a plan to steal the parts for a whole car, ONE PIECE AT A TIME, over several years.

The car in the song ended up having two headlights on one side and a single headlight on the other. The body parts were from different year models and nothing really fit together. The rear of the car had one tail fin. The finished product was an abortion of a car and everyone laughed at it.

Johnny's song reached number one on the Billboard Hot Country Singles chart.

Officers Jack and Pete were looking at a car that was obviously related to Johnny Cash's car. It had body parts on it from all the major car manufacturers. It was old and rusty. Where the parts didn't match up, body filler was used. Weld marks were everywhere.

Pete asked the driver:

"Exactly what kind of car is this supposed to be?"

"It's special construction."

No shit. So that's what you call it?

"Where are you headed?'

"Ahz be headed for the Willy Dalton off ramp."

"Just where is the Willy Dalton off ramp? There isn't an off ramp named 'Willy Dalton."

"Yez there is, that be my brother in law, and we going fishin'."

"What time you going fishing?"

"In a couple hours. I gotta find the Willy Dalton off ramp real soon. I been lookin' for it for hours."

At this point, Jack and Pete have an old guy with red, watery eyes, slightly slurred speech, not the best balance in the world, who is driving the ugliest car in the universe. Jack and Pete still don't smell any alcohol on the guy's breath.

"Let's open up your trunk and take a look at your tail lamps."

The driver opened the trunk. It was dirty and full of approximately thirty mostly empty, bottles of gin. Some of the bottles had some liquid still in them.

There's the reason why we didn't smell any alcohol on his breath. He's been drinking straight gin which is sometimes difficult to smell.

"How long you been looking for the Willy Dalton off ramp?"

"Since six o'clock tonight."

Uh, hate to tell you this partner but there ain't no Willy Dalton Off Ramp and it's two thirty in the morning. I think you're blotto drunk but you have a high tolerance for alcohol.

"There isn't an off ramp called the Willy Dalton Off Ramp."

"Yez there is, it's the Willy Dalton Off Ramp!"

Jack and Pete have a small side conference and Pete told Jack to just talk to Willy Dalton Off Ramp for a while. While Jack and Willy Dalton Off Ramp were talking, Pete walked up behind Willy

Dalton Off Ramp without him knowing. Pete just stood there, sniffing the air and then it hit him:

> *Bingo dude, I smell the gin. You are higher than a kite. You're not going fishing today and your piece of junk car is getting towed.*

Willy Dalton Off Ramp went to jail for driving under the influence. His blood alcohol level was .23, which is quite high and way over the limit.

Officer Jack attempted to call the real Willy Dalton and advise him his brother in law will not be joining him for deep sea fishing but there was no answer. He probably went fishing without him.

So, just to let you know, if you're on a strange freeway, lost, and drunk, you are looking for:

"The Willy Dalton Off Ramp".

I'M SO BITCHIN!

Police Officers are supposed to act and behave better than the general public. Sometimes, a cop screws up...

OFFICER MATT

Officer Matt was a very conscientious Officer. He was a good street cop and performed his duties as well as anyone else. He had one little chink in his armor: he was vain.

When Matt came to work, he was the poster boy for professional looking cops. His uniform was spotless. His leather gear and shoes were always spit shined. He didn't have a hair out of place. To ensure he looked good, he had a full-length mirror attached to the inside of his uniform locker door. He couldn't use the one in the men's bathroom.

Nope, the bathroom mirror is for second rate cops. I need my own mirror. I am superior and so is my mirror!

Yes, Officer Matt was vain, but you couldn't say he wasn't squared away. He was:

Mister Squared Away!

Cops usually joke around in the locker room when they are going on or coming off duty. One afternoon, Officer Nielsen, Officer Matt, and Officer Parker were getting ready for evening shift.

THE POLICE LOCKER ROOM

The locker room had several parallel rows of lockers. The lockers were about six feet tall and made of fairly heavy gauge steel. Between the rows of lockers were wooden benches.

Officer Nielsen's locker was located by the locker room entrance door. It was several rows away from Officer Matt's and Parker's lockers.

Matt and Parker had lockers in the same row. Matt's locker was in the center of the row and Parker's locker was located four lockers to the right of Matt's, near the walkway.

Nielsen was getting dressed at his locker when Parker entered the locker room to do the same. Both officers were early and there was no rush getting ready.

Parker opened up his locker and began putting his name badge on a fresh shirt when Officer Matt walked in.

HEAVILY ARMED

Matt opened his locker and Nielsen started giving him a hard time about always looking vainfully in his personal locker mirror.

"That's because you're jealous Nielsen. Excuse me but I have to transfer my weapons from civilian clothes to my uniform. Everybody please shut up!"

419

Matt started to remove weapons from his civilian clothes:

"This is the part I like most about coming to work, laying all my weapons on the locker room bench."

Matt took his six inch .357 duty weapon out of a shoulder holster and laid it on the bench, a second pistol from an ankle holster, a knife from the other ankle, can of tear gas from his belt, folding knife from a pants pocket, a sap from his back pocket, and another pistol that he had hidden somewhere on his body.

"There, that should do it."

Parker:

"Do you really carry all that shit with you wherever you go?"

"Of course, you never know when you're going to have to take care of business."

Matt got dressed in record time. He could hardly wait to get onto the streets and show the public just how bitchin' he was. Parker and Nielsen were taking their time.

Matt was looking all sparkly and pretty in his perfect uniform and perfectly groomed hair which he was meticulously combing into place with the aid of his full length vanity mirror.

Parker:

"Hey Nielsen, Matt is making love to himself in his mirror again!"

Nielsen:

"Don't you ever get tired of looking at your ugly face in that mirror?"

Matt:

"You guys are just jealous of me and my superior crime fighting abilities. You only wish you looked as good as I do."

And with that, Matt took out his six inch .357 and held it next to his head, barrel pointing towards the ceiling, admiring himself and his weapon in his full-length mirror.

Parker didn't like what he saw:

"Hey Matt, we're just kidding Bro, please put the gun away. We're just kidding."

Matt holstered his gun and then Nielsen started in again:

"Yeah, well you're just a pretty boy, that's all!"

Matt couldn't stand the ridicule. He had to do some more admiring of himself in his mirror.

"Like I said, you're all jealous!"

At this time, Parker was pulling up his uniform trousers; they were up to his knees when Matt unholstered his .357 again. He was once again raising it to the previous position of admiration but this time, he cocked the hammer back.

"Hey Matt, Nielsen is just kidding, please put the gun away, we don't need an accident."

Matt was lowering his pistol as he stated,

"I'm so bitchin!"

KABOOM! The pistol went off. Parker instinctively jumped around the corner of the lockers, with his uniform pants around his ankles.

Matt:

"OH FUCK!"

Yeah, OH FUCK IS RIGHT MATT! Told you to put the fucking gun away twice and then the fucking thing accidentally goes off because you are too bitchin! Now I can't hear anything. Thanks a lot fucker!

Parker slowly crept around the corner of the lockers back to Matt's location. Parker put his hands out in front of him to show Matt he was not armed. Parker's pants are still around his ankles:

"Matt, it's me; I don't have a gun, put the gun down."

Matt is just standing in front of his locker, staring at his pistol that had just gone off. The bullet went through Matt's locker door, killing his vanity mirror and entering the locker to the right of his. Matt had some minor blood on his gun hand, evidently, parts of the bullet shaved off when it went through the locker door and blew back into Matt's right hand. Matt had an "OH FUCK!" expression on his face.

Nielsen! What the fuck about Nielsen? Matt's barrel was pointed towards Nielsen! Shit!

Parker yelled out, partially because of the gun blast and loss of hearing:

"NEILSEN, YOU OKAY?"

When Matt's gun went off, Nielsen instinctively ran down the long hallway that led out of the locker room.

Parker heard Nielsen yelling from the far end of the hallway,

"Yeah, I'm Okay!"

Parker buckled up his uniform pants and walked over to Matt.

"You okay?"

"Oh fuck! Shit! I've got part of the bullet in my hand but it didn't go very deep. You're my witness!"

"Yeah, I'm your witness for sure."

Witness? Really? You want me to be a witness? Witness to what? Witness to you fucking around with your gun in the locker room and then the fucking thing goes off and we all lose our hearing? What a Dumbfuck!

The watch commander heard the gunshot and ran down to the locker room. He took Matt's gun away from him and told him to get up to his office.

The bullet from Matt's gun went through his locker door and through the door of the adjacent locker. That locker was assigned to a senior officer. After going through two heavy locker doors, the bullet went through a very expensive police dress jacket that had a bullet hole through the heart. The bullet then bounced around inside the locker and ended its flight. No chance it would have hit Nielsen but who knew? This had never happened before. We never had someone so bitchin turn the locker room into a police pistol range!

Funny thing about this whole episode is that Officer Matt did not get into too much trouble for the accidental discharge. Officers Parker and Nielsen were never interviewed about the incident (and didn't want to be). Officer Matt must have broken out his "superior" bullshitting skills and skated on this one.

But sometimes it just doesn't pay letting the rest of the world know how bitchin' you are!

BLAME ME PLEASE

Detective Bob was assigned a bank robbery case. The case wasn't too involved:

The robber went into a bank, pulled out a gun, demanded money, the cashier gave him money and the robber drove away. Witnesses wrote down the robber's vehicle license number and called the police, advising of the robber's direction of travel. The patrol officers received a radio call of a robbery suspect leaving the bank and found him on a main thoroughfare, about a mile away from the bank. The cops pulled over the robbery suspect in a B.F.G. "felony stop". The bank robber didn't want to get shot by the cops, so he cooperated with the cops and was arrested without his shit getting blown all over the road. Simple case, rather straightforward.

All felony cases are assigned to a detective even though they are already "solved". There may be additional investigative work, like, "How many times has the suspect been arrested in the past? Has the suspect committed other crimes", etc. The investigating detective is assigned the case and he prepares the paperwork for filing charges with the District Attorney's Office. The whole ordeal is laborious, but a good detective knows what is needed to get charges filed. They do it every day. Hopefully, the Deputy District Attorney reviewing the case has premium French Roast Coffee in their Office. If not, it's a simple trip over to Deputy District Attorney Wade's Office for good brew.

NO NEED FOR LONG, DRAWN OUT COURT CASES

Detective Bob went to the District Attorney's' Office and got a robbery charge filed against his bank robber. A week and half later, Detective Bob showed up in court for a preliminary hearing. Remember, this is just a hearing for the judge to establish "probable cause" that a crime was committed, and the defendant probably committed it: just a "mini trial." A full blown trial will follow if the defendant does not accept a "plea bargain deal" (A deal where the District Attorney's Office will usually offer a lightened sentence to dispose of the case quickly.); happens all the time.

THE PEOPLE OF THE STATE OF CALIFORNIA VERSUS JIMMY JONES

Bank robber Jimmy was assigned a Public Defender because he could not afford a private attorney (of course!). The Public Defender representing Jimmy was very good at his job. So good, the Public Defender's Office often had rookie public defenders sit in on his cases to get some experience. So Jimmy basically had two attorneys representing him.

The judge handling the preliminary hearing called the case and asked Jimmy how he pleads to the charge of robbery in the first degree. Jimmy, sitting at the defense table, stands up and says,

"Not guilty your honor."

The judge then directed the District Attorney to present their first witness.

The first witness called was the bank teller; a nice middle aged gal.

"So, on the day in question, what happened?"

"This guy came into the bank, pulled out a gun and told me, 'Give me all your money!'"

"What did you do?"

"I gave him all the money in my drawer."

"What happened next?"

"He ran out of the bank."

"Do you see that person here today in court?"

"Yes, I do!"

"Would you please point him out and describe his clothing?"

Pointing at Jimmy, sitting at the defense table, the bank teller stated:

"He's sitting right there, dressed in blue."

Jimmy was sitting at the defense table; he was dressed in blue jail coveralls. Sitting to one side of him was the lead defense attorney; he was wearing a blue suit. Sitting to the other side of Jimmy was the rookie defense attorney, also wearing a blue suit.

Must have been national wear blue clothes to court day...

YOU CAN'T FIX STUPID!

Defense attorneys have a hard job. They are supposed to defend their clients even when the evidence is overwhelming. Sometimes, they will raise objections in an effort to show their clients they are trying to do their job. The senior Public Defender stated,

> "Your honor, I do not believe that was a positive identification of the defendant because all three of us here at this table are wearing blue clothing."

And with that, everybody in the courtroom took notice, that in fact, everyone at the defense table was indeed wearing blue clothing.

Jimmy looked at himself and realized he was wearing a blue jail jumpsuit. He looked to his left and saw that yes, his lead Public Defender was wearing a blue colored suit. Jimmy looked to his right and saw that his assisting Public Defender was also wearing a blue colored suit! He thought for a second that everyone in the courtroom could be misled by who the witness is trying to identify.

They were all wearing blue colored clothing! What a screw up!

Jimmy, wanting to help out in court and have a semblance of honesty, raised his hand and blurted out:

"IT WAS ME!"

Everyone in the court bust up. Except the judge of course. He had to cover his mouth full of laughter because he has to remain professional at all times.

> *I hate it when funny things like this happen in my courtroom! I'm not allowed to laugh. It's inhumane! I have to call a recess and go into my chambers and laugh with the court reporter and court clerk after things like this happen! There should be a better way!*

When Jimmy blurted out that he had done it, the lead Public Defender held his head in his hands, looking down at his table. There was a pregnant pause. When everyone in the court room quit laughing, he asked the judge in a very calm business-like voice:

"Your honor, may we please have a short recess to reassess a plea offer from the District Attorney's Office?"

"Yes, we'll take a twenty-minute recess."

And with that, everybody had a story to tell their friends about stupid Jimmy admitting to a robbery when the Public Defender is trying to help him out.

Detective Bob was laughing his ass off and couldn't believe what had happened. When he walked out of the courtroom, he professionally told the lead Public Defender,

"It's not your fault, sometimes you just can't fix stupid!"

Sometimes preliminary hearings will take hours or even days depending on the seriousness of the crime. Detective Bob could now return to his station if he wanted to.

That was a fast hearing! No need to rush back to the office, I think I'll mosey on over to Deputy District Attorney's Wade's office for a cup of French Roast and some felony networking...You just can't fix stupid but you can drink coffee!

CANINE FERTILITY CLINIC

OFFICER JAMES

Officer James had been on the force about five years. He was in his late twenties, slim, trim, in very good physical shape, and loved his job even if it meant working the dreaded dawn shift once in a while.

James also had a beautiful wife and was happily married. They were trying to have kids for several years with no success. One dawn shift the plans for having children were terribly threatened.

At about one in the morning, Officer James and two fellow patrolmen received a radio call of a reckless driver at a shopping center. Dispatch advised the reckless driver was speeding all around the parking lot, crashing into shopping carts. Approximately a dozen shopping carts had already been killed and numerous others wounded.

Crashing into shopping carts? Who does that? Somebody who is either drunk or crazy, maybe both?"

AMERICAN SHOPPING CART ABUSE AND GENOCIDE

Sylvan Goldman was a self-service grocer in 1937; he conceived the idea of the shopping cart. It is estimated there are now between 20 and 25 million shopping carts in use in the United States.

Almost 2 million shopping carts are kidnapped each year. The food industry reports the annual loss per store is approximately $8000 to $10,000. It is an epidemic that most of the general public is unaware of. Many of these carts end up abandoned in fields and lots, left victim to the elements. They suffer abuse, rust, and die. 2 to 3 million shopping carts must be produced each year to replace the stolen and dead shopping carts in the United States and still, nothing is done to address this serious cultural issue.

Most shopping carts in high volume stores only live four to six years but some have been known to live until they are ten years old if they are well cared for. The cost of a new shopping cart ranges from around $90.00 upwards to $400 for specialty carts.

Because of cart kidnappings and cart genocide, some retailers use a radio frequency locking signal on one of the cart's wheels to prevent them from being kidnapped from their store parking lot. The system works fairly well but not all shopping carts are protected; the abuse and genocide continue. Congress refuses to act.

Officer James was assigned a call involving an active shopping cart terrorist. The shopping cart terrorist was driving into and killing shopping carts at a local shopping center.

No wonder the price of food keeps going up. It's because of assholes like you! You indiscriminately kill shopping carts! What did they ever do to you?

Officer James arrived to the shopping center and witnessed the shopping cart terrorist slam into and kill another cart.

Such violence!

The shopping center was littered with overturned, dead and wounded shopping carts. It was shopping cart carnage at its worst!

Officer James sped up to the suspect vehicle and activated his pretty red and blue overhead lights. The suspect vehicle took off. Officer James turned on his siren and the pursuit was on!

The shopping cart terrorist vehicle sped out of the shopping center and onto a main thoroughfare. Officer James was joined by two more black and white patrol cars. It looked like Christmas with all the festive felony red and blue lights from the patrol cars notifying Mr. Shopping Cart Terrorist that:

The cops are coming for you and you're not getting away!

Mr. Shopping Cart Terrorist was all over the road. It was obvious to Officer James that the terrorist was probably drunk and/or high on drugs. Mr. Shopping Cart Terrorist took Officer James and friends on a high-speed pursuit down city streets; he pulled into an apartment complex leaving his car running and took foot bail up some stairs to an apartment. Officer James noticed that Mr. Shopping Cart Terrorist is about thirty years old and average build. Officer James is hot on his heels:

433

One ass kicking coming up! Can't wait to slap the cuffs on you fucker! You kill all those innocent shopping carts and somehow in your deranged mind you think it's o.k.? You think you are above the law and don't have to stop for my siren and beautiful felony red and blue lights? You're not getting away with this behavior idiot, not on my watch!

Mr. Shopping Cart Terrorist ran into an apartment. The door wasn't locked, and he tried to slam the front door on Officer James as he entered the apartment. Officer James tackled Mr. Shopping Cart Terrorist on the living room floor and the wrestling match was on.

Sitting on the living room couch, watching the wrestling match was Mr. Shopping Cart Terrorist's brother and sister in law. They just watched the fight like they were watching T.V. they had no idea what Mr. Shopping Cart Terrorist had done, and they did not want to become a part of the ass kicking. Running around the living room was a rather large Pitbull canine and he was confused. The dog was barking, snapping at Officer James here and there as he wrestled with Mr. Shopping Cart Terrorist.

Officer Keith entered the apartment and was trying to help subdue Mr. Shopping Cart Terrorist who was fighting ferociously. The living room floor was cramped, and it was difficult for anyone to get the upper hand in the fight. The Pitbull continued to snap at Officer James. The Pitbull let Officer James know that he was not invited into the apartment to kick the shit out of Mr. Shopping Cart Terrorist.

The brother and sister in law yelled at the Pitbull to calm down and to come to them but the dog was confused. The more yelling, the more aggressive the beast got.

Officer James was trying to get a choke hold on Mr. Shopping Cart Terrorist while dodging attempted bites from the dog. Officer Keith punched Mr. Shopping Cart Terrorist with a couple of civil rights and a couple of civil lefts. The officers were finally able to get Mr. Shopping Cart Terrorist face down on the floor and handcuff him. The fight was over. Officer James stood up and the Pitbull lunged forward and clamped onto Officer James' crotch.

Ouch!

Officer James and everyone except for Mr. Shopping Cart Terrorist were yelling at the dog to let go. The brother and sister in law finally got the beast to release its hold on Officer James' private parts and he grabbed his crotch. He was in a lot of pain to say the least.

Officer Keith took Mr. Shopping Cart Terrorist to jail. Another patrolman took Officer James to the local emergency room. No one knew how serious Officer James' injuries were. The department notified Officer James' wife of his injuries and she responded to the emergency room. Mrs. James was very concerned to say the least. This current situation could prevent the couple from ever having children of their own. No one was happy, especially Officer James.

THE EMERGENCY ROOM

Officer James was made to wear one of those fairy looking emergency room gowns. He was assigned a bed and his wife joined him at his side.

The emergency room was not busy that night and the E.R. doctor thought it would be better if he personally treated the wounded officer.

The E.R. doctor was very professional and asked what happened. James went into the whole story about how Mr. Shopping Cart Terrorist was murdering innocent shopping carts, led them on a high speed pursuit, ran into his brother's apartment, fought with the officers while the Pitbull went crazy and then after the fight, the Pitbull latched onto his private parts.

Mr. E.R. Doctor lifted up James' gown and inspected the damaged area:

"You're lucky, usually when a Pitbull latches on, they don't let go until everything is totally destroyed. From what you told me, you definitely have some injuries but you should make a complete recovery. You're very lucky."

"Well, the dog was choking."

James' wife:

"On What?"

"The dog was choking on my privates and the thick reinforced crotch area of my pants!"

I don't think I like your comment!

The E.R. doctor chuckled to himself:

"Well, let's get you patched up. You'll be off from work for a while and no sex until you're healed!"

The E.R. doctor went to work putting this back together and putting that back together. Use your imagination on this one.

GOOD ENDING

If you will remember, Officer James and his wife were trying to have children for many years with no results. Two months after he got bit in the crotch by the Pitbull, Officer James' wife became pregnant with their first child. It was a Pitbull miracle! Everyone knew that the Pitbull must have jostled something around inside Officer James' private parts to get everything going for the production of little kiddos.

Sometimes a little violence is a good thing?

THE WALKING DEAD RANCH

MARIO AND SEAN

Mario and Sean lived in a farming community in a large southern California county. They were school friends, played on the same sports teams and liked to go on hikes together in the hills surrounding their community. They would take their BB guns, a canteen of water, and wander off and discover new places. They were two ten year old inquisitive young boys and enjoyed their adventurous expeditions. They were like Lewis and Clark but on a smaller scale.

One summer's day, they decided to go on one big, massive hike, several miles from their homes, further than they had ever gone. The boys met up early in the morning and took off on a long trek. The hiking was harder than usual because the temperature was reaching 100° but they eventually wound up on a ranch they had never seen. It was a beautiful ranch, well-manicured with large valley oak trees surrounding it and a huge barn that looked like it was 100 years old.

The ranch had cattle and horses, but no ranch house. Except for the cows and horses, it appeared abandoned to the two young boys.

SECRETS OF THE RANCH BARN

There wasn't anything happening at the ranch. Everything was quiet. No people, just horses and cows. Just one thing needed exploring: THE RANCH BARN.

Sean:

"Hey, want to look in the barn?'

"Yeah but I don't want anybody to see us."

"Me either, let's be careful."

The boys just hatched a conspiracy to look into a barn they didn't own because it would be "exciting and fun!"

Sean walked up to the main doors of the barn. They were huge double doors closed shut with a locking hasp but they weren't locked. A stick was wedged in tight into the hasp and Sean was having a hard time taking the pressure off the doors to release the stick:

"Help me, it's stuck!"

Mario came up and threw his weight into the heavy doors and between the two of them; they were able to remove the stick. The barn doors were big and heavy. Both boys pulled until they opened. Slowly, the doors creaked open.

It was a bit dark inside the barn but there were several barn windows that allowed some light in. When Mario pulled open the barn doors, the boy's had to refocus. They saw barn owls flying around inside.

They opened the barn doors a little bit more to get more light inside. They stared in horror of what they saw on the opposite side of the barn:

Three decaying corpses sitting in old wooden chairs, covered in spider webs, obviously killed by some sick, deranged, psycho mass killer! THE WALKING DEAD! Except they were now, "The Sitting Dead" and have been for some time.

"Ahhhhhh!"

Mario and Sean ran as fast as they could, back towards their homes. After about three hundred yards, where they felt safe, they stopped to catch their breath:

"THEY'RE DEAD!

"I KNOW, KEEP GOING!"

The boys went home, told their Mothers what they had seen, and called the Sheriff's Department. Everyone was horrified!

Sheriff's dispatch sent Deputy Brady out to the call. He had been on the force about four years. Following directions provided by the boys, Brady located the walking dead barn. He knew how to handle police calls but he was not prepared for what he was about to see.

The barn door was left ajar by Mario and Sean. Brady drew his pistol and kept it by his side:

Just in case the psycho mass killer is still in the area. Better safe than sorry...

Brady peeped into the barn. No suspects or footprints in sight. He saw the three decaying corpses on the other side of the barn.

How sick! Somebody is really deranged here! This crime scene is going to be one for the books. Shit!

Being the keen observer that Officer Brady is, he then saw something almost as disturbing as the corpses: on the ground, in front of the sitting dead was an old wooden box that was labeled:

DUPONT EXPLOSIVES
EXTRA DYNAMITE
60% STRENGTH

The box itself wasn't too much of a worry except, out of one front corner, it was leaking nitroglycerin onto the ground.

ALFRED NOBEL

In 1867, a Swedish Chemist named Alfred Nobel invented dynamite. Dynamite consisted of mixing nitroglycerin (a very unstable and dangerous clear liquid explosive) and Diatomaceous earth. Dynamite was safe to handle and required a blasting cap to detonate it.

Old dynamite that has been sitting around for years will eventually start to leak liquid nitroglycerin, which is extremely unstable. Just touching it can detonate it and ruin one's day.

Deputy Brady was thinking to himself about how many different department resources were going to be needed for the call he was on: Bomb Squad, Homicide Detectives, Crime Scene Investigators, Fire Department in case the bomb squad screws up and the nitroglycerin explodes, paramedics (just in case), and a Public Information Officer in case the press finds out about the call.

Heck, we're going to have one big department reunion out here!

Brady's Patrol Sergeant, Sergeant Walker arrived at the Walking Dead Barn:

"What ya got Brady?"

"Sarge, three decaying corpses in the barn. Some sicko put them on chairs and they're sitting around a box of dynamite that is leaking nitroglycerin! It's a major crime scene and I ain't going in that barn because one, it's a homicide scene, I don't want to disturb it, and two, I don't feel like getting blown up!"

Sergeant Walker walked over to the barn doors and took a peek inside:

"Oh Yeah! Good call Brady. I'll call headquarters and let them know what we have. Go ahead and set up the crime scene tape, we don't want the scene disturbed."

What sick son of a bitch would do something like that?

"I'll get the tape up and start a log of all the personnel entering the scene."

Brady has done this before. He knows what is coming: one big giant Sheriff's Department reunion at the Walking Dead Ranch.

Send in the Big Boys!

INCIDENT COMMAND SYSTEM

Many law enforcement agencies utilize an Incident Command System, or, I.C.S. for handling major incidents. I.C.S. is an organized protocol for the handling of big or unusual situations.

CAPTAIN AL

Captain AL has been on the department almost thirty years. He's a no-nonsense type of guy and is well liked. Captain AL is a people person and knows how to relate to fellow cops. The Sheriff's Department sent Captain AL to Incident Command System training. The end result was that whenever a major incident occurred, Captain AL was sent out to initiate "I.C.S." and ensure that all resources are coordinated and the scene was handled correctly. Captain AL was "Mister I.C.S.". No major incident was too big for Captain AL: train derailments and plane crashes were simple child's play for Captain AL.

Captain AL received a phone call from the watch commander about the Walking Dead Ranch Corpses and the leaking box of dynamite. In less than an hour, he was in the passenger seat of the Department Command Post, a huge, state of the art motorhome with big, beautiful Sheriff's Stars on all sides and antennas bristling from its roof. His driver was Deputy Bart. Also along for the ride was a senior dispatcher, Judy. Both Bart and Judy knew what their respective jobs were. They liked Captain AL and his emergencies. They felt needed and important when they assisted him on his tragedies.

Usually when Captain AL responded to a scene where he had to initiate I.C.S., numerous people have already been killed or injured. Captain AL has three murder victims in the barn and a very volatile box of dynamite. Captain AL cannot afford to have additional victims; each move by Captain AL has to be done in a safe and methodical manner.

Before he left the station, Captain AL dispatched a deputy to the local subway restaurant to pick up enough sandwiches for about forty personnel. This is not Captain AL's first rodeo:

You have to feed your cowboys and cowgirls if you want them to perform and be happy!

On the way to the Walking Dead Ranch, Captain AL made several phone calls. He called the bomb squad, the homicide boys, the fire department, and the crime lab. Everybody but the swat team and hostage negotiators.

444

The weather was hot and Captain AL knew that nothing could be done until the bomb squad boys cleared the leaking box of dynamite out of the barn. The hot weather by itself could set of the nitroglycerin. It is a very dangerous job.

Once at the ranch, Captain AL directed Deputy Bart not to park too close to the barn. If the box of dynamite in the barn exploded, Captain AL did not want any flying debris hitting his beloved command post motorhome. Bart found a shady spot underneath a huge valley oak tree, well away from the Walking Dead Barn. Captain AL was pleased.

Just for the heck of it, Captain AL called the department air unit to have a helicopter get photos of the Walking Dead Ranch and to search the surrounding area for any morbid mass graves of additional Walking Dead; and, to make sure that *"My Friend, Some Dude, and Some Guy"* weren't lurking somewhere on the property.

"Judy, while I'm trying to coordinate all of this, would you please call the Homicide boys and ask them to have a representative from the District Attorney's Office respond out here? They're not going to be happy if they don't know about this from the get go."

"Aye-Aye Captain, one District Attorney coming up!"

"Bart, call the Crime Analysis Unit downtown and get me all calls for service for the ranch and the surrounding area. I want intelligence info on this place."

The crime analysis unit had a computer data base for all calls for service, crimes, and incidents occurring anywhere within the county.

"Already have a call into them Captain, waiting for a call back."

"Outstanding!"

Everything was running smoothly. Judy, without being asked to, called the station to have extra water delivered to the scene. It was hot!

The homicide boys arrived. The bomb squad would be late because they had to pick up their bomb disposal trailer which was getting new tires installed on it. The Fire Department and the paramedics showed up. The public information officer showed up. A District Attorney showed up, and ten extra detectives responded to assist in whatever way they could. Everyone waited for the bomb squad.

"Captain, Crime Analysis only has reports of illegal hunters on the property during hunting season and way back in the 1970's, a group of hippies tried to set up a commune out here and we ran them off. None of the contact phone numbers for the current owner are any good."

"Good job Bart."

The Crime Lab C.S.I. unit showed up with their crime scene van with their special C.S.I. cameras, the laser blue light, and all the other fancy equipment you see on T.V. They were happy to get out of their stuffy office and be out in the open air for a change. It was beautiful summer's day and they couldn't wait to process The Walking Dead!

This incident is going to be on AMERICA'S MOST WANTED and we want to be a part of it!

The Sheriff's Air Unit completed their photo mission and search of the Walking Dead Ranch. There was no sign of *"My Friend, Some Dude, and Some Guy"*. The air unit landed their helicopter in a nearby field and joined Captain AL at the command post.

The bomb squad showed up with their bomb trailer. The trailer was about twenty feet long and had a huge upright cylinder/barrel in the middle of it that is referred to as the "bomb tube." The bomb tube is made out of heavy gauge steel and is about four or five feet high and about 42" in diameter. When bombs are recovered by the squad, they use a winch on the trailer to put them inside the bomb tube. The bomb tube has a heavy lid to cover the bomb tube. The bomb is then driven to a safe location for disposal.

Sergeant Luke of the bomb squad took a peek inside the barn and the old wooden box of dynamite:

"Oh Yeah!

"Captain, hope you don't mind but I asked a friend of mine from the ATF to come out here. They have a special technique, a solution to treat old dynamite with and making it inert on scene. He's bringing a special crew out here with him. I also called county HAZMAT (Hazardous Materials) to come out in case we need a cleanup crew."

Captain AL, sarcastically replied:

"No - Luke, Captain AL doesn't mind... You go ahead and invite as many of your little friends as you want to *my* party. The more the merrier."

"Knew you'd be happy."

"Judy, we're going to have more guests for dinner!"

"More sub sandwiches and drinks on the way Captain!"

A couple more patrol Deputies showed up to help out. Sergeant Walker used them for security, including directing all vehicles to stay parked well away from the barn.

Deputy Bart set up shade tents and tables for all the party attendees: the command post is well equipped. Bart was thinking:

Man, I should just get a Bar-B-Que fired up and we could have the Sheriff's Department Annual

Summer BBQ out here...This is a beautiful ranch. All we would need is some adult beverages, a little music, a Jolly Jump for the kids and we'd be set...

Quit daydreaming Bart!

Five County HAZMAT personnel arrived. Captain AL now has over 40 personnel on scene. Everyone is lingering in front of the department mobile home command post. It was, as Deputy Brady predicted, one big Sheriff's Department reunion.

The county road that accesses the Walking Dead Ranch could be seen from the command post. One of the officers in the crowd in front of the command post pointed towards the road and stated,

"Hey, I think the ATF is here, look at all the vans."

There was a Congo line of vans approaching the Walking Dead Ranch. The first van was just a regular white van. The other six vans were equipped with numerous satellite dish antennas on their roofs. As they came closer into view it became apparent where the other vans came from: the sides of the vans proudly displayed: Channel 2, Channel 4, Channel 5, Channel 7, Channel 9, and Channel 11.

Captain AL didn't want to deal with the media. He immediately assigned Sergeant Walker to make sure they stayed off the ranch. Captain AL also sent the Public Relations Officer over to talk to the reporters. Three news helicopters appeared in the sky but they were careful not to overfly the scene. Captain AL yelled:

"Okay, who called the press? I want to know who called them!

IF YOU CALLED THE PRESS, YOU'RE FIRED!"

Of course Captain AL was joking, but he didn't want to deal with the press or have them on scene. He could do without them for now; this situation could turn to shit if the dynamite exploded. Captain AL had too many issues to deal with. Every time Captain AL was sent to an I.C.S. situation, his reputation and career was on the line.

You can have a hundred "Atta Boys" under your belt but it only takes one "Aw Shit! To wipe them out!

"Sergeant Walker you're in charge of keeping the press by the road. The further away the better. If they give you any problems, tell them jail food tastes like crap!"

Sergeant Luke walked up to the command post with two ATF agents, Agents Cassidy and Jones. Luke introduced them to Captain AL.

Captain AL:

"Okay, I heard you have some new solution that makes the dynamite inert?"

"Yes Captain. What I would suggest is we send our robot in there to give us a good video feed of the box of dynamite. Then we'll go in with the bomb suits and soak down the box with the neutralizing solution. After that, just for extra safety, we'll have the robot place the box of dynamite in the bomb tube and take it to a remote, offsite location. Then, your homicide team can go in and do their thing. How's that sound?"

"Sounds good, be careful."

Agent Cassidy had to have a little fun with Captain AL:

"Oh, did anybody do a pre-detonation test on the box of dynamite?"

"What's that?"

"A pre-detonation test: someone has to go inside the barn and kick the box of dynamite. If it explodes, it's unstable. If it doesn't explode, it's stable."

Without missing a beat, Captain AL, so accustomed to fellow law enforcement smart asses, with his most sarcastic tone, replied:

"No Agent Cassidy, we haven't received that specialized training, please demonstrate for us..."

"Sorry, it's an ATF joke. I couldn't resist. We'll send the robot in now."

BOMB ROBOTS

British Army Lieutenant-Colonel 'Peter' Miller invented the first bomb disposal robot in 1972. Several British Explosive Ordinance Disposal (E.O.D.) soldiers had been killed by car bombs in Northern Ireland and a solution was needed. Millers' robot was basically an electrically operated wheelbarrow made to carry a hook device that could be attached to a car to safely tow it away. Since that time, the robots have evolved into complex machines comprising of disruptors, pincers, and jammers.

Today's Bomb Robots cost around $200,000 and in addition to handling bombs, have been used to disarm suspects, and in one case, to shoot an armed suspect that refused to surrender to police.

The newer bomb robots are so sophisticated; they are capable of mixing refreshing cocktails after performing their bomb disposal duties. Not really, just threw that in there to see if you were awake.

The ATF bomb robot was sent into the barn and took some nice video of the dangerous box of dynamite. The video confirmed what everyone already knew: lots of nitroglycerin was leaking from the box of dynamite.

Cassidy and Jones got into their bomb suits. The suits weigh approximately 80 pounds and can get really hot inside. An optional cooling system is available for the suits from the manufacturer.

We're so glad the agency purchased the bomb suit cooling system...

The bomb robot was left inside the barn to video the next moves by Cassidy and Jones. If the dynamite exploded while it was being soaked down, the bomb technician world would have another training video of "How not to do it." If the dynamite did not explode, the bomb technician world would have another video of "This is how the big boys do it."

The ATF bomb boys entered the barn with their cumbersome bomb suits and all their equipment for spraying down the box of dynamite and making it safe. They began spraying the nitroglycerin that was leaking from the bottom of the box and nothing was happening to it. It appeared to have somehow solidified and was not reacting to the neutralizing solution. Something was wrong. Cassidy and Jones backed out of the barn and met with Captain AL:

"Something's wrong, the solution is not doing its job for some reason. I don't know what it is. I'll need to call the office and check a couple of things."

"O.K., do what you have to."

Sergeant Walker walked up to the command post with an old cowboy looking fellow:

"Captain, this is Mister Stevenson; he owns the ranch."

Captain AL didn't know if he should draw down on Mister Stevenson or just talk to him like a normal person. Stevenson didn't appear to be a threat.

Is this the sicko in control of The Walking Dead Ranch?

"Thanks for showing up Mr. Stevenson."

"Boy, you folks sure got some big production going on out here. Is there a problem or are you just shooting a movie?"

"Is that your barn?"

"Sure is."

"When was the last time you were in it?"

"Oh, I'd say a couple of weeks ago, why?"

"Because of what's inside it."

"Oh, you mean my friends? Is that why all of you are out here?"

Friends? The corpses are your friends? Looks like we have a mass murderer psycho cowboy on our hands. What a weirdo...You're going to the State mental hospital for the rest of your life partner!

"Those are your *friends*?"

"Sure are, there's Jimmy, Suzie and Peetey. Couple years ago we had a movie shoot out here and the movie folks forgot to take all their mannequins with them. They've been my drinking buddies ever since. Hah, this is funny."

"What about the dynamite?"

"That's a movie prop too. Safe as hell, it's fake but looks real. Those movie folks really know how to make things look real."

You have got to be kidding me! Everything is a movie prop! We've spent thousands of dollars of taxpayer resources and everything's fake! Shit!

We were following proper protocol with the information we had. We were better safe than sorry. Fooled all of us because it was so 'life like', or 'dead like'. It looked real!

The press is going to chew us a new asshole if I don't handle this right. I have to turn this into a positive or we'll look like idiots for sure…

"Mr. Stevenson, thank you for coming out here and straightening all of this out for us. Two young boys went in your barn earlier today and reported decaying corpses to us and then we found the box of dynamite and we had to respond accordingly."

"I understand, no problem. They look real! Ha!"

"Please have some sandwiches and water or whatever else you want. We'll be out of here in a while."

"Don't mind if I do, thank you."

"Sergeant Walker, get everybody over here for a debriefing except for your troops keeping the press at bay."

"Got it."

Captain AL assembled the Walking Dead Ranch Response Team and told them the new information he had. Most everyone was cracking up. Captain AL then allowed his entire team to have a photograph taken with Jimmy, Suzie, and Peetey. The crime lab photographers were on scene and might as well use them.

CAPTAIN AL COURTS THE PRESS

After a quick update phone call to headquarters, Captain AL instructed his Public Information Officer to hold a quick press conference with the press who were still waiting outside the ranch.

The press is going to eat us alive for using so many resources on a "non-crime." But, I'm going to turn this around. Today is: "Press Appreciation Day". Once they see how life like the mannequins and box of dynamite are, they'll be on our side and happy we played it safe. Nobody was hurt!

The Press Information Officer held a short news conference explaining that the corpses and box of dynamite were movie props. He then asked all the news crews to turn off their cameras and microphones because he had some good news to tell them:

"I just want to let you all know that Captain AL, because he's always enjoyed such good rapport with the press (even though he didn't want you here in the first place), is going to allow each news crew to take photographs of the mannequins and box of dynamite.

Now here's more good news: since we have so many resources already here, Captain AL wants to give all of you a personalized tour of the bomb squad's equipment, the Fire Department's equipment, the crime lab's equipment, the Sheriff's helicopter and let you speak to all the personnel involved so you will know how they all work together at scenes like this. We also have plenty of refreshments for you."

The Sheriff's Department Mobile Home Command Post was stocked with extra snacks: boxes of candy bars and chips to go with the sub sandwiches. Dispatcher Judy placed all of those on the tables Deputy Bart had placed out. She also called headquarters and ordered iced teas, iced coffees, and sodas. This was not Dispatcher Judy's first rodeo; she came from a big family and knew how to entertain.

After the press viewed the "homicide scene" and took their photos, they thoroughly loved their little tour of all the law enforcement resources. They got to look in the bomb tube, got a bomb robot exhibition, saw the laser blue light being demonstrated in the dark barn, the high tech cameras of the crime lab; they also got a close up look at the modern fire trucks, the state of the art paramedic van, the Sheriff's helicopter and visit with the homicide detectives, some of which they already knew from other crime scenes. Yes, the press was having a field day and loved getting to have their very own law enforcement and fire department resource exhibition. No one ever treated them as well as Captain AL!

Captain AL, you're the best! No one has ever taken the time to show us all these resources and explain everything to us! Thank you so much! We loved the bomb squad, laser blue light, fire trucks and the air unit!

Dispatcher Judy ordered more sandwiches and drinks...

While the news crews got to explore the Walking Dead Ranch and the resources employed there, Captain AL and ATF Agent Cassidy were able to visit a little. It was Captain AL's turn to have some fun with Cassidy:

"So, How many did you bring?"

"How many what?"

"How many automatic weapons?"

"What are you talking about?"

"I thought you were an ATF Agent?"

"I am"

"Well, 'ATF' stand for 'Alcohol, Tobacco, and Firearms'. So, when you respond to one of our scenes, we expect you to show up with alcohol, beer preferably, tobacco, I like cigars, and firearms: my guys and gals like to shoot automatic weapons."

"I was in a hurry to get out here. Sorry about that. You'll all just have to show up at the annual ATF Bar-B-Que."

"Send us an invite! And next time, don't forget to bring the Alcohol, Tobacco, and Firearms; we'll bring the chips!"

The two had a good laugh.

"Thanks for coming out Cassidy, even if it was a dry run."

"No problem, I thought it was real. I think we all learned something new today."

Once the News crews got the whole story of the Walking Dead Ranch, they ended up praising the

Sheriff's Department, the Fire Department and the ATF for their professionalism and careful approach to the issue:

"At about 11:00 o'clock this morning, Sheriff's Deputies responded to this remote ranch because they received a report of three decaying corpses in the ranch barn. It appeared to be a scene of a gruesome multiple homicide. When Deputies arrived, they also discovered an old box of dynamite that was leaking nitroglycerin which is very unstable and can explode any second. Numerous officers responded to the ranch to process the scene. The corpses and box of dynamite turned out to be old movie set props but the Sheriff's Department had no way of knowing that at the time. They played it safe and no one got hurt.

As you can see, these movie set mannequins look like real corpses. It's scary just being near them. Years ago this ranch was used as a movie set and the film crew left the decaying corpses and dynamite box here. The land owner has been waiting all this time for the movie crew to reclaim their props but they were found by two young adventurous boys instead.

Even though there was no actual crime here, it's good knowing our Sheriff's Department, Fire Department and Agents from the Bureau of Alcohol, Tobacco and Firearms are well prepared and capable of handling situations like these. Had this been an actual crime scene, it would have been handled correctly and no one would have been injured...

Live from the Walking Dead Ranch, Connie Stuart, Channel Two Action News...*"*

MERRY CHRISTMAS!

SPECIAL ENFORCEMENT DETAIL

Many departments have a "Special Enforcement Detail" or, "S.E.D." The name and function may vary among departments.

Patrol officers aspire to get assigned to S.E.D. because it entails a variety of fun work assignments: conducting surveillances, assisting detectives with search warrant service, serving arrest warrants on bad hombres, monitoring gang members, and any other "special" situation that may need addressing by the police department.

When not engaged in any special details, the S.E.D. officers team up in two man plainclothes units and patrol the city streets during evening shift in the hopes of finding a bad guy and arresting him. They will stop almost anybody for any misstep of the law to ascertain if that person is up to more than just a mere infraction of the law. Oftentimes the S.E.D. officers stop regular everyday citizens who merely committed a traffic violation. These citizens are usually sent on their way with a warning. If the backseat of their car is full of burglary tools or drugs, the person stopped and the S.E.D. officers will become well acquainted with one another and somebody is going to jail...

OFFICERS STEVE AND JEFF

Officers Steve and Jeff were assigned to S.E.D. for over a year. Their team consisted of six officers and one Sergeant. All the team members loved being a cop and working plainclothes patrol in the city. One never knows what criminal act one may stumble upon. That's part of what makes working S.E.D. so interesting. Steve and Jeff especially like working plainclothes because *"My Friend, Some Dude, and Some Guy"* can't tell they are cops: they are dressed in civilian clothes and driving a car that appears to be an everyday car.

The special enforcement team was very close knit and all the members enjoyed working with one another. They were so close knit, their Sergeant always threw them a Christmas poker party!

CHRISTMAS IS IN THE AIR

It's two weeks before Christmas and everybody is getting into the Christmas spirit. The secretaries at the police station have the offices well decorated; they are also making preparations for the annual Christmas pot luck: a favorite with all the department employees, the weather is cold and the city streets are decorated with holiday decor.

Yes, Christmas is in the air…

Sometimes, things aren't going right for the S.E.D. unit and people are too well behaved. If one wants to enjoy one's job during the slow periods, one must become inventive with fun new ideas. Fun ideas like the ones Officers Steve and Jeff invent.

TONY

Tony was in his early twenties. An average

guy, had a job, family lived in town, no criminal record, no traffic violations on his record. Just an average guy who wanted to go over to his girlfriend's house to visit one night. Just two problems: Tony was speeding a bit too much and failed to signal while turning. Tony warranted a stop by Officers Steve and Jeff because most criminals are notoriously bad drivers. Besides that, "Tony" could very well turn out to be *"My Friend, Some Dude, or Some Guy"*.

We don't know until we stop him!

Officers Steve and Jeff pulled Tony over for the violations. Officer Steve approached the driver's door while Officer Jeff stayed on the passenger side of Tony's car, illuminating it with his high intensity flashlight. Officer Jeff checked out Tony's car for contraband. None is seen.

Officer Steve:	"Good evening sir, police department (Officer Steve showed Tony his badge), may I see your license, registration, and proof of insurance?"
	Tony handed over the documents.
Tony:	"Was I going too fast?"
Officer Steve:	"Just a little. Where are you going in such a hurry?
Tony:	"My girlfriend's, she lives right up the road."

464

Officer Steve: "Please wait here."

Officer Steve walked back to his plainclothes patrol unit and ran a background check on Tony. Tony was super polite, was sober, and had has nothing suspicious in his car. He appeared to be an upstanding citizen that was just driving shitty; squeaky clean.

Officer Steve tells Officer Jeff:

"Operation Jingle Bells!"

Officer Jeff: "10-4."

Officer Steve walked back up to Tony's driver's door:

With a very serious cop tone to his voice,

Officer Steve: "Tony, will you please exit your vehicle and step over to the curb?"

Tony got out of his car and walked over to the curb where Officer Jeff is standing.

Officer Steve: "Tony, do you have any idea how

465

expensive traffic tickets are?"

Tony: "I heard they're a lot"

Officer Steve: "They are; not to mention your insurance will also go up and you'll have to take a day off from work to show up in court."

Tony: "Do you have to give me a ticket?"

Officer Steve: "Not always. I'm going to let my partner explain to you how you may possibly qualify for just a warning."

Officer Steve walked up to Officer Jeff. Tony could barely hear the two mumbling something about a "Christmas Traffic Warning Program" and maybe Tony qualifies.

"Tony, this may be your lucky day, I don't know for sure but my partner is going to explain to you about a special Christmas Traffic Warning Program, or, "C.T.W.P." we have for bad drivers like yourself."

Tony: "Really?"

Officer Jeff: "Yes Tony, you see, during the holiday season, the Chief has authorized us to give out a limited number of warnings to drivers that qualify.

Do you promise never to drive bad again?"

Tony: "I promise!"

Officer Steve is nodding his head up and down in a sign that, so far, Tony qualifies for the Christmas Traffic Warning Program.

Officer Jeff: "So far, you qualify. Do you like Christmas?"

Tony: "Yeah, I do."

Officer Steve is nodding his head up and down again.

Officer Jeff: "Do you know how to sing? You can't get a Christmas warning unless you know how to sing."

Tony: "I can sing, my family says I'm pretty good."

Officer Jeff: "What do you think partner?"

Officer Steve: "Sounds like he qualifies."

Officer Jeff: "O.K. - Tony, do you know the words to 'Jingle Bells'?"

Tony: "Yeah."

Officer Steve is nodding his head up and down that Tony definitely qualifies for the Christmas Traffic Warning Program...

Officer Jeff: "Okay Tony, to claim your warning as part of the Christmas Traffic Warning Program, let's hear, 'Jingle Bells'."

Tony lets it go with one of the best renditions of Jingle Bells Officers Steve and Jeff have ever heard. He sounds like Bing Crosby!

"Dashing through the snow. In a one-horse open sleigh. O'er the fields we go. Laughing all the way

Bells on bob tails ring. Making spirits bright. What fun it is to laugh and sing a sleighing song tonight

Oh, jingle bells, jingle bells, jingle all the way. Oh, what fun it is to ride in a one-horse open sleigh"

While Tony is singing, Officers Steve and Jeff are nodding their heads up and down in a sign that Tony is seriously earning his warning through the Christmas Traffic Warning Program.

Officer Jeff is secretly recording Tony's wonderful performance. It is definitely a contender to be illegally broadcasted over the police radio band in violation of FCC rules when the time is right to entertain the entire department.

Officer Steve: "Tony, that was wonderful! You get to leave with just a warning and have saved hundreds of dollars in fines, penalties, and increased insurance rates! Are you happy?"

Tony: "Yeah!"

Officer Steve: "Good, we like happy customers. Here's all your paperwork back. Drive safe."

Tony: "Thanks. Bye."

Officer Steve: "And Tony?"

Tony: "Yes?"

Officers Steve and Jeff in unison:

"MERRY CHRISTMAS!"

Tony: "Merry Christmas!"

At midnight, while driving back to the station at the end of their shift, Officers Steve and Jeff just couldn't wait to play Tony's wonderful rendition of Jingle Bells over the police radio. They knew that they would probably win the Christmas Traffic Warning Program award for the best performance.

The other guys would have to stop Dolly Parton or somebody else of that high quality to win the award and the chance of that happening are slim to none.

As they drove to the station, there weren't any emergency calls going out over the radio. Officer Jeff played Tony's recording over the police radio band.

All the other police cars clicked their radio microphones on and off in a sign of approval. They enjoyed Tony's wonderful rendition of jingle bells. They also knew it was Officers Steve and Jeff who played the recording.

The watch commander that night heard it too and thought it was wonderful. He didn't care that some of his officers were once again goofing off. No, the watch commander was not going to damage department morale by making a big deal about the illegal use of the police radio for the spreading of positive holiday cheer.

Yes, Christmas, was in the Air!

BATMAN AND ROBIN

Circa early 1990's

Quite often, cops form very strong friendships with each other and later they both end up in calls that become infamous. This is one such story:

OFFICER KEITH

Officer Keith had been on the department about ten years and was assigned to the patrol division. He was hard charging and loved police work. He enjoyed having fun on the job when he could. Also, he let all of his fellow officers know that he did not drive a "patrol vehicle"; he piloted a "Crime Apprehension Sled".

OFFICER ANTONIO

Officer Antonio was a new officer on the force. Fresh out of the academy, he was assigned to work the jail. It was there that Officer Antonio met Officer Keith and the two became good friends. Whenever Officer Keith booked a prisoner into the jail, he received platinum treatment from his friend, Officer Antonio. Antonio was yearning to finish his jail assignment and get out to the patrol field. Until then, he would listen to Officer Keith's stories about the exciting life of a patrol officer. Even though Officer Antonio was not yet assigned to patrol, the department allowed officers from the jail to "ride along" with patrol officers from time to time. Antonio rode along with Officer Keith on a regular basis and it helped break up the monotony of working in the jail.

471

During these ride alongs, the friendship between Officers Keith and Antonio grew stronger. The ride alongs provided Antonio with advanced patrol training. Antonio was a good listener and easy to teach. When the time finally came for him to leave the jail and go to patrol, he would have an easier transition than the average officer. Officer Keith also greatly benefited from Antonio riding along with him: he had instant back up if he needed it.

CRIME FIGHTING DUO

Both Officers presented a positive image of the department: their uniforms were immaculate, and they were very professional. Officer Keith was tall and stocky. Officer Antonio was in good physical condition too, but he was a bit shorter than Officer Keith and had an average build. When they rode together in their Crime Apprehension Sled, it gave one the impression the felony team is working today. Because of the height difference in the two Officers, images of Batman and Robin came to mind. Add some Ray Ban sunglasses to their wardrobe and no crooks in their right mind would mess with the Crime Fighting Duo.

GOODBYE JAIL, HELLO PATROL

Officer Antonio was thrilled the day he was notified that he was being transferred out of the jail and to the patrol division. He wasn't transferred to the same station as his friend Officer Keith but at least he was going to patrol.

Antonio spent a couple of months in field training and was finally released to work on his own. He was then as Officer Keith would describe an official: "Crime Fighting Road Warrior"!

Antonio was so happy about completing his field training that one evening shift he invited his very good friend, Officer Keith to ride along with him. The department allowed Officer Keith to ride along, but only in civilian clothes; otherwise, the department would have to pay Officer Keith for his time and the department was not willing to pay him to volunteer his time and bullshit with his friend, Officer Antonio.

Officer Keith arrived early at Officer Antonio's station and attended the patrol briefing. Officer Antonio was assigned the beat area and call sign "7C31" ("Seven - Charles - Thirty-One"). Afterward, the two went out into the patrol vehicle parking lot and Antonio inspected his crime fighting sled. He was happy in that the vehicle he was assigned had only 5,000 miles on it and still smelled brand new.

We'll be fighting crime in style partner! We've got a new crime fighting sled with tons of horsepower; ain't nobody getting away from us!

Even though Officer Keith was on a "ride along", he brought all of his patrol equipment with him.

You never know when the shit is going to hit the fan. Better to err on the side of caution and bring all the tools of the trade then to be caught with your pants down...

It was the middle of summer and Antonio was thoroughly enjoying having his friend, Officer Keith on the evening shift ride along. The two made some traffic stops, had a couple of report calls and the shift was going quite well.

And then, three quarters of the way through the shift, it happened: the adrenaline packed emergency radio call:

> "Seven Charles Thirty One, assist Four Charles Thirty One: Numerous subjects fighting, wedding reception, possible weapons involved."

"Subjects fighting, wedding reception" was polite police language for big assed drunken Mexican American wedding brawl. Keith had been to one before. Antonio was a virgin to wedding brawls but that was about to change.

BIG FAT BEAUTIFUL MEXICAN AMERICAN WEDDING

Rosa and Alfredo had been planning their wedding for almost a year. They came from two large families and had many, many friends and family members. Several male relatives on both sides of the families did not always see eye to eye but hopefully they would put aside their differences for the couple's happy day.

The happy couple rented a large ranch barn outside the city limits for the wedding reception venue. The ranch was a common wedding venue, had ample parking, and the barn was decorated as well as any five-star hotel banquet room. Almost two-hundred guests were invited to their wedding. Over one-hundred fifty attended.

Everybody was dressed to the nines, even the children. This was a very important occasion, and no one wanted anyone to think they didn't know how to dress for formal affairs.

The ranch barn had beautifully decorated tables for all the guests: flowers, beautiful candle place settings, and various other wedding decorations.

The bridal party table had approximately twenty seats and boasted numerous bottles of champagne.

Off in one corner of the barn was the hosted bar with plenty of refreshments to help get the party started. Next to the bar were three large metal tubs full of ice and every beer known under the sun. No one was bashful about getting a drink and the three bartenders were kept very, very busy.

Sometime during the reception, a couple of the male guests got into a heated argument over by the bar with words being exchanged. The argument moved to the center of the reception area and before you knew it, almost everybody was yelling and cursing at one another; especially the Uncles and the cousins of the bride and groom.

The fists flew, the legs kicked, and the beer bottles crashed upon heads. About half the guests were either yelling and or fighting in the melee:

Yay! Rosa and Alfredo were officially married!

A ROAD TOO FAR

Although Antonio was off of field training, he was not familiar with the roads leading to the wedding reception ranch.

After receiving the fight call, Antonio stopped his crime apprehension sled for Officer Keith to get all of his field gear out of the trunk. He also got out a map book to guide them to the disturbance; GPS and all that good stuff wasn't available back then.

Officer Antonio pressed down on the accelerator and headed for the ranch which was several miles away. Keith guided him down long semi-rural roads. After one minute, the station advised:

"Seven Charles Thirty-One, respond code three (pretty red and blue lights and siren), reporting party states subject with a gun, one subject shot, several subjects stabbed."

Officer Keith thought:

Holy Shit! The Big Fat Mexican American Wedding has just turned into a Big Fat Mexican American Riot! Everybody got drunk and somebody from the Bride's side pissed off someone from the Groom's side and now everybody wants to kick ass on each other! Sure glad I brought my field gear!

Keith schooled Antonio:

"Partner, you haven't been to one of these before but I have. We do not leave each other's side. We have to stay together. There are going to be too many drunk assholes to handle. We'll go for those posing the biggest threat and take them down first."

"Got it."

Antonio picked up the speed to over 80 miles per hour.

These roads are fairly straight and the traffic is light. Eighty should be a good speed, after all, this is an emergency call and we've received the green light to haul ass!

There have been so many accidents involving police cars rolling "Code Three" (lights and siren) that police academies have made a special effort to hammer into the heads of police recruits that many members of the general public don't see or hear police car lights and sirens. If a cop runs a red light at high speed, there is a very good chance there could be an accident. If that happens, the purpose of sending a cop to an emergency is obviously defeated. Cops have to master their adrenaline and arrive at the scene safely, even if that means slowing down and creeping through busy intersections with their lights and siren. No one is supposed to get hurt responding to emergency calls.

Officer Keith put on his seatbelt. Antonio forgot to do the same. The emergency "Code Three" radio call was Antonio's first since he left field training. Antonio is driving fast but he is on a road in which he has the right of way and visibility of all crossroads is good. He is not driving beyond his capabilities.

Keith directed:

"There's a three-way intersection up ahead, go straight, you'll be going over some railroad tracks."

Everything is going smoothly except for the contour of the road. Ahead of our crime fighting duo is a railroad crossing with a speed limit sign of 35 miles per hour. No trains are within view and the train crossing lights are off. Smooth sailing, Antonio doesn't have to slow down. Unfortunately, the railroad crossing was constructed "back in the old days". The crossing appeared to be flat. It wasn't. Just before the railroad tracks, the road sloped upwards, just enough to resemble a launch ramp the Dukes of Hazard would be honored to jump but it was an optical illusion and appeared flat. Neither Antonio nor Keith were prepared for what happened next.

Antonio's crime fighting sled hit the launch ramp at 83 miles per hour and catapulted his police car twelve feet into the air. While sailing through the air, Officer Keith was so scared; he made his peace with God and was prepared to meet Saint Peter.

The patrol unit sailed 92' from the launch ramp and landed with a huge solid crash. Officer Keith did not sustain any injuries when the police space craft returned to earth. Officer Antonio was not wearing his seat belt and fucked up his back during re-entry.

The police space craft landed so hard, it sustained major damage: the frame was bent in several places, the suspension was destroyed, and the rims had flat spots. The car body was twisted and bent here and there; smoke and steam were coming from the engine compartment. The windshield was cracked, the red and blue light bar on the roof had broken off on one side and the light bar was almost diagonal across the roof. The crime fighting sled was making weird noises and limping along at a top speed of 30 miles per hour.

Yeah, we're rolling code everybody, just a little bit slower than normal!

Antonio radioed to headquarters that he was having "mechanical difficulties" with his patrol car:

"Station one, seven Charles thirty-one, be advised our ETA (Estimated Time of Arrival) is unknown; we're having mechanical issues with the unit."

Really Antonio? "Mechanical issues?" How about, you just played Dukes of Hazard with an almost brand-new police car. You turned it into a spacecraft, and you landed without a parachute. Congratulations Antonio: you transformed your police car into a piece of scrap metal shit!

Despite all the damage to their police car, Antonio and Keith were the first two officers on scene. Their police unit limped into the Big Fat Mexican American Ranch Wedding Reception Riot Parking Lot.

It was quite a scene: an almost totally destroyed police car that looked like it had been through World War Three, slowly driving up to the ranch barn at now, barely ten miles an hour and its crooked red and blue light bar and a siren that sounded like a moaning cat. The police car was a scary sight.

As Antonio pulled into the barn parking lot, a Truckload of Mexicans was driving away with all of the occupants in the truck bed pointing towards the ranch barn, obviously advising our crime fighting duo where the problem was.

Chalk one up for the Truck Load of Mexicans – this time they're helping!

Batman and Robin got out of their patrol car and ran into the barn to find all the shot and stabbed participants. They didn't find anybody shot or stabbed but they did find violence at the bridal party table: The groom was holding the cake knife in his hand and attempting to stab a subject he was holding down on the bridal table. The bride was wielding two empty champagne bottles in both hands and hitting anyone that came near her husband. Antonio and Keith saw her score several well placed direct hits. From time to time, she would add a smack to the head of the subject being held down by her husband. If this continued, the guy being held down by the groom would be killed for sure.

Antonio was shocked by what he saw:

I haven't been to one of these before. You gotta be shitting me! People really act like this? Somebody really pissed off the bride and groom. What a violent wedding!

Batman took out his nightstick and smacked the knife out of the groom's hand. A leg sweep and a wristlock and the husband was cuffed nicely. The subject getting his ass kicked by the groom slid off the bride's table and onto the floor. Robin grabbed the wife, folded her against the table and cuffed her. Robin got on his radio and called for an ambulance and backup. Batman and Robin held fast at the bride's table because they had a wall to their back. They weren't going to move their prisoners until they were absolutely sure it was safe to do so. Batman had the groom face down on the ground and used a knee on his back to keep him there. He was then able to monitor the subject who was getting his ass kicked by the lovely bride and groom; he appeared to be drunk and half-conscious but at least he was breathing.

Sirens could be heard in the distance. A short while later, additional officers arrived. A couple more drunk guests were arrested. Ambulances arrived and treated several guests. All the arrestees were put in the back of the police cars.

The backup officers at the call were looking in amazement at the damaged Batmobile:

"What happened?"

Robin:

"It's a long story – we hit a bump in the road while enroute to the call."

"Is that thing safe to drive?"

Batman, sarcastically:

"Of course, it's just cosmetic…"

Robin's back was hurting him, and Batman volunteered to do the driving back to the station. The Batmobile limped back to the station at less than 10 miles an hour. It was quite a sight to passing motorists, seeing a totally destroyed police car limping along the roadway with what was once a nicely dressed bride and groom in the rear seat.

The bride's mascara was all over her face and her lace headpiece was torn and hanging down the left side of her face. The groom had a big lump from a fist on his left cheek and his tuxedo shirt was torn around the neck area. But, other than that, they looked great!

By the time the Batmobile made it back to the Bat Cave, it was limping along at only 6 miles an hour. The noises from the engine had increased and the loss of fluids that were steaming out of the engine compartment had taken their toll on the Batmobile; it was almost dead.

After booking their prisoners, Robin was instructed to fill out a vehicle repair slip for the Batmobile.

Okay, how do I fill this repair slip out in such a way that it sounds like I didn't destroy the police car?

Guess what Antonio? There is no way in hell you can write up a vehicle repair slip for a car that is totally destroyed without saying exactly that. You didn't know the roads and it's not completely your fault but you were the one driving...

After the prisoners were booked, the reports written, and the vehicle repair slip filled out, Officer Keith told Officer Antonio:

"Hey Antonio?"

"Yeah?"

"In five minutes, meet me at my car in the back of the (police) parking lot."

"O.K."

Antonio was leaning up against Keith's personal vehicle when Keith walked up, carrying his bag of police patrol gear.

Keith:

"Got somethin' for ya to help take the edge off."

"Yeah, what's that?"

Keith reached into his patrol bag and pulled out two bottles of champagne from the wedding reception:

"I found some abandoned property at the ranch and I was always taught not to waste anything."

Keith pulled out two plastic cups from his bag and pulled the cork on the first bottle of champagne.

"They're going to fuck you on this one Brother. They don't like it when their cars get damaged like that. Don't get pissed off or anything. Just let them do what they will do, within reason, and this whole thing will blow over in a year or two. The Police Union will guide you through the process to make sure the department doesn't fuck you over too much."

Except, down the road, I'm going to make fun of your ass whenever I can! It's gonna be so much fun making fun of you launching your cop car off the Dukes of Hazard ramp and turning it into a spacecraft for five seconds. Now is not the time for that but I'll get you later!

"And, make sure you fill out a first report of injury for your back getting screwed up and get treated by a doctor. You're probably going to get a lot of back injuries during your career and you need to document all of them"

"Thanks Keith but I think I'm going to need more than one bottle of champagne to ease the pain."

"Who do you think you're dealing with, a fucking rookie? I've got two more bottles in my bag! I'm here to help! Don't ever accuse me of that again!"

The two had a good laugh. Antonio needed it. His back ached and the champagne helped take the edge away of some of the pain.

Epilogue

No one at the wedding reception was actually shot or stabbed. The person who called the police told that to the dispatcher to get the cops to the scene faster than normal.

Antonio's patrol car was deemed a total wreck and went to the scrap yard. He received "days off" (days off without pay) as punishment for turning his patrol car into a spacecraft and crashing it in the process. Antonio had the distinction that year of destroying more dollars' worth of department property than any other officer.

Congratulations Antonio, You Won!

The department tried to punish Keith for his role in the affair but he politely reminded the department he was in a "ride along" status, not paid for "working", and not subject to "on duty" discipline. Keith received no discipline.

After Antonio's launching of his patrol car, the railroad intersection was thereafter affectionately referred to as "The intersection of Antonio and Keith".

BIG FAT BEAUTIFUL MEXICAN AMERICAN WEDDING CHARGES FILED WITH THE DISTRICT ATTORNEY'S OFFICE

When charges are presented to the District Attorney's office for filing, a police Detective gives a "Reviewing Deputy District Attorney" all the police reports involved plus criminal histories of all the defendants involved. If they exist, a really good detective also provides criminal histories on the victims and witnesses involved. The "Reviewing Deputy District Attorney" does not prosecute the crimes being filed for court. They only review the charges to ascertain if they have merit for prosecution in court and if so, the case is passed on to a Deputy District Attorney for prosecution. The Reviewing Deputy District Attorney fills out a "case review form" which contains a synopsis of the crime for the prosecuting attorney. This form is a short version what happened.

About a dozen "suspects" had charges filed against them for their part in the wedding riot: lots of Uncles and cousins.

The Reviewing Deputy District Attorney wrote on the case review forms for all the defendants:

"Big Fat Mexican American Wedding Reception: Alcohol, Fight, and Cops."

That kinda sums it up...

Keith and Antonio are now retired and remain good friends. They stay in touch and yes, the launching of the Batmobile is discussed whenever they get together. It was a day that lives in infamy!

Antonio's injured back still bothers him to this day but he is glad he has such a wild, fun story to tell his family and friends. Whenever he can, Keith still loves to throw the launching of the Batmobile story in Antonio's face: IT'S FUN!

I HAVE PERMISSION OFFICERS!

HAPPY

"Happy" was almost twenty years old. He received his street name because he was just that, "happy" most of the time. He had an eighth grade education and a bunch of friends that were always in trouble. They were always getting caught by the cops for stealing, getting drunk and other forms of disorderly conduct. Happy followed in the footsteps of his friends and he too was always having run in's with the cops. The local cops were sick of dealing with the likes of Happy and his stupid friends.

OFFICER DADE

Officer Dade had been on the force about twelve years. He was street wise and diligent in the performance of his duties. He was a senior, veteran officer and although he seemed a bit too serious most of the time, if he could have some fun on the job, he would.

Officer Dade was assigned to Dawn Shift and began his shift by fueling up with coffee at the local coffee shop. He was wide awake and patrolling his beat, looking for *"My Friend, Some Dude, and Some Guy!"*

Dade pulled into an apartment complex and started patrolling the parking structure surrounding the complex. Around one bend in the driveway he found Happy holding a rubber hose which he was using to siphon gas out of a mini school bus and into a plastic gas can. Dade radioed to headquarters that he was stopping a suspicious subject in the apartment complex.

It's my old friend Happy! So good to see you again dumbshit! I can hardly wait to hear your explanation about your theft of gas...

Another patrol officer, also wide awake on coffee, stopped to back up Officer Dade. This second officer was a new guy and would only assist Dade if he needed physical back up. It was Officer Dade's show.

"Happy, nice to see you, I see you can't sleep and just had to get out of bed to steal some gas!"

"I'm not stealing gas Dade, I've got permission. I know the driver of the bus and   they   said   I could have some gas for my Chevy. I ran out of gas. Serious man, I've got permission..."

"At fucking twelve thirty at night, Happy?"

"Yeah man, well, I couldn't get down here earlier. This was the only time..."

Yeah, sure, you dumbshit!

Dade always said he could tell when Happy was lying: Happy only lied when his lips were moving.

Dade knew where Happy lived and that he owned a late '70's Chevrolet. Dade also knew that

Happy has a gas station within one block of his house but he decided to walk another quarter of a mile past it to steal gas.

What a lazy, stupid fucker!

Dade used his flashlight to inspect the mini school bus, the siphon hose and plastic gas can.

Happy continued to siphon gas as he further explained that the school bus driver, "*My Friend*", gave him permission to take some gas.

"That's really nice that your friend from the school district let you get some gas out of their bus. I heard they only use very clean gas. You should send them a 'Thank You' card for all the nice gas."

"Yeah, they are really nice."

The new backup officer looked at Officer Dade with a look that said:

Aren't you going to arrest this lying, thieving piece of shit? Man, you caught him in the act, you got him!

Dade understood the look he had received from his younger backup officer. Dade shook his head in the negative and winked at his backup officer. The younger officer did not understand at the time why Dade wasn't arresting Happy but he knew there was definitely a reason for not doing so. The new officer would not interfere with Dade's handling of the incident.

After Happy got a couple gallons of gas out of the school bus, he walked away with his gas can. The younger backup officer was fuming... He could not understand why Dade had let Happy steal the gas and just walk away. Officer Dade had just allowed a petty theft to take place and refused to affect an arrest!

What incompetence! And, from a senior officer!

After Happy left with his gasoline, Officer Dade invited the new officer down to the parking lot of the local coffee shop. The two officers spent about half an hour drinking coffee to stay awake. Dade did most of the talking. Dade got the newer, younger officer up to speed on Happy and his friends and what a pariah they are to society.

After Happy got home, he thought he would be able to start his car with fresh gas in it.

For over six months, Officer Dade and the newer patrol officer would drive by Happy's house and monitor if Happy was able to start his Chevrolet or not. Happy was spending almost all his time working on the car. It never got fixed, it never moved. Weeds and windblown trash were accumulating underneath the car. Happy feverishly replaced this part and replaced that part. His Chevy just wouldn't start!

It was all Officer Dade's fault. He wanted to have some fun. And, he did! Officer Dade let Happy steal the gas from the school bus because above the school bus gas filler tube was a little horizontal sticker from the factory that read:

DIESEL FUEL ONLY

Poor little Happy thought he outsmarted the cops by telling them he had "permission" from "*My Friend*" to take gas from the school bus; he enjoyed every second pouring stolen diesel fuel into his gasoline fueled Chevrolet. Happy ruined his engine!

YOU CAN'T FIX STUPID!

And that is how a "THEFT IN PROGRESS" turned into "FUN IN PROGRESS!"

WHAT A PITY

YOU

Have you ever been ripped off? Has your home ever been broken into and your prized possessions been taken from you? Has your car ever been broken into and someone stole your belongings? Chances are most of you have been ripped off by some asshole at one time or another in your life. This story is dedicated to YOU!

COP CYNICISM

Cops get cynical throughout their career. They don't want to be cynical, but the nature of the beast is that cops are trying to help good people, "YOU", from getting fucked over by bad people! Cops handle calls where shitheads attack and steal from the citizens that are trying to enjoy a normal way of life and cops don't like it when a shithead fucks over a good citizen. That is the cold hard truth; plain and simple. Is that so hard to understand? No, it isn't.

OFFICER LUCAS

Officer Lucas has been a patrol officer for seven years. He had a foul mouth and didn't mince words. If you were stupid or an asshole, he'd let you know. Very seldom did he smile. If he smiled, he was thinking something sinister. He was tied for first place in being the most cynical cop on earth. He hated crooks and wanted to waste them all and bury them all in an unmarked mass grave in nowhere land

493

(wherever that was). But, Officer Lucas was very diplomatic with the people he protected.

Lucas didn't work in the ghetto. His beat area was a nice up and coming bedroom community. But crime knows no zip codes and is everywhere. For several years, Officer Lucas had been writing many a burglary report where some shithead had been enjoying himself by violating the sanctity of the family homes and stealing them blind while they were away from their castle. Most of the burglaries occurred during the day while the victims were working. They had something called a "JOB", they worked for a living. Something Lucas' nemesis would never know anything about:

MIKEY THE BURGLAR

Mikey had a nice home, but he did not have parental supervision. His parents did not get along and somehow, Mikey was falling through the cracks of parental care and guidance. Mikey entertained himself by shoplifting. Soon, he graduated to burglarizing homes. Mikey wasn't gifted intellectually but he learned that many people leave the doors and windows of their homes unlocked. It was easy takings and Mikey enjoyed ripping off his neighbors.

Mikey didn't have a car, but he did have a noisy street legal dirt motorcycle he enjoyed speeding around town on. Whenever he drove past Officer Lucas, he would give him a sarcastic wave as if to throw it into Officer Lucas' face:

You can't catch me!

COPS CAN'T BE EVERYWHERE

One day, Mikey ended up getting arrested for possession of stolen property. Officer Lucas did not take part in Mikey's arrest, but he sure wished he had:

I'd love to throw the cuffs on that scumbag and maybe break a hand or something in the process...

The stolen property Mikey was caught with was taken from a home that Mikey had burglarized but, the cops couldn't prove that little Mikey broke into the house and stole the property. Therefore, Mikey was only charged with possession of stolen property when he went to court. The original charge was a felony but it was reduced to a misdemeanor to get Mikey to plead guilty and expedite the legal process. Mikey did a couple days in jail and was put on three years "informal probation". This meant, Mikey was not supposed to break the law again or he could be thrown back into jail. Mikey was subsequently released from jail to continue his rape of the city.

Officer Lucas was furious about Mikey getting let off so lightly:

A couple of days in jail when this fucker has burglarized so many fucking homes? Really? I'll give you a couple of fucking days in jail...How about I take the fucker into a vacant lot and put him in a fucking hole in the ground? I'll take care his shit! Fuck him!

Of course, getting rid of Mikey is just a daydream of Officer Lucas'. Lucas didn't want to spend the rest of his life in prison for committing such a horrible crime. Still, the dream lived on in Lucas' mind and sometimes he thought:

Only if I got caught though...

Cops can't be everywhere. They handle a lot of calls. While they handle traffic accidents and other incidents, Mikey, *My Friend, Some Dude, and Some Guy* are out there doing their thing: ripping off the public.

Officer Lucas scoured his patrol beat when he could, trying catch Mikey in the act of burglarizing a home. This cat and mouse game went on for years. Officer Lucas did his best to catch Mikey the burglar in the act, but Mikey had the advantage of when to time his crimes.

KARMA

And then it happened, one beautiful summer evening shift: Officer Lucas had just started his shift and arrived in his beat area when he received a "Code Three" call to an injury traffic accident. Police dispatch advised it was a:

"Vehicle versus motorcycle, fire and ambulance are enroute."

Lucas rushed over to the injury traffic accident scene which was a driveway entrance to an office building complex parking lot. Lucas used his police car to block off the entrance and make it inaccessible to any other vehicles.

A young rookie Police Officer showed up to assist Lucas. This young officer was gung-ho and ready to help out in any way he could. The young officer also respected Lucas, even though Lucas often displayed a shitty attitude towards people and things in general.

Lucas surveyed the crash site:

One motorcycle crashed into one compact car in the driveway of the office center. The motorcyclist was lying on his back. He couldn't talk, he could only moan because it appeared his back was broken. Three young gals hovered over the motorcyclist. They were well dressed and appeared to be secretaries who had just gotten off work.

"Lucas, you want me to lay out a flare pattern?"

Lucas, pissed off at the question:

"No."

"You want me to get out the first aid kit?"

Lucas, pissed off again after being asked another stupid question:

"No. Fire and ambulance are on their way. We let them do first aid."

Lucas spoke to a couple of witnesses that saw how the accident occurred. They told him the young man on the motorcycle was making a left turn into the parking lot and he sped up to beat oncoming traffic and the driver of the small compact car was trying to exit the parking lot and couldn't avoid hitting the speeding motorcycle.

The rookie officer that was assisting Lucas on this call was having a real hard time reading Lucas' mind. Lucas appeared to not give a shit about the injured motorcyclist.

The hovering secretaries were trying to console the motorcyclist:

"It'll be okay, you'll be alright..."

"Help is on the way..."

"Try not to think about the pain..."

Lucas stood near the secretaries, staring expressionless at the motorcyclist, with his hands on his hips like he had just finished up a big work project.

The rookie officer, who by now had figured out that he was not needed at this tragic scene, walked up beside Lucas:

"Hey, since I'm not needed, I'm going to take off."

Lucas turned his head toward the rookie officer, he was smiling!

This is freaking weird. First Lucas acts like a complete asshole and now he's smiling! What the fuck is going on here?

Lucas looked back towards the motorcyclist who was moaning louder than before. In a monotone voice, while staring at the downed motorcyclist, Lucas told his rookie partner:

"That is Mikey the burglar. This couldn't have happened to a better person. What a fucking pity, this is Karma.

He probably won't be able to walk for years. I feel like giving the gal that ran him over a big hug. I love her."

Lucas, smiling from ear to ear, looked his rookie partner in the eye, and with a voice with just a tinge of laughter in it:

"This is a good day for America partner. I'm buying beers at the end of shift."

I've never seen Lucas happy, let alone THIS happy.

Cranky Officer Lucas was finally in a good mood. No one could believe it. It was so out of character for him to be happy, especially at work. Lucas spent the rest of his shift contacting his fellow patrol officers to advise them he was buying beer for everyone after work.

When their shift was over, Lucas and team mates met in a secret location, a vacant field. The trunk of Lucas' personal vehicle was full of beer on ice. Lucas told the story about asshole Mikey the burglar getting run over and how he probably may never walk again. Lucas was in a beautiful, positive mood. He was actually being nice and polite to his fellow officers; they could not believe that Lucas was capable of being happy.

"Lucas, can't believe you are in such a good mood?"

"It was a tragic, tragic accident, so tragic...Please have another beer!

What a Pity..."

The End

Made in the USA
Monee, IL
15 May 2021